Andrew Dibben's
NORFOLK
WATERSCAPES

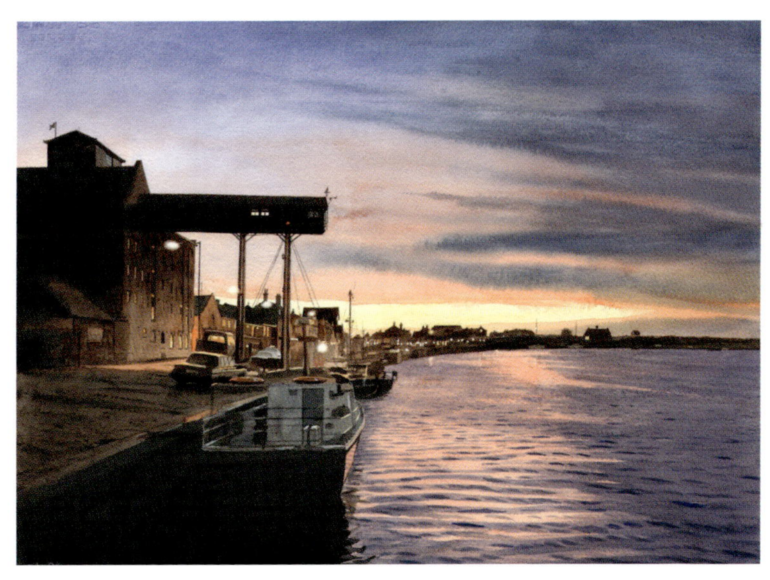

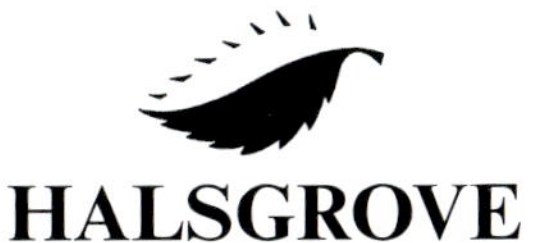

HALSGROVE

First published in Great Britain in 2005

British Library Cataloguing-in-Publication Data
A CIP record for this title is available from the British Library

ISBN 1 84114 349 9

HALSGROVE
Halsgrove House
Lower Moor Way
Tiverton, Devon EX16 6SS
Tel: 01884 243242
Fax: 01884 243325
email: sales@halsgrove.com
website: www.halsgrove.com

Printed and bound by D'Auria Industrie Grafiche Spa, Italy

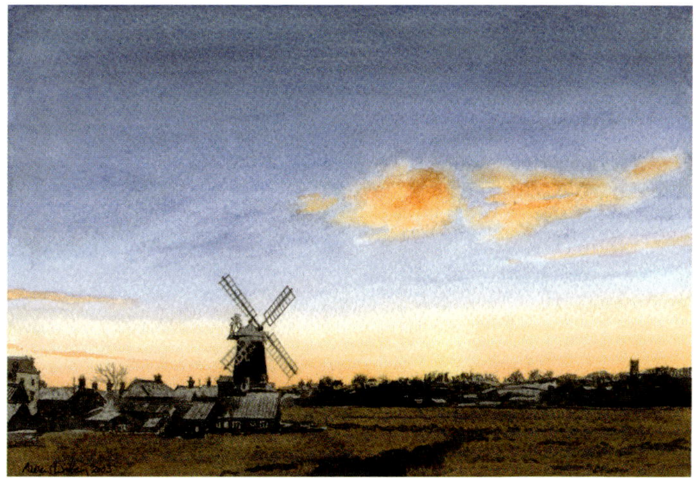

Cley Sunset – Winter 7" x 10" 2003

FOREWORD

by Keith Skipper

The old Norfolk trick of dangling one foot in the sea while the other clings to dry land may explain the number of veterans wandering round places like Cromer with rheumy eyes, rolling gaits and revived ambitions.

Andrew Dibben, it seems, has mastered the art after no more than 35 years of an apprenticeship designed to convince him and remind us that special talents can blossom and flourish on The Road to Nowhere. That's dynamic progress by Norfolk standards – especially for a lad from Somerset.

His first volume, crammed with enticing Norfolk landscapes and published three years ago with a foreword by Dame Norma Major, simply underlined a fast-emerging reputation as a watercolour communicator of rare class. Now he presents a stunning array of waterscapes (with this friendly nod of a foreword by Skipper Minor) as an encore with extras.

Andrew has sought out and saluted some of the county's more wild and remote places, not least to acknowledge their naturally therapeutic qualities at a time of renewed shrill cries for thousands of new homes relatively close by. This precious collection adds fresh urgency to the perpetual clash – vibrant economy versus fragile ecology.

It is a measure of the Dibben standing in such a debate that his work is being cited as much as a timely warning of what we can lose all too easily as it is a beckoning finger to savour 'undiscovered' delights. Yes, that straddling trick again – and it is given to very few to strike the correct balance.

When we set up the Skipper family home in Cromer in 1988, it soon became obvious how potent an influence the Norfolk coastline would exert on our busy lives. The stretch between Weybourne and Wells has become a firm favourite for gentle reflection, especially in winter, but we are aware of other siren calls from either side.

Sea Palling, Waxham and Winterton can stir the soul on branch-bending days when light is rationed and strolling is a tricky pastime. Brancaster Staithe, Burnham Overy and Holkham Beach constantly demand longer stays than we can manage at any time of the year. Hunstanton cliffs, as Andrew declares, are surely entitled to a far louder song of praise.

Even so, it is his evocative dip into Thornham waters that stands out for me in this creative tour de force. I have dropped anchor here in the lost harbour many times in all seasons, freely allowing emotions to be towed towards barnacled and broken ribs in a coastal graveyard where boat coffins live on mud and seagulls sweep the sky clean above.

Andrew called at the end of January with snow on the marshes and dunes, and even on part of the beach. Crunching ice and gusting winds added to a wintry cocktail before a wonderful Norfolk sunset lit the scene. Poetry and painting nuzzling up to each other for warmth. This eagerly-adopted son of Norfolk has produced another sumptuous book. Long may he dip his brushes into our enchanting waters.

Keith Skipper
Cromer, 2005

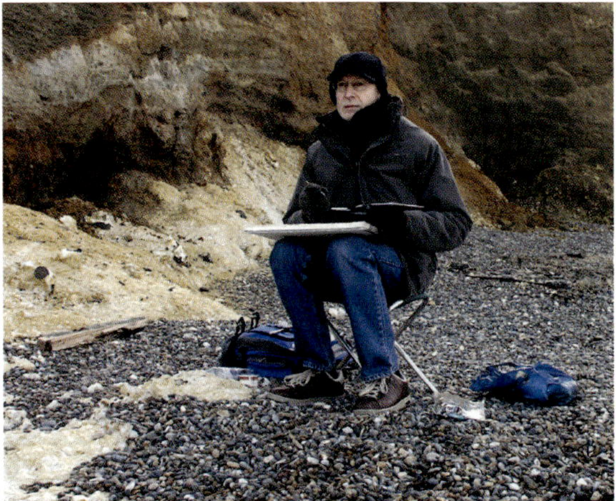

The artist on Weybourne beach, March 2005

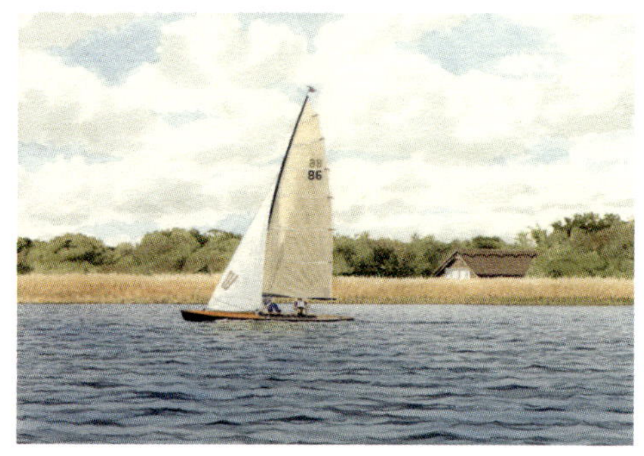

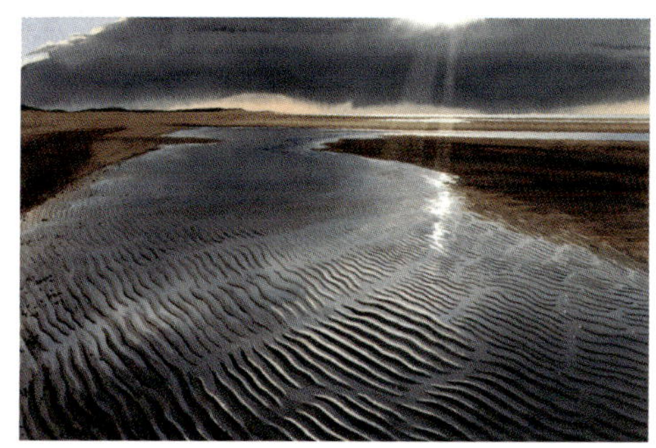

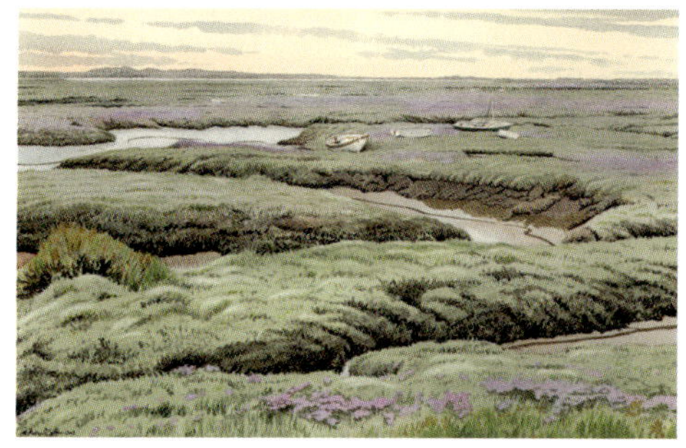

CONTENTS

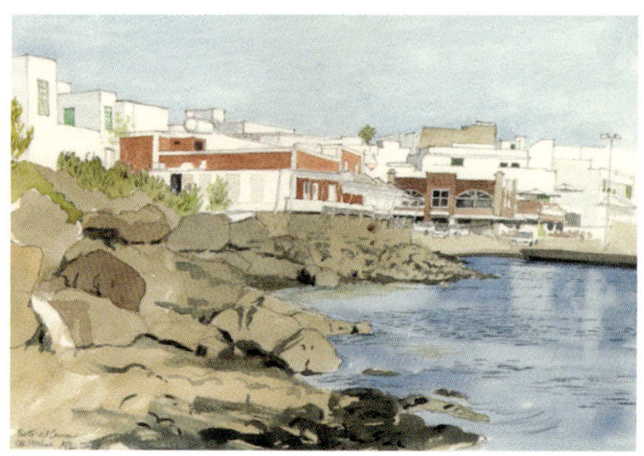

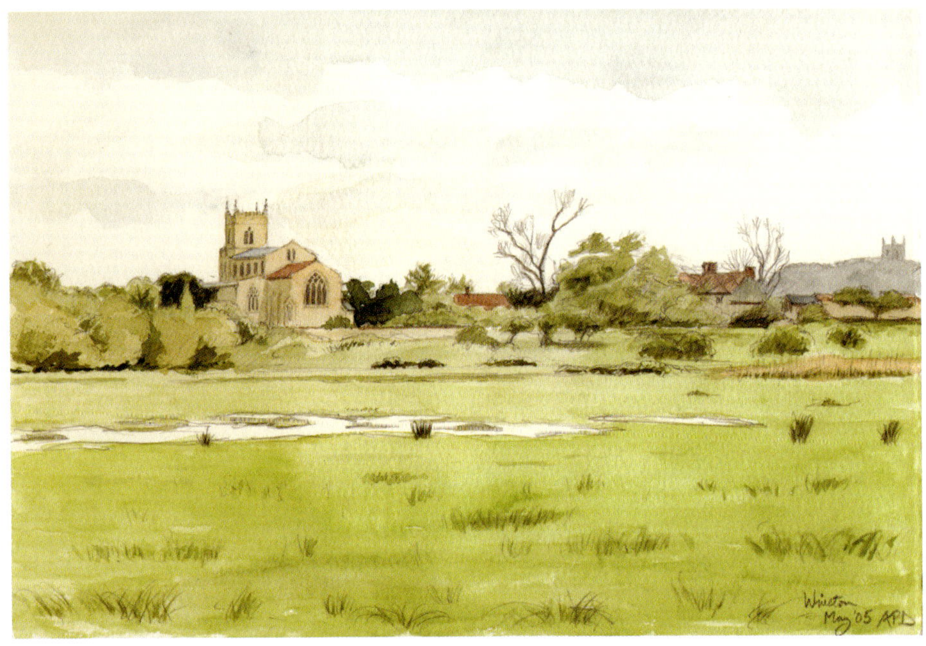

Flooded Meadow, Wiveton (7" x 10") 2005

For all who love water.

ACKNOWLEDGEMENTS

I would like to thank all the following for their help in the production of this book:
The irrepressible Keith Skipper, for his Foreword.
Simon Butler and Denise Lyons, and all at Halsgrove for their encouragement for a second volume.
Jonathan Neville, for information gleaned from his amazing Norfolk Mills website.
The owners or neighbours of several watermills, for permission to work on their land.
My wife, Ann, for continued tolerance and support.

INTRODUCTION

When I was trying to think of a suitable subject and title for a sequel to *Andrew Dibben's Norfolk*, the idea that first came to my mind was to work on the theme of 'Norfolk Rivers'. But even this apparently wide-ranging topic seemed too restricting after a time. I keep being drawn back to painting the coast and the sea, despite my love of the Norfolk Broads. 'Norfolk Waterscapes' then came to mind as a more general theme, which could encompass both fresh and seawater environments. This led me on to ponder about the remarkable attraction that water has for me, and also, it would seem, for most of humankind. Why is it that people will sit by the sea or a river, and just watch it for hours; or, in a mountainous area, why will they walk enormous distances to find a waterfall to stare at? Transpose to an urban situation, and it will be a fountain that draws a crowd; just think of Trafalgar Square, the new Princess Diana memorial fountain in London, or the Trevi fountain in Rome…

I suppose that our affinity with water should not be such a mystery; after all, our bodies are composed of some 60% water by weight, an average of an amazing 48 litres. We now understand that all life on Earth originated in the oceans, that nearly all life on Earth depends on water for its survival, and it would seem that most major groups of animals still live in water. Water itself can very often seem to be alive; in the natural world it is moving in some way most of the time, whether it be a river flowing, or the sea constantly breaking on the shore, no matter how still the wind. The tides can seem rather like the effect of the oceans' gigantic slow breathing, in and out, incessantly, while

the seas also appear to have varied moods; writers often refer to the fury of the sea on a stormy day. Water also appears to have a voice; it murmurs or babbles when it is a little brook, while the sea can roar in the most frightening fashion. The ocean is potentially a very dangerous environment, subject to quite sudden changes of state, so that no seafarer ever takes it for granted or ventures on it unprepared. Its destructive potential is almost limitless, as has been seen many times on a low-lying, fragile coastline such as ours in Norfolk. The Indian Ocean tsunami of 26 December 2004 was a terrifying demonstration of the power of water. The quality of danger makes the sea all the more exciting somehow, and more of a challenge for those people who like their courage to be tested; it is the unpredictable, sometimes friendly old adversary, while at the same time, on these islands, until the building of the Channel Tunnel, it was the warder that also kept us imprisoned here, as well as our stout defence against invasion.

On the other hand, water is also a life-giver and a cleanser. It provides us with food, in the form of aquatic plants, fish and crustaceans. It brings new life to plants that appear to have died, refreshes people and animals, helps revive the tired and ill, and assists healing. Few forms of cleaning will not involve water at some point, thanks to its ability to dissolve most substances, given enough time. It is hardly surprising therefore that water has been the subject of worship in various civilisations, or been seen as the source of all life, or the place where the newly-departed will find immortality by being set adrift in a boat. Water can also be a source of play, relaxation, or sport,

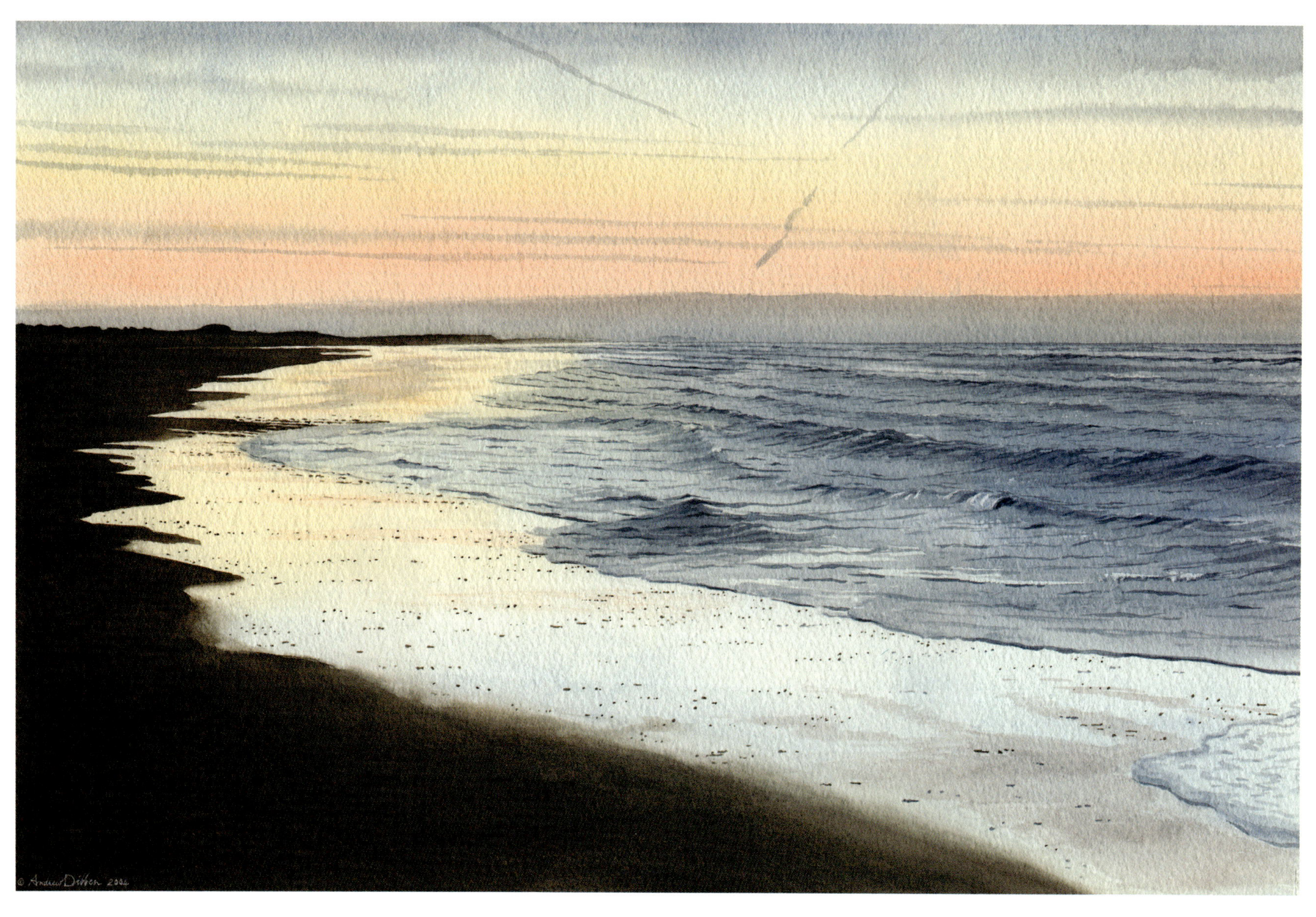

'The unpredictable, sometimes friendly old adversary'

depending on your predilection. You can swim in it, dive into it, sail or row on it, go fishing in it, or simply spend time admiring its indigenous wildlife.

Norfolk is a very watery county; it has a coastline of over 90 miles, with portions facing all directions of the compass except south (unless one counts the southern shore of places such as Blakeney Point!) It is also blessed with a large number of fine rivers, countless drainage dykes of varying sizes, as well as the renowned series of small shallow lakes collectively known as the Norfolk Broads. Broadland and the Fens began as great swamps that covered huge tracts of the east of England, and provided the ideal habitat for a variety of wildlife far greater than can be seen today. The hand of man changed the appearance and size of these environments. The Fens were drained thanks to the energy and genius of Dutch engineers, while the Broads were formed as a result of the accidental flooding of ancient peat-diggings, as sea levels rose, and forced river levels to rise as a consequence. Drainage work was undertaken later on the margins of the Broads area, while more recently, some of the Broads have gradually silted up, as they have become less important for transport, or for growing the reeds for thatched roofs.

It is a profoundly sad fact that the future of these areas looks very bleak; the tectonic plate upon which sits the British Isles, continues to rise in the north-west, unburdened of the weight of the last ice-sheet, while here in the south-east it is slowly settling into the sea. At the same time, global warming, whatever its cause, is making sea levels rise by melting the ice caps and glaciers at an increasingly faster rate. The latest predictions warn that the North Sea may be 82 centimetres higher in 100 years' time. Such a rise would undoubtedly cause a huge change in the appearance of the low-lying areas of East Anglia, coastal or riverine. There would seem to be little appetite in government circles for defensive measures; the cost is astronomical, while the affected population here is relatively small. The logic is sound, unless you happen to be one of those affected, in which case it can seem like the end of the world, or *your* world at least. So, water, the life-giver that is also prone to unpredictable moods and acts of violence, is about to strike at this peaceful corner of the world, and there is little we can do but enjoy what we have while we can. There is no doubt that, if the predictions are correct, the effect on the Norfolk Broads will be catastrophic. The sea can advance from two directions; it can raise the levels of the rivers trying to drain the land, causing them to burst their banks, and it can also breach the eastern coastal defences where the land is very low lying in places which, paradoxically, are far upriver and yet very close to the coast.

The paintings reproduced in this book are not necessarily all about water, nor do they even all feature water. There is however a loose theme of water, or of waterside places, throughout. Some readers may feel that there has recently been a slight change in the way I paint; I certainly feel that my work *has* gradually evolved. It is important for an artist to try to evolve, or to constantly give themselves new challenges or goals. Over the last three or four years, I have tried to find subject matter that appears at first sight to be simpler, less cluttered. Having spent some years painting numerous pictures of our best-known villages, I felt that I wanted to depict another aspect of the same area. These are still pictures of Norfolk, but they feature more of the natural environment of the county which is so wonderfully varied. It is fascinating that, while this south-eastern corner of Britain is really very crowded, it is nevertheless still possible to find places within it which can seem very wild and remote.

Naturally, if you walk along the beach, particularly in a non-urban setting, then you benefit from the immensity of the sea on one side to help achieve that sensation of remoteness. On the north Norfolk coast, it can make a difference knowing that there is no land at all to the north, only the North Pole. (A northerly wind can be quite raw here!). The various marshes, whether they be salt or fresh water, have a very strange quality to them too. Even in summer, in Norfolk it is not that difficult to find a stretch of marsh devoid of people; distances then become difficult to define, because there are so few familiar objects on which the eye can focus.

It is very comforting to be made aware of these wild places, when so many of us live in overcrowded conditions; indeed the recognition that there is in people an innate need to see wild areas was one of the reasons for the creation of National Parks. The wild fringes of our region are likely to find themselves increasingly valued for their recreational and therapeutic benefits if plans to build an additional 70 000 homes in Norfolk come to fruition. I have to admit that I hate the thought of such large-scale building plans; the county has changed dramatically over the last thirty years, and one is only too aware that once fields are built on, they will probably never revert to agriculture or woodland. I am very worried about the environmental impact of the proposed Norwich Northern Distributor road, which looks set to cut through a lovely section of the Wensum valley near Ringland. Then there is the likelihood of the dualling of the Acle straight. There seems to be a constant nibbling away at the countryside, and no end to it in sight. Some of this feeling is undoubtedly 'not-in-my-back-yard' syndrome, but it is difficult to avoid, particularly if one is old enough to be able to remember how things were in the 1950s. They were by no means a golden era, but space has contracted considerably since then, and pollution has increased immeasurably. If we continue to build large scale low-density housing developments, massive trading estates, and sweeping highway 'improvements', and then find that a large chunk of the county becomes covered by water permanently, then we will have lost an irreplaceable part of our children's heritage. We cannot beat nature, but it *is* possible to change our own ways.

My research into watermills, when I became interested in the idea of painting a series of pictures of them, unearthed the fact that there were 580 watermills in Norfolk at the time of the Domesday Book. Only 52 remain now. It occurred to me that an opportunity has been lost by not using these sites for generating electricity, instead of building some of the controversial wind generators.

FRESH WATER

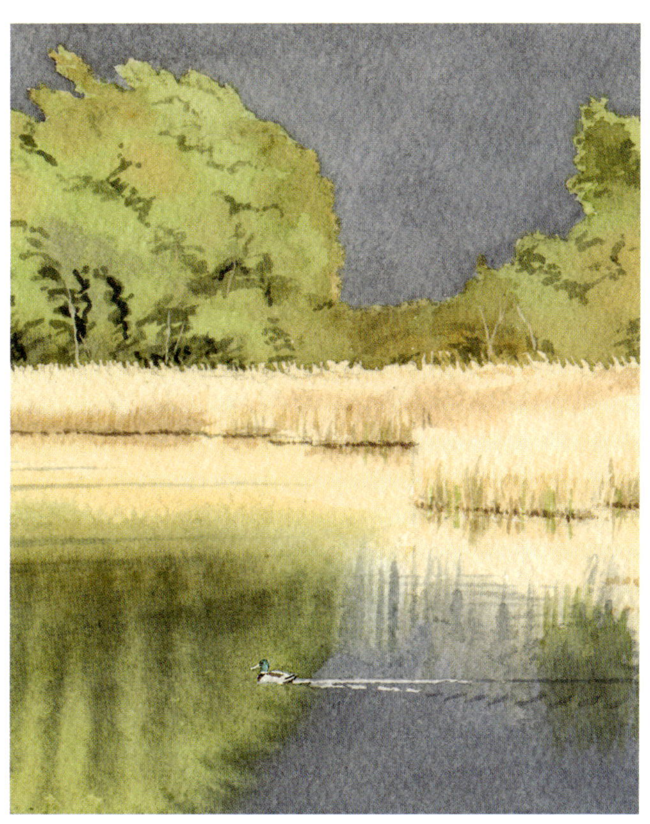

CRUISING THE BROADS

We used to own a small sailing craft on the Norfolk Broads, and enjoyed many weekends exploring the delightful waters of the Ant, Thurne, and Bure, until my new career necessitated a tightening of belts, and the sale of the boat! In May 2003 we decided to reacquaint ourselves with the rivers by hiring a boat, like the countless thousands who have enjoyed boating holidays on the Broads since the hire industry began, early in the twentieth century. I wrote a short account of our trip to send to a number of friends, some of whom live overseas, and it seemed appropriate to reproduce the piece, slightly embellished, in this book.

We spent a week in May 2003 on the Broads aboard the valiant little vessel *Broadland Moon II*. She is a slightly elderly 25-footer, fitted with a forward saloon with a sliding roof, forward controls, a well fitted little galley, separate toilet and shower compartments, and an aft cabin with a fixed double berth. There is standing headroom throughout, though I did hit my head a number of times in the doorways! We enjoyed quite good weather, with a rain shower on just one day; the start of the week was positively warm, and we enjoyed several beautiful sunsets.

The Broads system comprises a network of six rivers that provide 200 miles of navigable waters, and they flow through a number of small shallow lakes (Broads). These are rarely more than a mile and a half long, with the exception of the only one to be named differently, Breydon Water, which is between 4 and 5 miles long. Breydon is close to the sea entrance to the system at Great Yarmouth, and due to the flat terrain and extensive nature of the rivers, this stretch of water is very tidal. The system is divided in two at Great Yarmouth, and so to navigate from the northern rivers to the southern rivers, one has to pass through Yarmouth and Breydon Water, and time one's passage to coincide with low tide in order to pass under two low bridges. It just adds to the fun and excitement, but then, I gain pleasure from quite small things! Passing through Breydon Water certainly adds an extra dimension to a boating holiday on the Broads, as one is very aware of the sea's influence there, and the brackish nature of the water. I once travelled through Breydon at night, and was delighted to see phosphorescence in the boat's wake; a lovely sight. There is also a huge lifting bridge at one end of Breydon Water, and coasters occasionally pass through this on their way up to Cantley or Reedham, although this traffic is ever diminishing. Large yachts make more frequent demands on the bridge nowadays. Back in 1989, when I gave up my job to become an artist, one of the things I had planned to do was to make frequent visits to Carrow Bridge in Norwich, to photograph and sketch the coasters coming through to moor in the Port of Norwich. Alas, I was already too late; the last coaster to visit Norwich had left in September 1989. Since then, a new fixed road bridge for the southern bypass has prevented any further ship traffic.

We spent three days on the northern rivers. Setting off from Stalham, we motored down the River Ant and through Barton Broad, admiring the amazing riverside residences in Irstead, Wroxham and Horning, many of them thatched, and enjoying a couple of good meals in two of the many excellent riverside pubs. In Wroxham, we negotiated the frighteningly low and narrow medieval bridge; it seemed far too tight, but the gauge is there to tell you there is enough clearance, provided you aim straight! Upstream of the bridge, we looked at the little Bridge Broad, completely tree-lined, and with water lilies at the edge.

Opposite: *Yacht on the Ant* 14½" x 10½" 2003

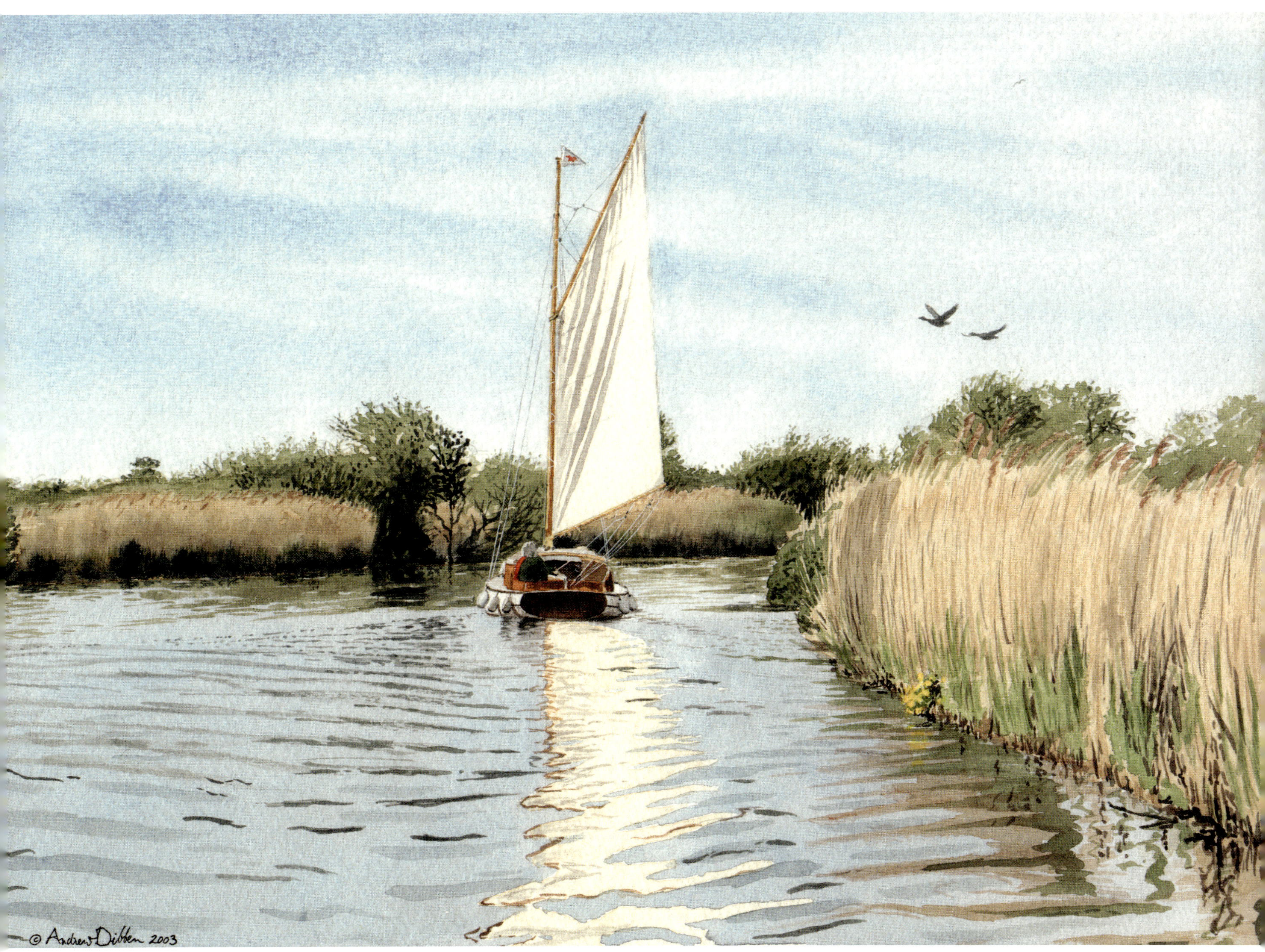

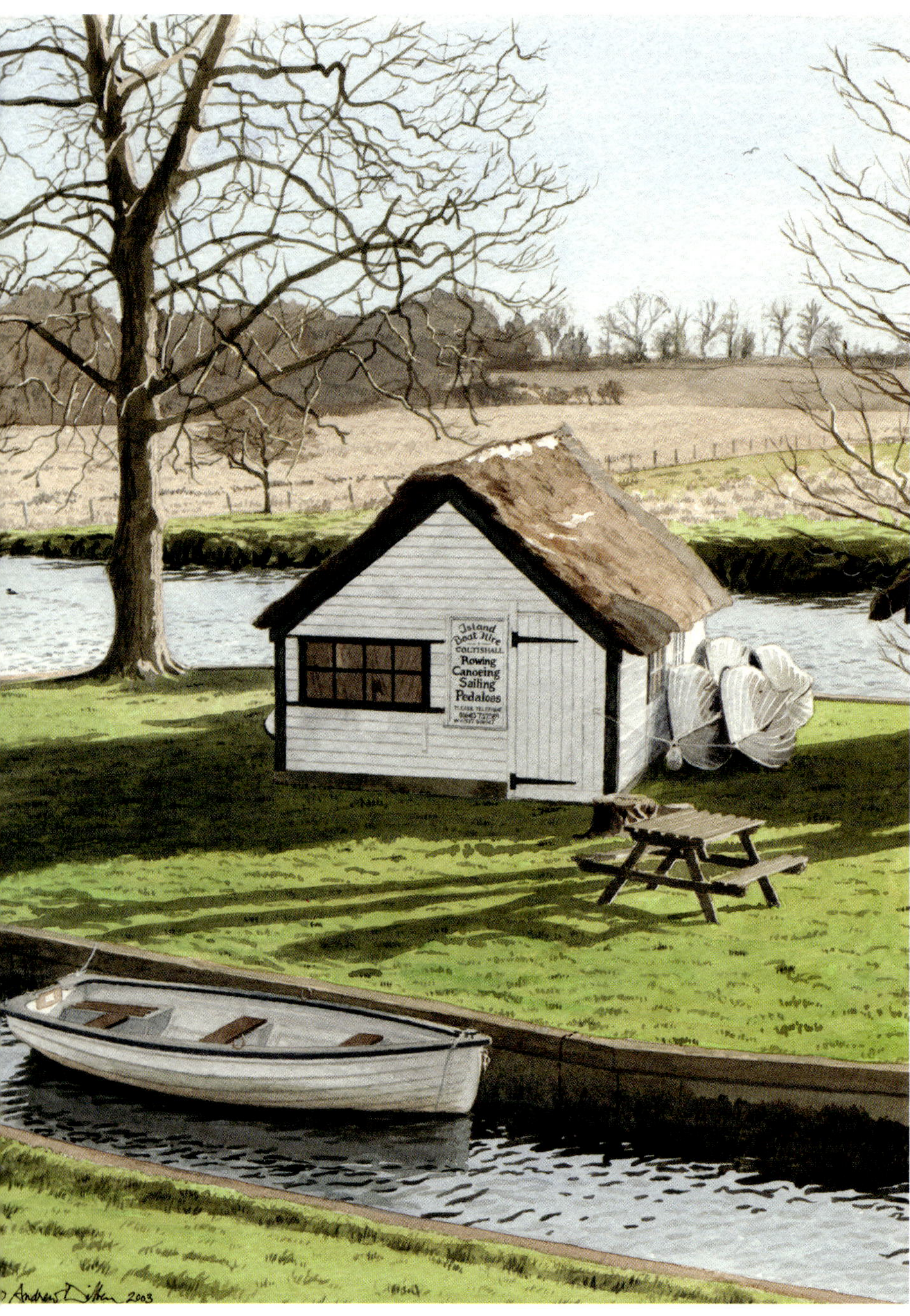

Coltishall Island 14½" x 11½" 2003

The River Bure

The Bure begins its seaward journey in North Norfolk, just south of Melton Constable and flows south-east through Corpusty and on towards Coltishall where, after taking a leap over the weir, it becomes navigable. The upper reaches are a delight, being markedly hilly, and are worthy of exploration on foot to discover the watermills and attractive landscape along the valley.

The pretty village of Coltishall offers sailors a couple of attractive waterside pubs and a lovely expanse of meadow to moor alongside, among other attractions. If you have hired a boat, it pays to take it as far as possible up the narrow section upstream of Coltishall Green, below the many overhanging branches of this quiet stretch, by way of experiencing a complete contrast to the bustling lower reaches, beyond Wroxham and Horning. As the River becomes ever narrower, and turning back would seem to become impossible as the trees and undergrowth close in, there is a feeling that you have arrived at a place that time has forgotten. Twigs and leaves brush the decks, while the propeller churns the silt just below your keel. Finally, you reach the head of navigation, where the weir forbids further progress, but it is just possible to turn a boat around.

This painting shows the little island by the Green, from where it is possible to hire rowing boats.

Then we passed through Belaugh, a tiny village built on the side of a steep escarpment overlooking the river, before arriving at Coltishall with its broad riverside green, pubs, and beautiful thatched church. Just past the village, we reached the head of navigation of the Bure, in the form of a large weir. We turned round, and headed back to Belaugh to moor up for the night. Early the next morning we set off to catch the tide downriver to Yarmouth; this means cruising down the whole navigable length of the Bure, which is over 40 miles of very attractive countryside. We stopped overnight in the pretty village of Stokesby, enjoying a meal in the riverside pub there. This close to Yarmouth, the tide's effect is very powerful; the river flows upstream quite strongly for a couple of hours with the flood, so it pays to consult the tide tables to avoid standing still! We set off again next morning with the tide virtually slack, soon reaching Great Yarmouth's slightly industrial northern edge. We passed under the fixed bridges, and arrived at the junction with a much wider stretch of river, which is the Yare; turning right, upstream, the large bulk of the Breydon (lifting) Bridge came into view, and beyond it the wider expanse of Breydon Water. We motored up the slightly choppy Breydon, whose broad channel is marked by very large red and black wooden posts (red to port, black to starboard when going upriver) and stopped at the northern end to visit the impressive Berney Arms wind pump. This had just had a new cap fitted, and was awaiting its new sails later in the year. The numerous windmills are a familiar and popular feature of the Norfolk Broads area, and several have been beautifully restored.

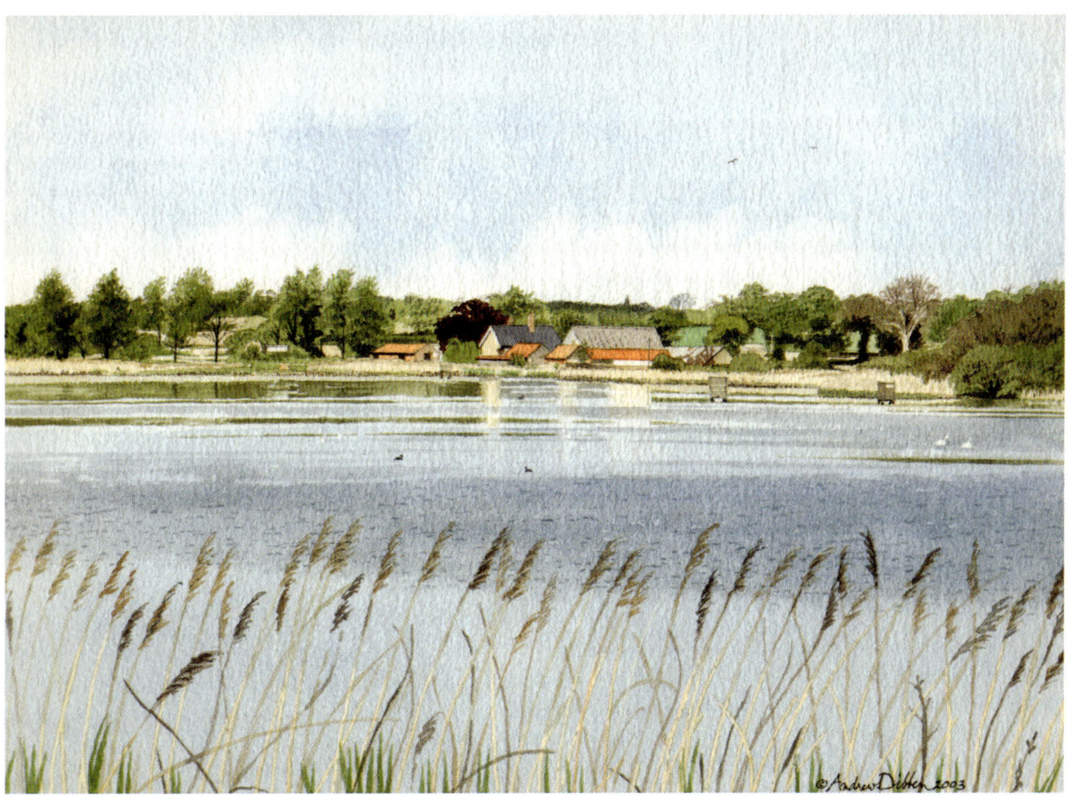

Hardley Flood 9" x 12" 2003

From here, we travelled on up the Yare to visit the attractive village of Reedham, built on a slope overlooking the river, then turned up the narrow and winding river Chet, to stay a night in Loddon. This is a very picturesque village, the staithe (quayside) being sited just downstream of a fine watermill. Another superb sunset followed, but we were woken early next morning by several cockerels, which appeared to live just next to the staithe! I understand that the local authority has since removed them after they attacked a young girl. After exploring a little on foot, we travelled back down the Yare to Reedham, then took the New Cut, a man-made shortcut between the two rivers, through to the River Waveney.

East of Reedham, the Yare flows through marshland, until it arrives at Breydon Water, and the confluence with the Waveney, which, for much of its course, marks the boundary between Norfolk and Suffolk.

Sailing up the Waveney, we stopped at Burgh St Peter marina for lunch and a walk to the quaint little thatched church, with its ziggurat-shaped tower. Continuing upstream, we passed Somerleyton, with its swing-bridge (for the railway) and the very fine Herringfleet wooden smock mill. Near here, we saw a pair of marsh harriers hunting together; they are among the largest British birds of prey, and we were fortunate enough to see several on this trip. The wildlife is another feature of the Broads; we saw over thirty species of birds in our week, most of these being aquatic fowl. Dedicated and knowledgeable birdwatchers would undoubtedly see more.

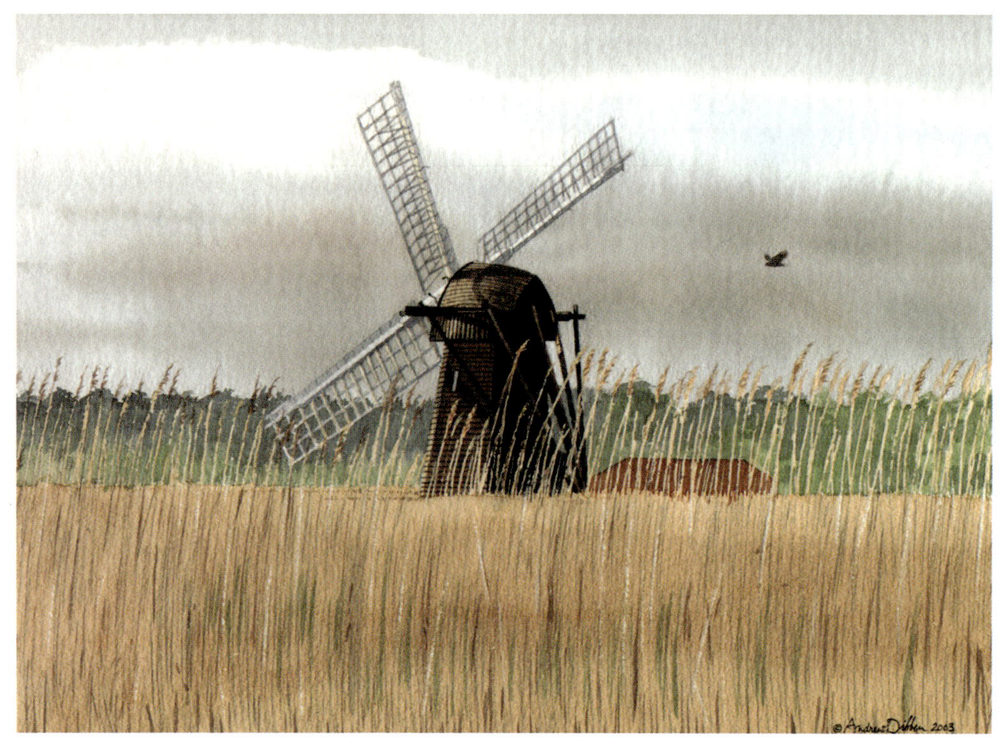

Herringfleet Smock Mill (River Waveney) 9" x 12" 2003

Opposite: **Marsh Harrier** 11½" x 14½" 2003

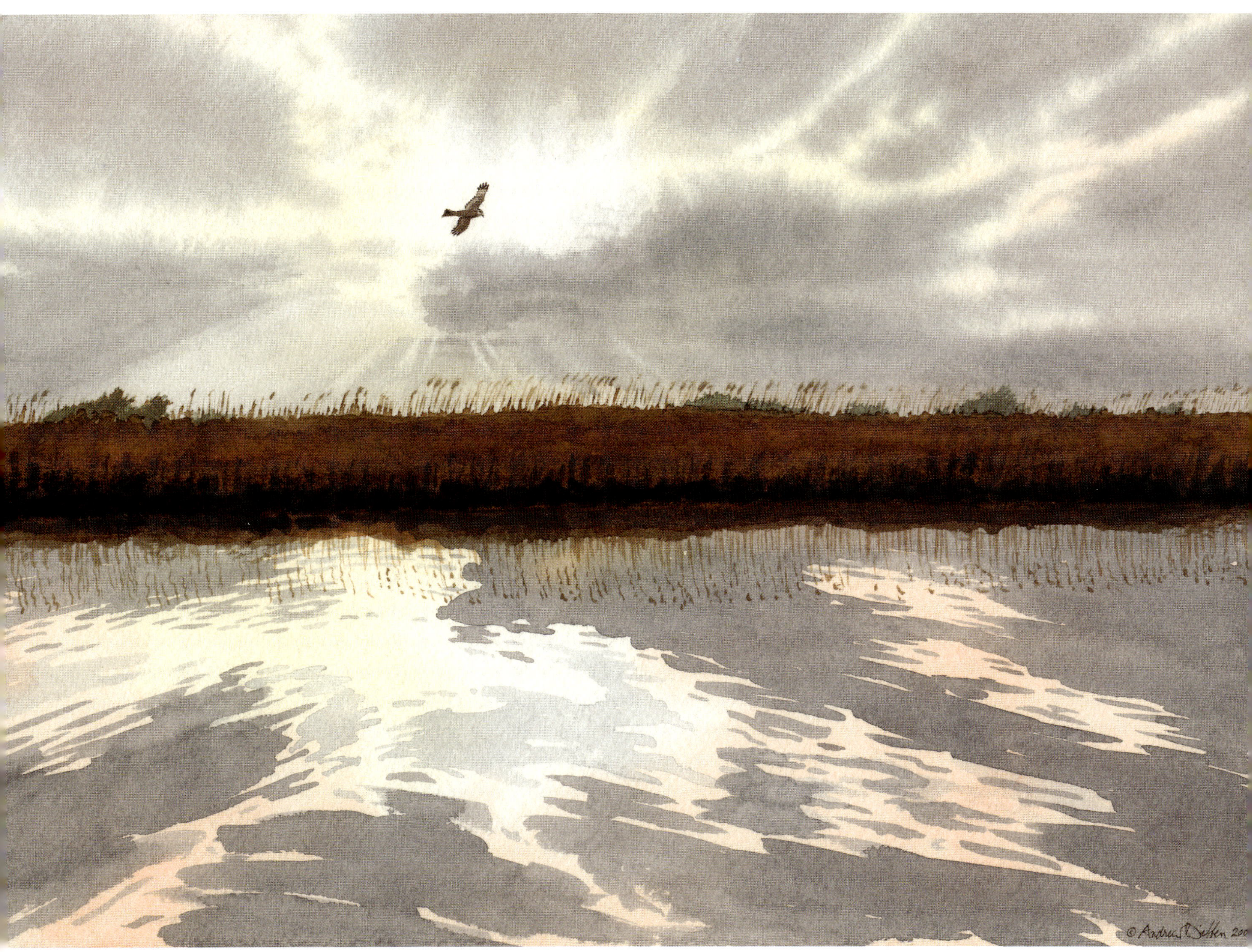

Continuing up the Waveney, we came to the little town of Beccles (on the Suffolk bank of the river), where Ann and I had begun our married life, and motored very slowly through, trying to recognise places we knew. It started to rain here, and since time was short we didn't stop, but turned around to head back towards Great Yarmouth. We stopped for the night in the village of St Olave's, where we enjoyed an excellent meal in the Bell Inn, the oldest pub in Broadland, a lovely half-timbered structure. Just downstream of the low fixed bridge, the *Cariad*, a beautiful 2-masted schooner from Philadelphia, was moored up. Late that night, there was a commotion and bright lights, as a large sea-going cruiser moored up astern of us. We spoke to the owners next morning, and it seemed that their boat needed 11 feet of clearance to pass through the bridge (compared to our 6'6"), so they had been forced to stop and wait for low water in Yarmouth. For the same reason, we hastened on down river so we could pass through the two low bridges at Great Yarmouth, going through Breydon Water once again, and returning to the northern rivers. The trick here is to arrive at the confluence of the two rivers just as the tide is turning; that way, your boat has been carried downriver with very little effort, and similarly, after 'turning the corner', you will be helped upstream by the flooding tide. This procedure is particularly important for the few remaining yachts that have no auxiliary engine, such as those hired out by the County Sailing School at Ludham. For them, getting it wrong involves a good deal of back-breaking work with the 'quant', a long pole with a forked business end, and a shoulder pad at the other; this device is used to propel Broads yachts through bridges (with the mast lowered), or in windless conditions.

Once back on the Bure, and after stopping for water at the yacht station, we continued upriver, this time turning up the River Thurne. We stopped at Potter Heigham, where the bridge is so frighteningly low and narrow that in fact you are obliged to use the services of a Bridge Pilot to go through. This service is free to hire-craft users, as the Hire Industry reckons it is cheaper to offer the service than to continually repair their boats! The gauge at the side of the bridge appeared to read no more than 6' 8" when we moored. I strolled over to the Pilot's office, and asked whether it would be possible to go through that afternoon. 'What's the name of your boat?' he asked. '*Broadland Moon II*,' I replied, adding 'It says 6'6" air draught by the helm.' He took a great fat book, with the records of all 1200 hire boats, and looked up our craft. 'Well, it says 6' 7" here,' he said, showing me the hand amended inscription on the page. 'Well, it should just about be all right; we'll give it a go, shall we?' he said casually. Butterflies fluttered in my stomach.

We walked back to the boat, and he asked us to untie her (before even having started the engine!) then took hold of the controls, and headed us for the middle of the river. "Right, can you slide the roof back, and you and your wife stand up here in the saloon please," he asked, explaining that bringing everybody forward helped to lower the boat's highest point, the windscreen. We complied, and then he put the engine to a moderate speed, stood squarely on the centre-line of the boat, and headed for the tiny arch, one hand on the wheel making jerky little corrections this way and that, until we were feet from the bridge and there was no possible way back; the corners of the flimsy windscreen frame cleared the 500-year old stonework by about 2 inches each side! "There you are," he said with a little smile, "just drop me off over there, would you?" On the way back, the next day, we had a different Pilot, but, it was the same courteous service; one got the impression that they loved their work, although as he told us, it gets really busy at times as there are only certain times of the day when the water is low enough, and there can be as many as 100 boats to take through on some days.

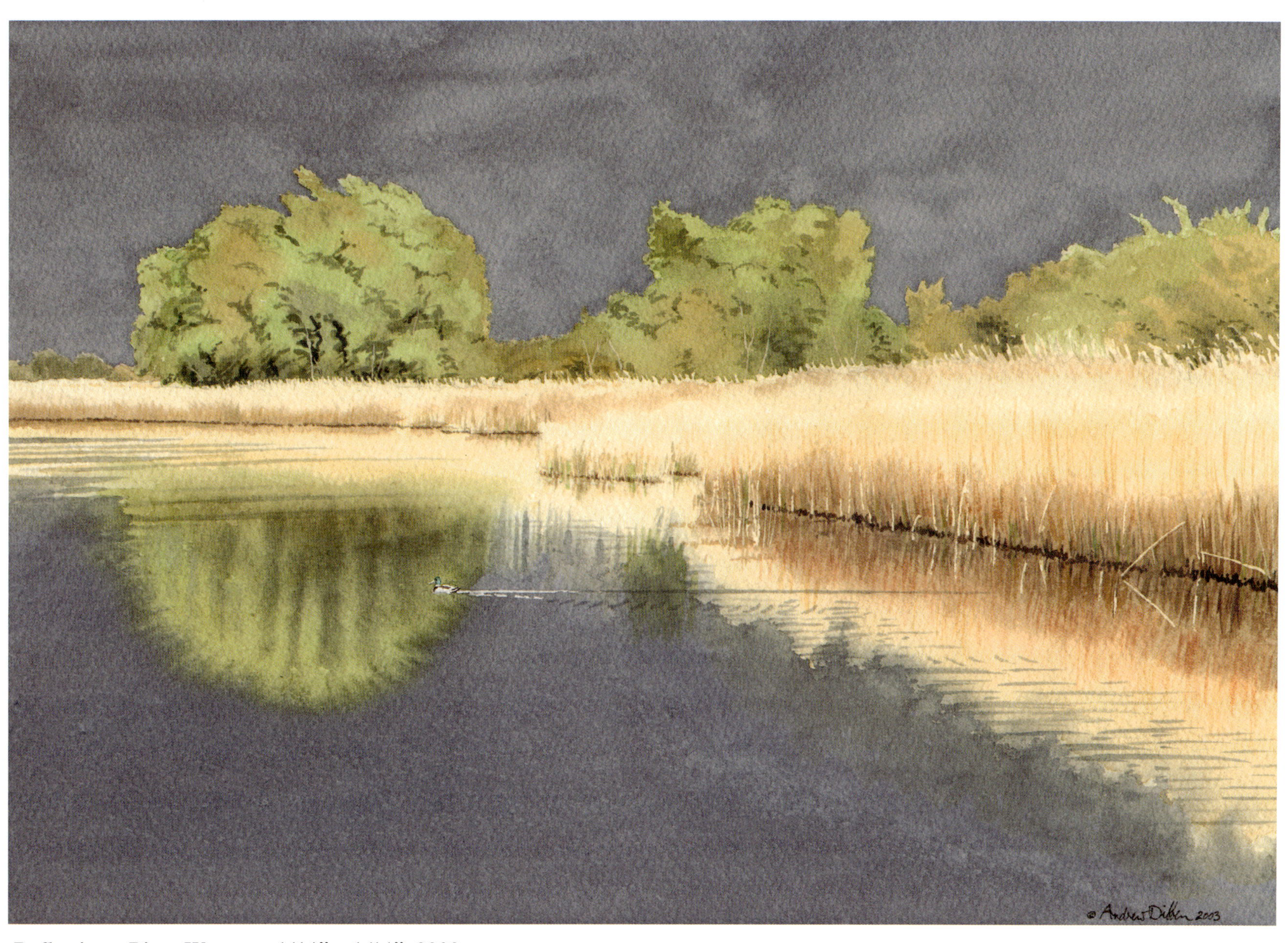

Reflections, River Waveney 11½" x 14½" 2003

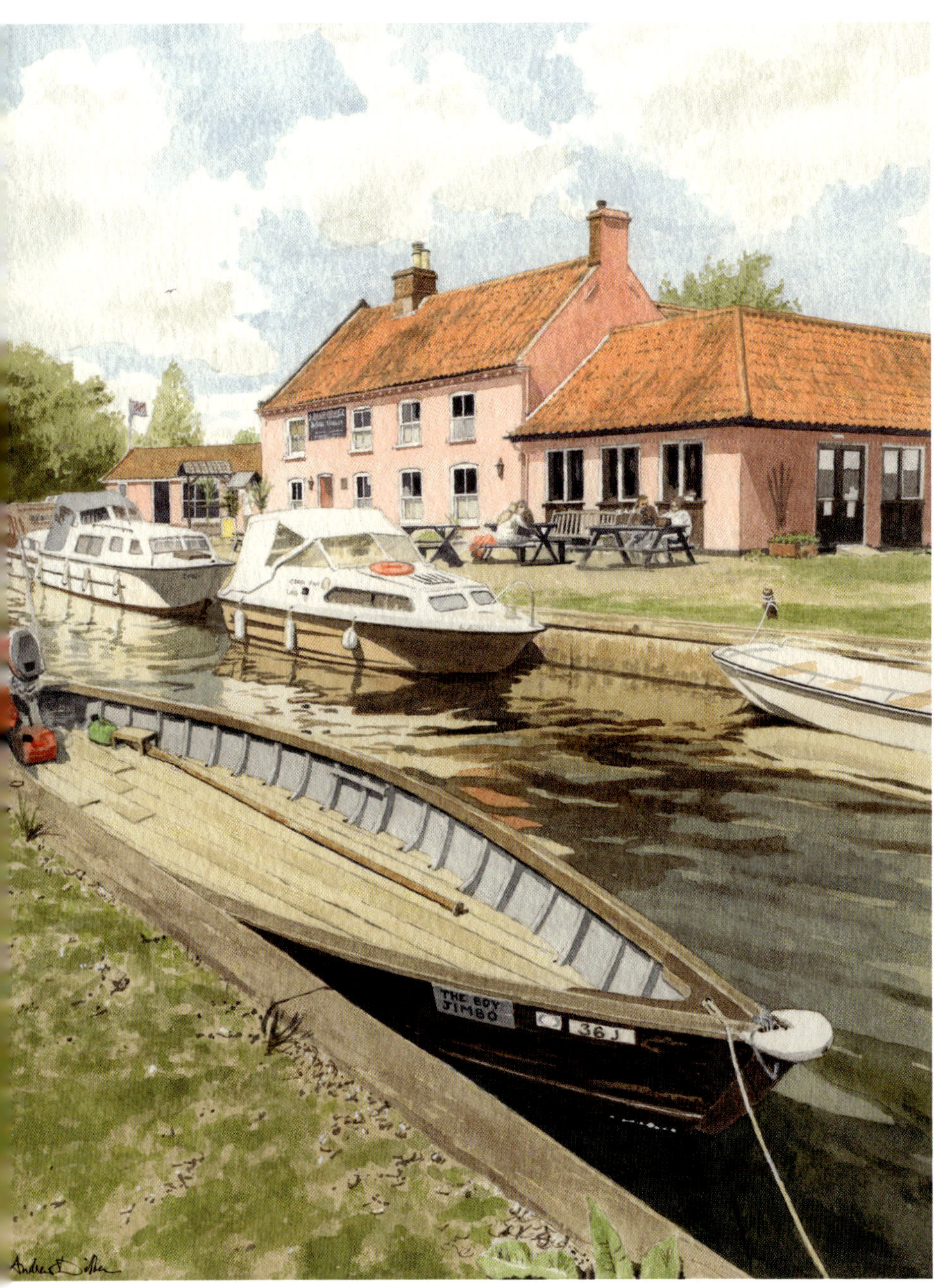

The Pleasure Boat Inn, Hickling 14¹/₂" x 11¹/₂" 2005

From Potter Heigham, we continued up the Thurne until reaching the fork near Martham, where you can either go up to Martham and West Somerton, or to Hickling Broad and Horsey Mere. We decided to make for West Somerton, as we had never been there by river, and stop there for the night. Another lovely sunset followed. Next morning, we realised how incredibly clear the water is here. One of the problems in the Broads today is water quality; fertilizer run-off from nearby farms, and innumerable propellers stirring the mud, have resulted in rather murky water in most places. Huge efforts have recently been made to clean Barton Broad, with hundreds of tons of silt pumped out, and effluent being diverted away. But here the water looked as clear and pure as in a new aquarium; we peered down at the lush fronds of water weed, and soon spotted hundreds of tiny fish, then slightly larger ones, and finally, a couple of young pike waiting to ambush the small fry. Seeing these defenceless creatures, it is worrying to think about how precarious an environment all this is; the sea is very close to the Broads system at this point, a mile or so north-eastwards beyond flat farmland and a fragile dune. It would be so easy for a big storm-driven tidal surge to break through to the Broads again; it happened in 1953, and there was a near repeat in 1978. Even assuming that the damage to the protective bank or the dunes is not too great, it still takes years for the freshwater environment to recover. Then there is also the projected rise in sea levels to consider.

Setting off again, we headed up for Hickling Broad, the largest of the Broads, and also the wildest. The approach to the Broad, known as Heigham Sound, is gorgeous, with such vast horizons, and great golden reed-beds swaying gently in the breeze. Many boats cannot pass under Potter Heigham bridge, so that restricts the traffic a bit up here, although at weekends, there can be quite a lot of yachts and dinghies racing on the Broad.

It was almost lunchtime by the time we reached the far end of the Broad, and most of the racers had stopped for a liquid lunch at the Pleasure Boat Inn in the village of Hickling. We headed for the same place, mooring up in the dyke before going for a very pleasant exploratory walk. There are many thatched houses and boat-houses here, as well as a large sail-less windmill; it is all quite picturesque. We indulged in a drink and some nuts and crisps in the very homely inn, and then returned to the boat to start back for our appointment with the tide at Potter Heigham Bridge.

Once safely through the bridge, we spent an idle half-hour going round Latham's store, then looked at the boats which were on sale in Herbert Woods' yard, before untying again to wend our way downstream and back to the Bure. We passed the two windmills at Thurne, and I took numerous photographs, then we turned right, up the Bure, and on as far as the confluence with the Ant, with just a short detour to the lovely South Walsham Broad. There are two parts to this broad, divided by a constriction in the land; passing through the 'straits', one arrives in the privately owned inner broad. Navigation is permitted here, but no mooring. There are woods all around the broad, and the grounds of the Fairhaven Gardens slope picturesquely down to the water's edge, making it worth a detour.

Thurne Windpump 14½" x 10½" 2005
This Broads landmark was rescued from dereliction in 1955 by Mr R.D. Morse, and the sails were replaced in 1962. I had the pleasure of meeting Mr Morse sixteen years ago, when I was sitting in front of the mill, sketching it. He came to see what I was doing and made some very generous comments about my scruffy drawing; what a delightful gentleman!

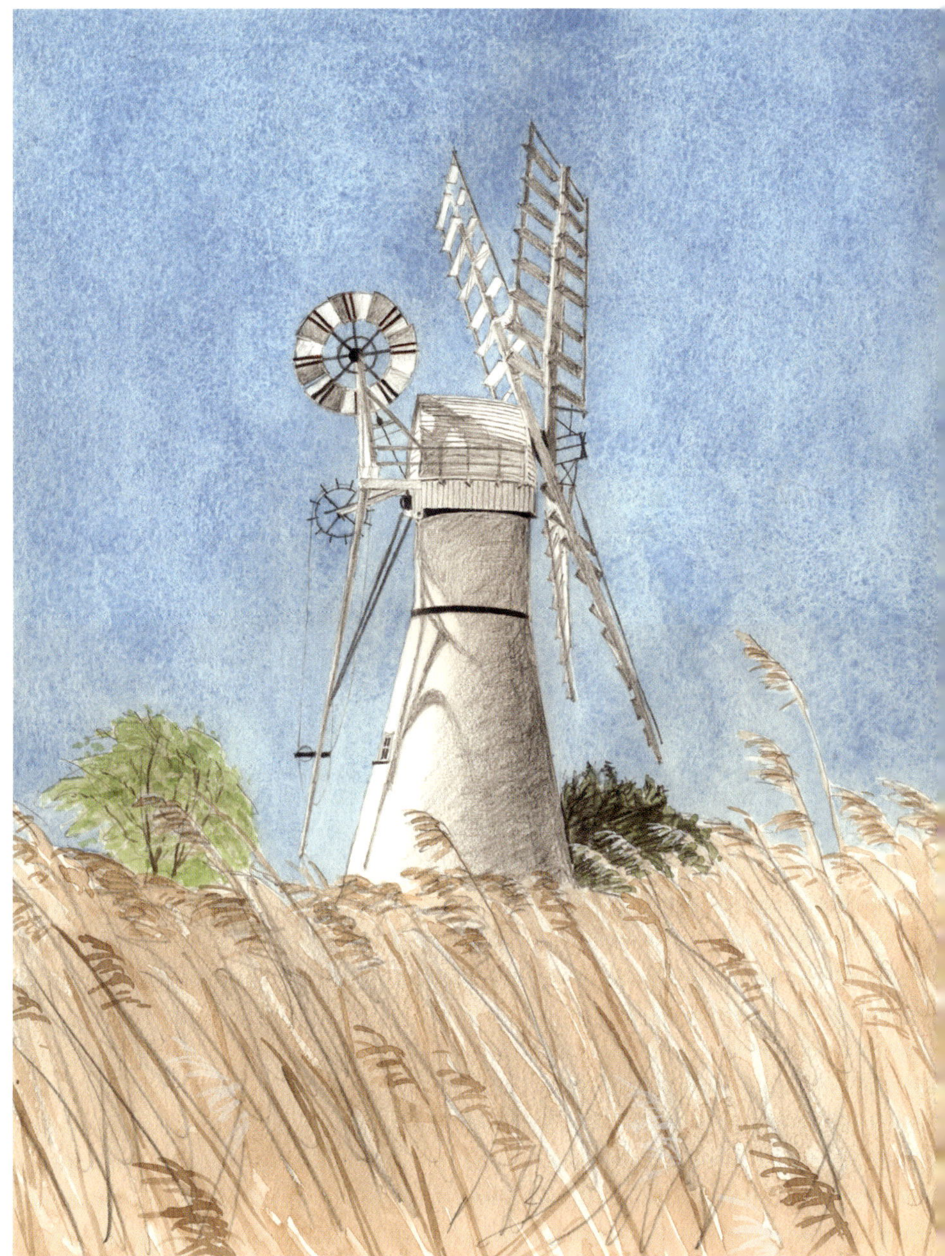

We had planned to stay the night at the village of Neatishead, which is very pretty, but there was no vacant mooring to be found, and so we dropped our mud-weight (substitute for an anchor – which is not legal on the Broads) close to the entrance to Barton Broad, in a nicely sheltered, tree-lined spot. And so here we had our last meal aboard, as the next morning we were to hand the boat back to the yard in Stalham.

On returning home, the house seemed bigger than before we left; the bathroom particularly, which I have always felt was rather small, at first seemed remarkably spacious! It's just another of the benefits of a boating holiday.

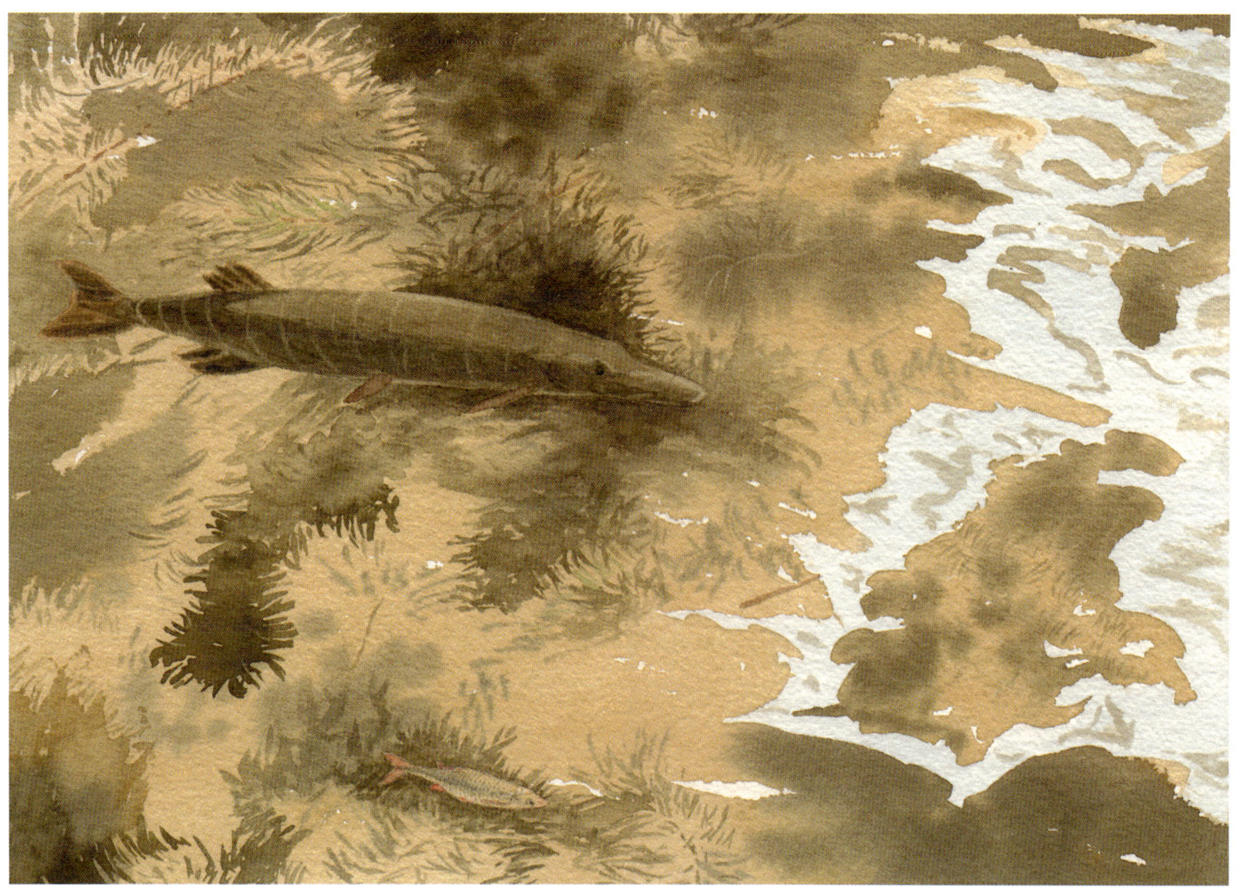

Jack Pike and Small Fry 11½" x 14½" 2004

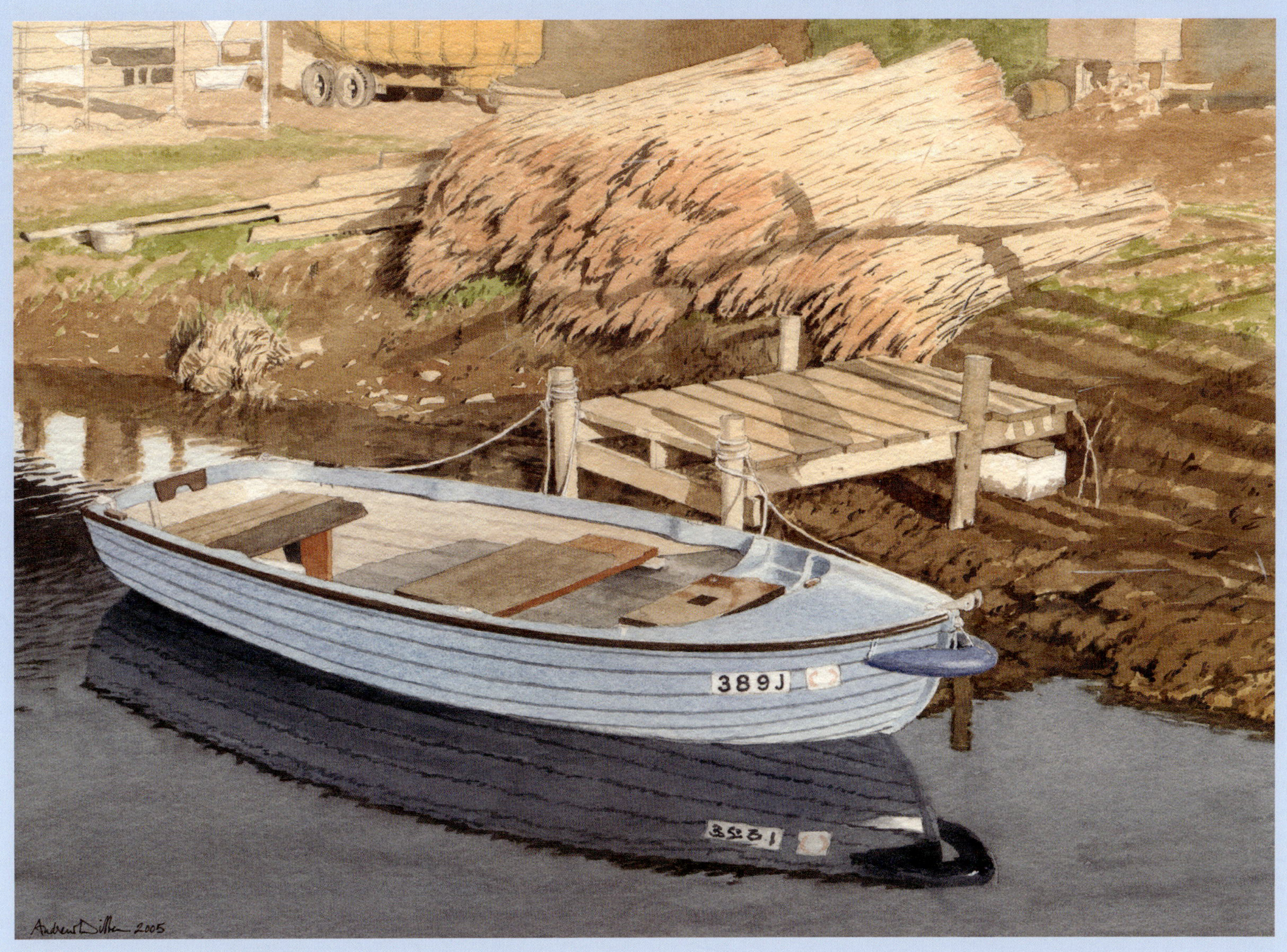

The Reed Harvest, Martham 11½" x 14½" 2005

A HERON FISHING

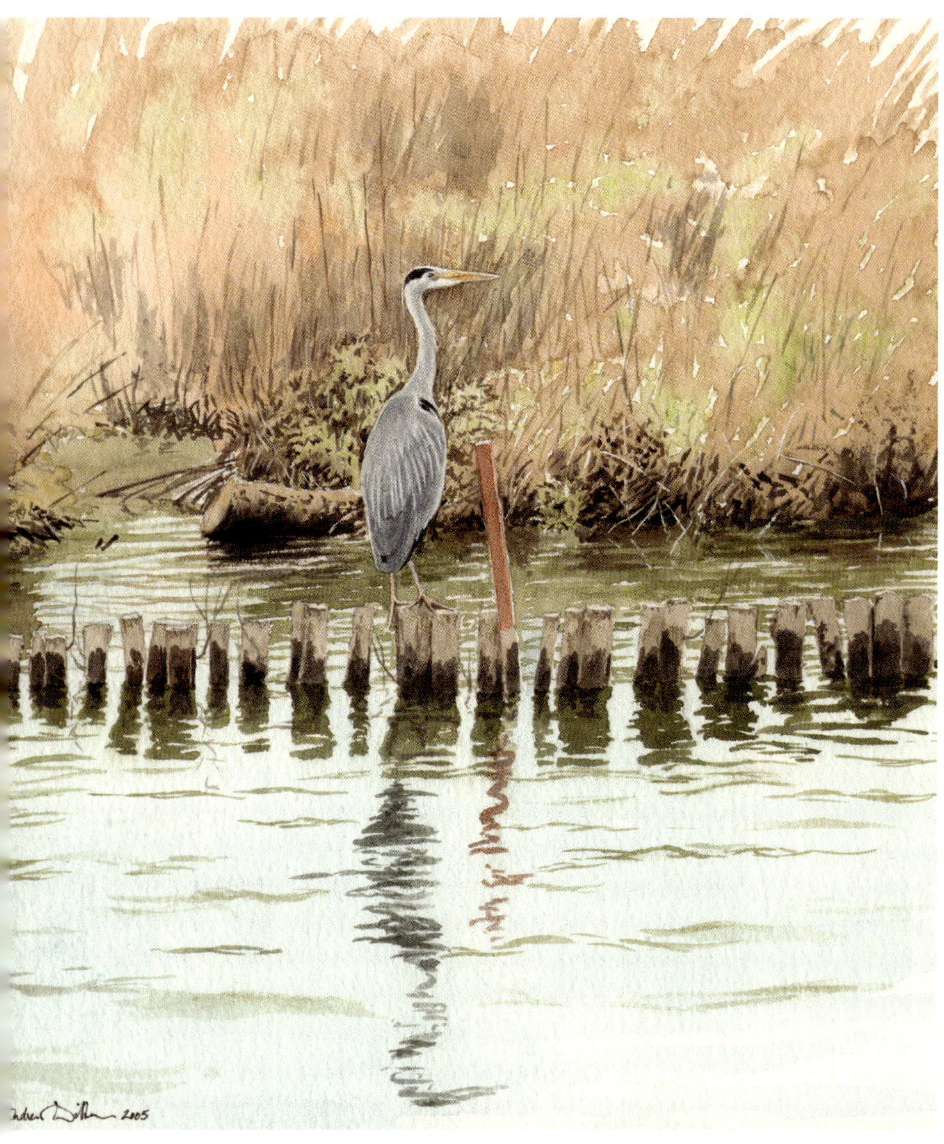

The sight of a heron waiting patiently for a fish to come close enough for it to pounce is one that is familiar to all who visit the Broads. Despite being relatively common, they are still a magnificent sight, especially when they take off revealing the full extent of their huge wingspan. They are certainly more welcome among fishermen than the increasingly common cormorant, a large and somewhat evil-looking black bird with a voracious appetite for fish. Normally sea-going birds, cormorants have taken increasingly to fresh waters in recent years in their quest for food.

Martham Broad is no longer an open expanse of water in the way one expects a 'Broad' to be, being little more than a wide channel. Nonetheless, it is a delightful place; a peaceful backwater with excellent water quality and abundant wildlife, set in the midst of great expanses of swaying reeds.

Left: *Heron Fishing* 12" x 10½" 2005

Opposite: *Martham Broad* 11" x 14½" 2004

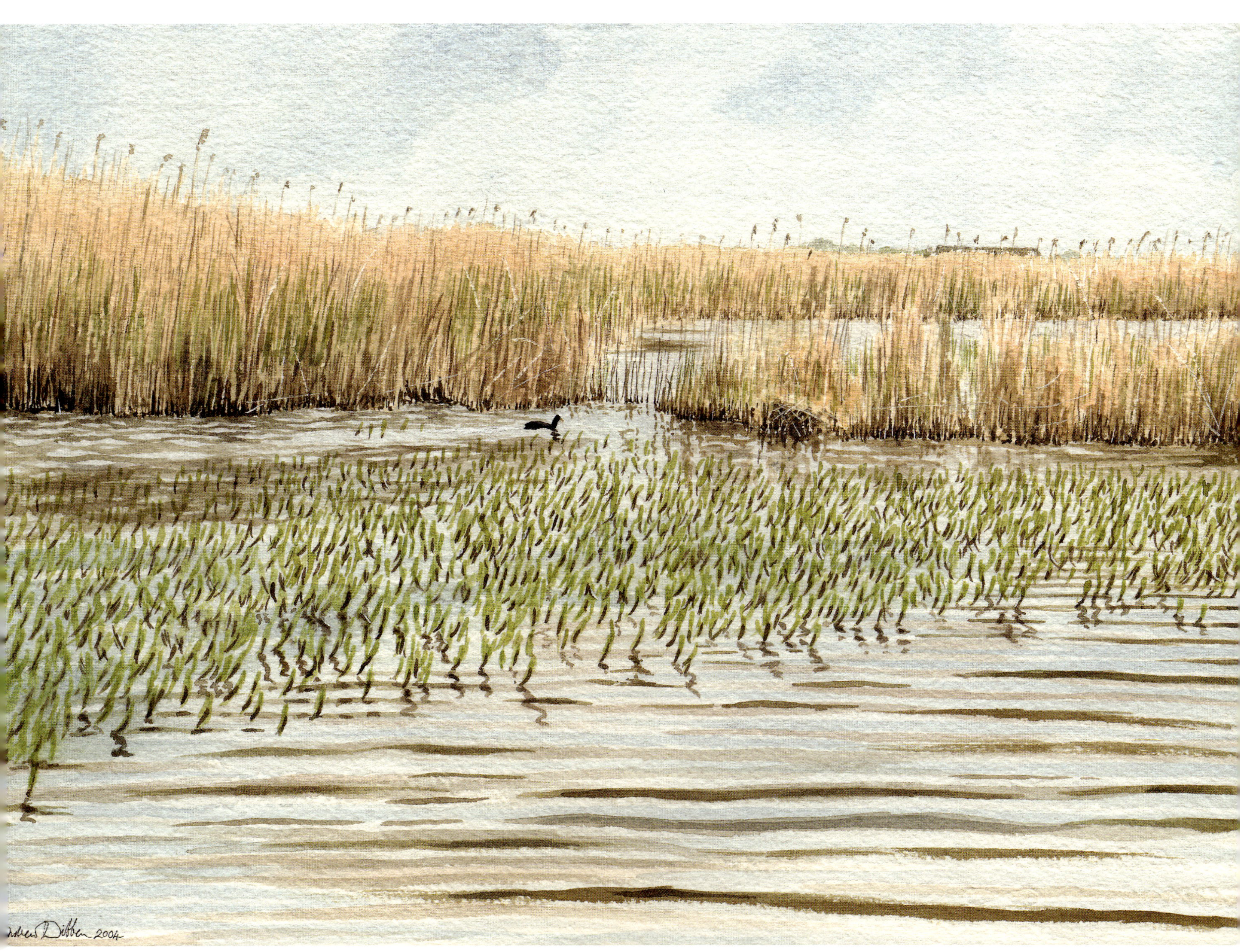

SAILING ON THE BROADS

This is *Wood Anemone*, a typical Norfolk Broads yacht from the renowned County Sailing Base, at Ludham. Many of the Ludham boats have no auxiliary engine, and rely on the crew's skill to keep them moving in all conditions. Broads yachts are perfectly adapted to the local environment, having evolved over more than a century into this highly ingenious general shape. The rig maximises the mainsail area while avoiding an unwieldy tall mast, which would cause problems when 'shooting' bridges. However, a topsail can be rigged, filling the triangular area left between the yard and mast, and rising higher than the mast, thus giving the boat even more sail area for light airs, and catching the breeze above the branches in tree-lined stretches of river. The small foresail, with a jib-boom at the base, allows more efficient tacking on the rivers. The mast is pivoted just above the cabin coach-roof, and counter-balanced at its foot. A long narrow hatch in the fore-deck allows the mast foot to swing up when the mast is lowered. Lastly, the cabin coach-roof rises on canvas sides, rather like a concertina, to give more headroom when moored up.

The Norfolk Punt is another locally evolved class, developed for pure speed. Slender bodied, and with a tall, powerful rig, the boat depends on the crew's agility on the trapeze to provide the all-important human ballast.

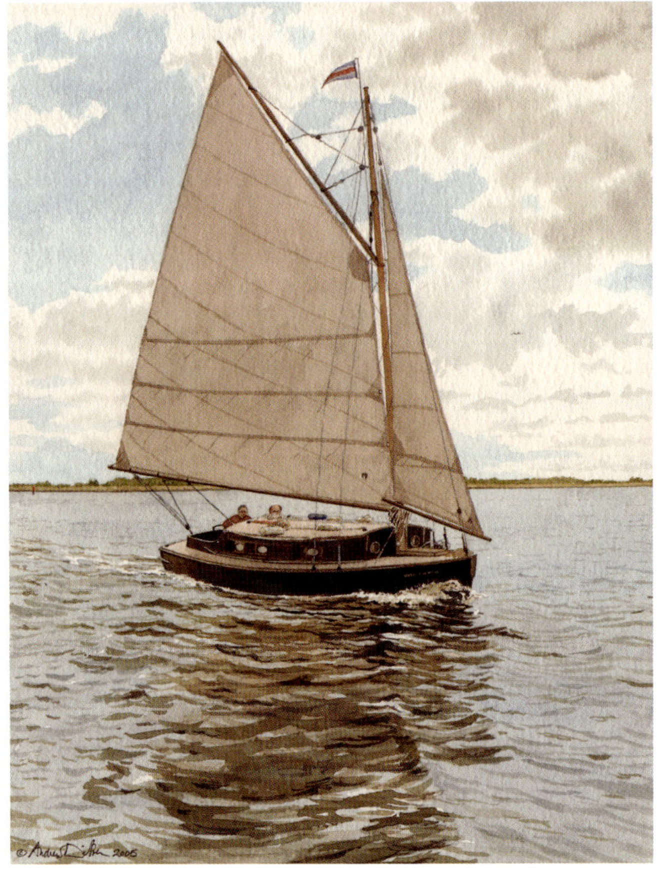

Right: Wood Anemone *on Hickling Broad*
14" x 11" 2005

Far right: *A Norfolk Punt on Hickling Broad*
14" x 11" 2005

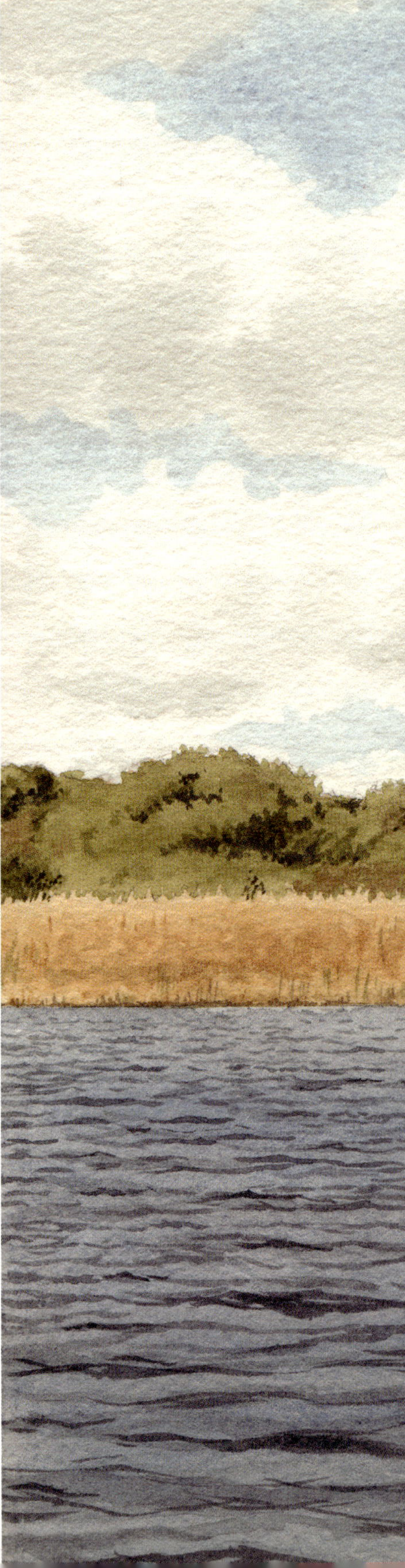

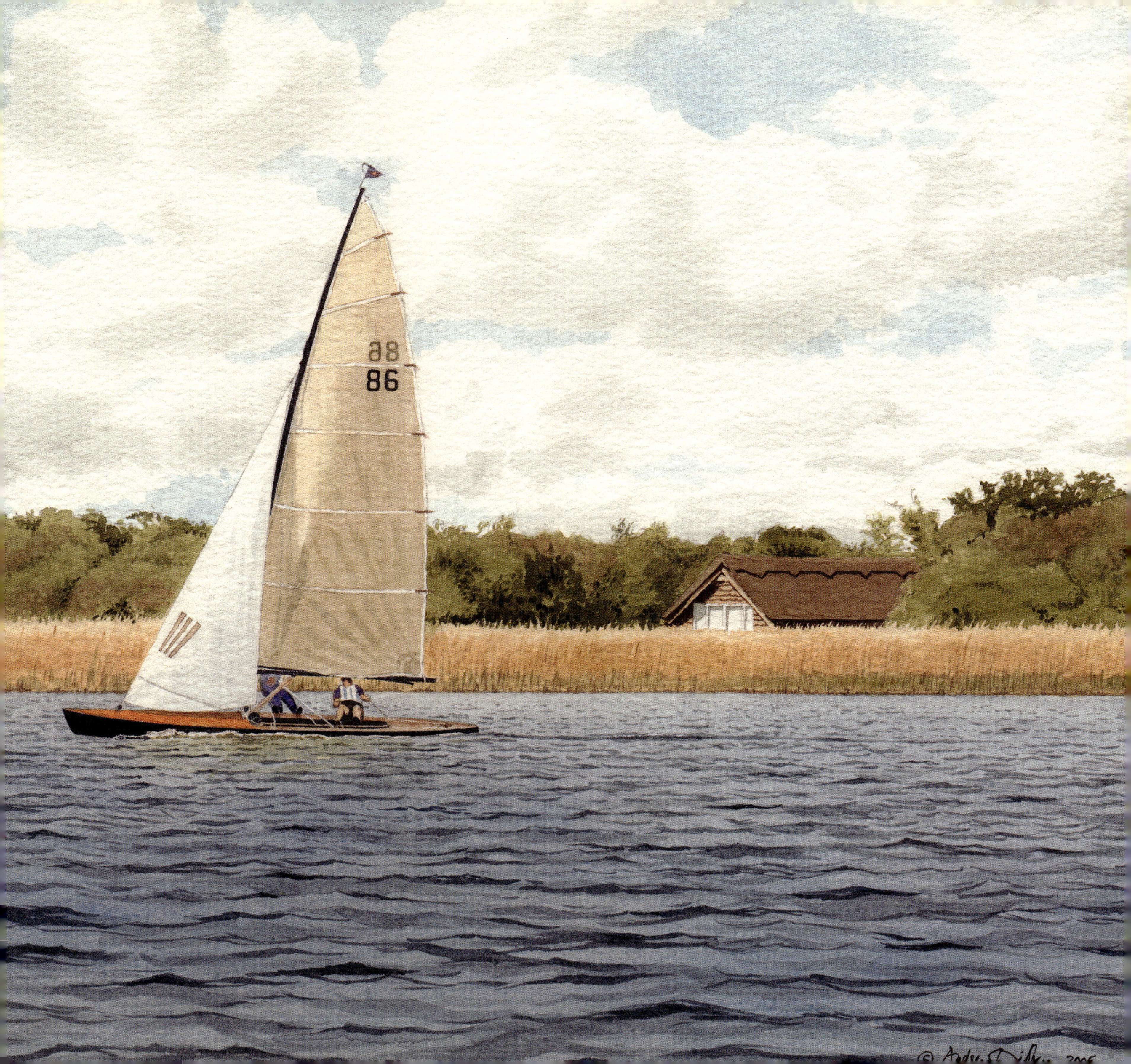

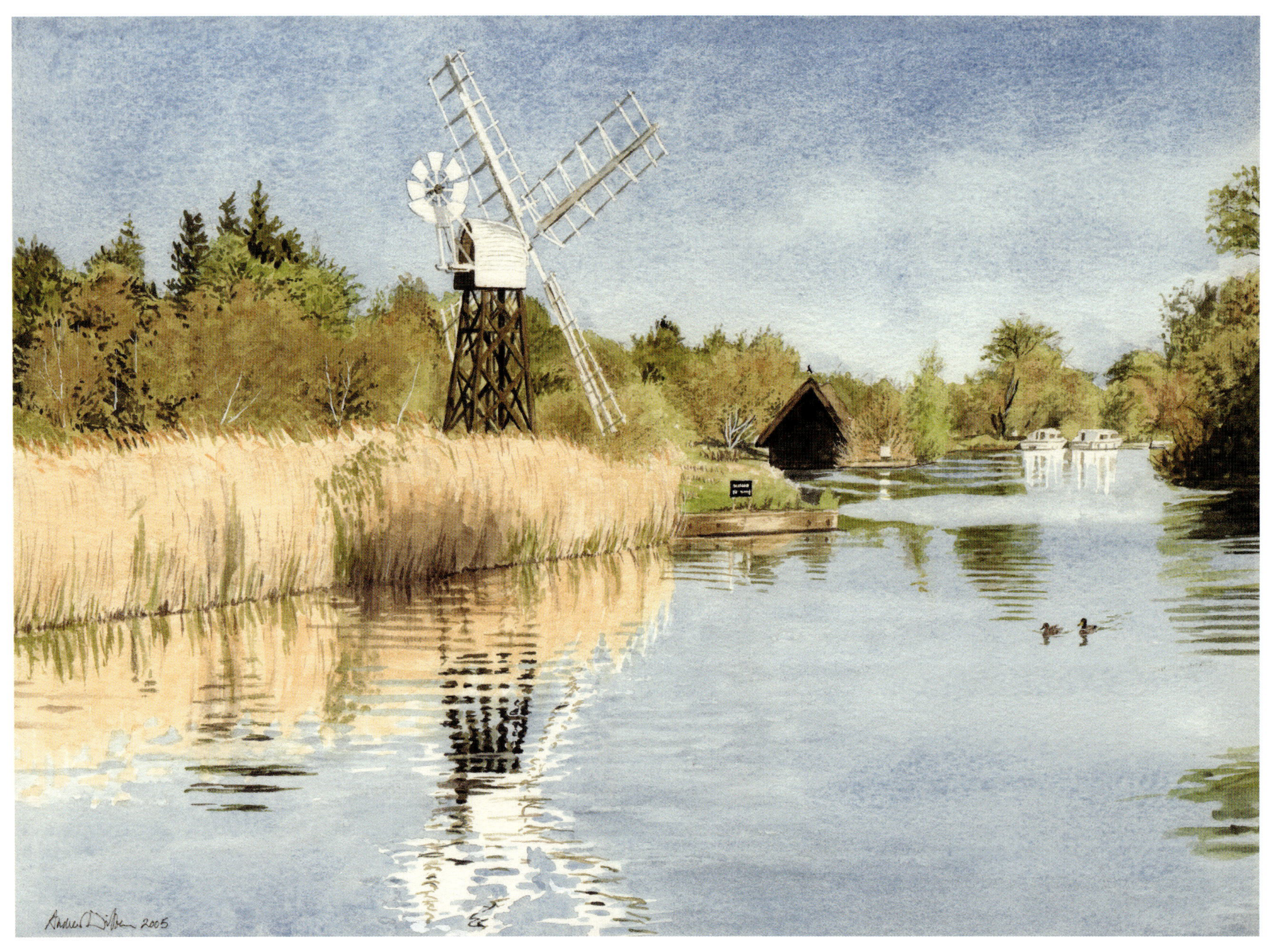

Boardman's Mill, How Hill 14½" x 10½" 2005

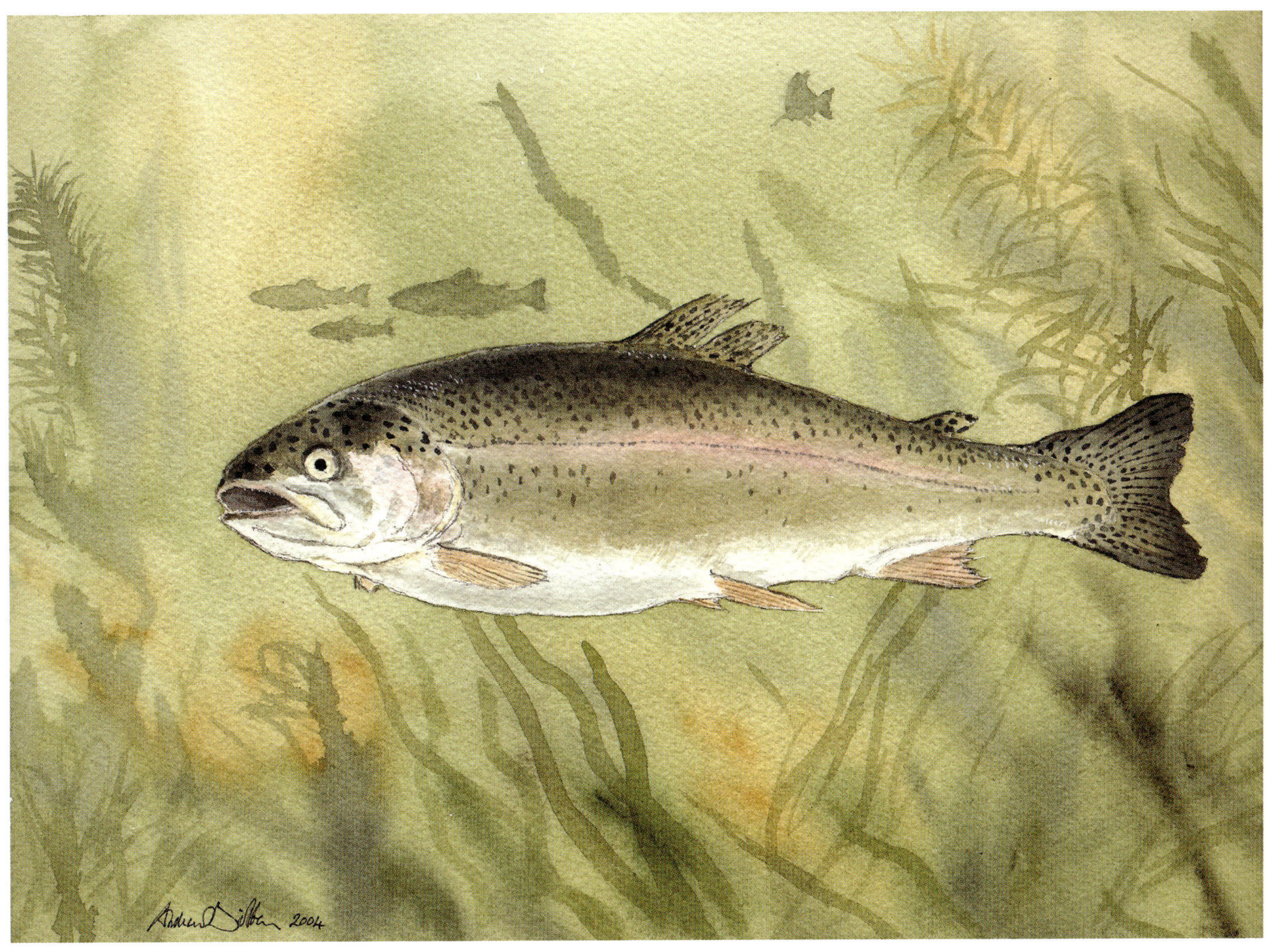

Rainbow Trout 11" x 14½" 2004

This fish has nothing to do with the Broads really! This is a portrait of a rainbow trout caught at Swanton Morley by my neighbour. He has given me a number of trout in recent years, and I decided to paint a picture of one of them to thank him. I found the subtle shape extremely difficult to render accurately, but an interesting exercise. The dorsal fin of this specimen appears to have been attacked at some point. There are a great many stocked fishing lakes in Norfolk, most of which are the result of excavation of sand and shingle for the aggregates industry.

WATERMILLS AND UPPER REACHES

Amazingly, for such a reputedly flat county, there were some 580 watermills in use in Norfolk in the eleventh century; this fact alone helps to illustrate the watery nature of the county. At the time of writing, only 52 mills remain standing, and just 20 of those still retain any of their machinery. There is only one working watermill remaining in Norfolk, and that is the one at Letheringsett, on the river Glaven. Most mills had stopped working by the nineteenth century, due to the advent of steam and then electric power, which meant that machinery could be positioned anywhere, rather than having to be by a river, or on top of a hill in the case of windmills. Most of the remaining watermills have now been turned into very desirable houses or apartments, highly sought after thanks to their attractive clapboarding and enviable river views. The very attractive mill at Buxton has recently been restored, and converted from a restaurant into housing.

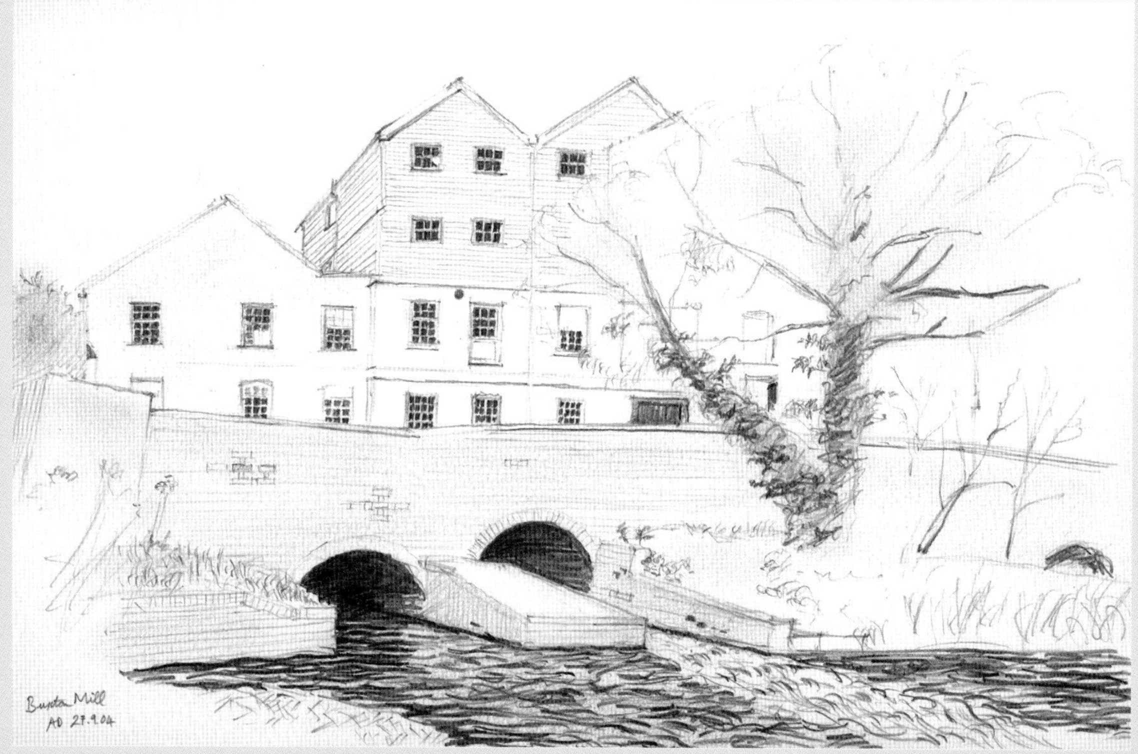

Buxton Mill Pencil Sketch 7" x 10" 2004

Opposite: ***Buxton Mill and Tail-Race*** Charcoal and Pastel 33" x 23½" 2005

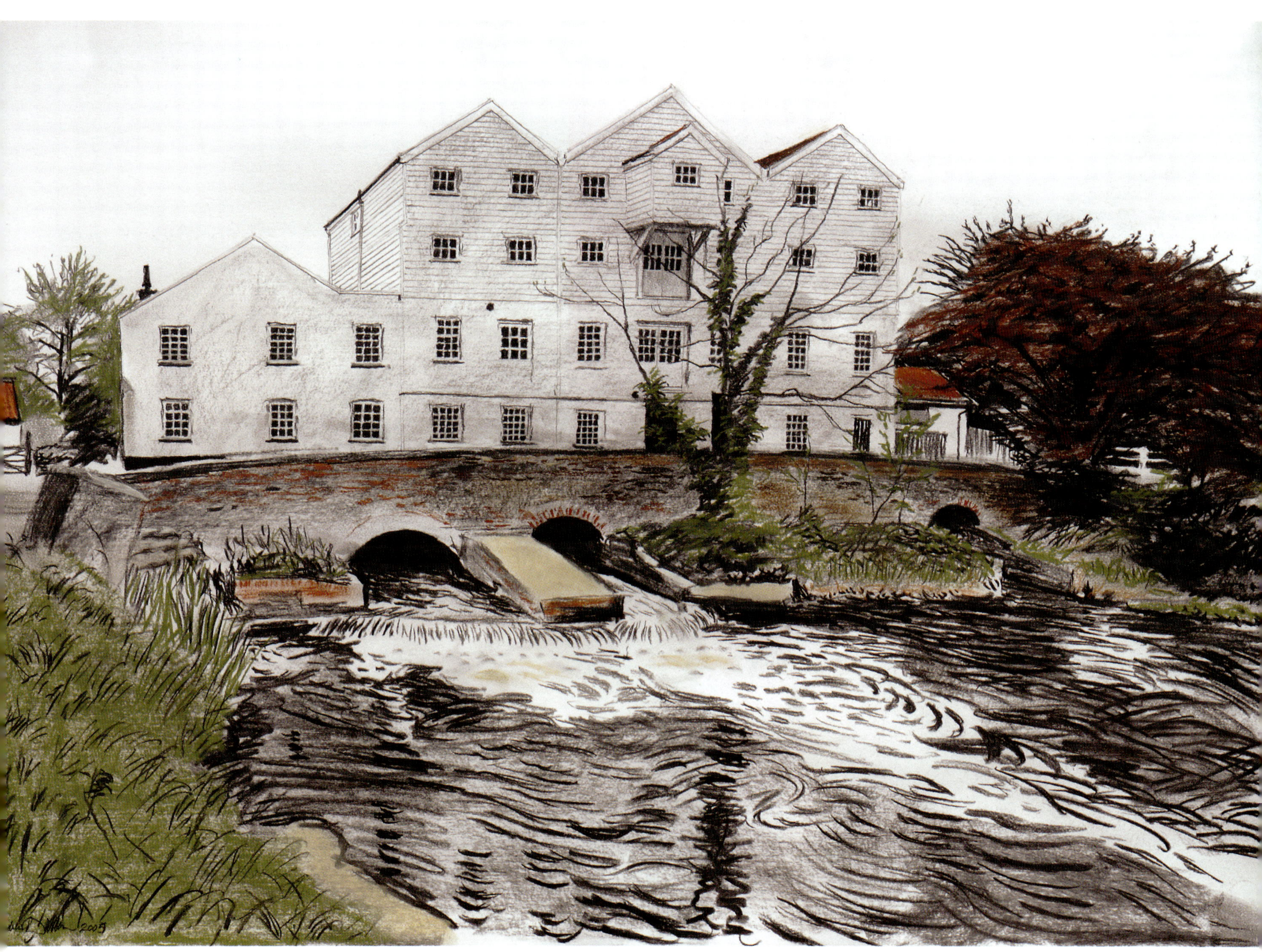

Bintree Mill

I decided in 2003 that it would be interesting to do a series of studies of watermills, but, with various other projects ongoing, I didn't really pursue the idea until the following year; even then, progress was rather spasmodic. Finally, early in 2005, I made a determined effort, and took myself back to Bintree Mill, on the River Wensum, where I had made a pencil and wash study in September 2004, and made a series of sketches over several days. The landscape here is particularly attractive, the river valley having fairly steep sides, so that the mill buildings are viewed against a backdrop of high ground. Together with the lovely sound of cascading water, it is all quite enchanting, and further enhanced by the very pleasant manner of the delightful landowner, Paul Seaman, who assured me that I could visit whenever I liked, and go anywhere. Although some of the days were very cold, I was lucky to have at least a brief glimpse of sunshine every day; this helps a great deal with depicting the modelling of buildings, especially when they are all white! The overhanging gantry (or 'lucam') on the end of the mill, together with its supporting struts, casts a marvellous shadow in mid-afternoon. Bintree was used by the BBC, with various temporary alterations, for the filming of *The Mill on the Floss* in 1996.

The joy with watermills is the marvellous juxtaposition of a rugged old building with a powerful watercourse. Mills were often positioned where there was a change of gradient in the riverbed, and sometimes an embankment was created to make a millpond. On the downstream side, there is rushing water at the exit from the mill (the 'tail-race'), and frequently a waterfall or sluice nearby where excess water in the millpond can be released downriver in times of spate. Wonderful patterns of swirling waters are created, which add greatly to the visual feast.

I wanted to try various media on a fairly large scale, including charcoal, which is an expressive medium that encourages a less detailed pernickety approach that I yearn to develop. It is surprising just how attractive a picture can be when produced with what is essentially a piece of burned wood! Charcoal comes in a graded range of diameters, in sticks about six inches long; with the side of a fat stick, it is possible to cover a large area quite quickly, smearing it with the fingertips to produce an even, medium tone, pressing hard to make black marks, or sharpening the tip with a knife to produce fine lines of remarkable delicacy. The other medium that I have mixed into some of the pictures in this series is pastel; by spraying the charcoal drawing with fixative, it is then possible to add colour with pastels over the top. Sometimes I worked charcoal into the pastel again afterwards to give stronger darks. This is a very messy process, which should really not be attempted in a carpeted living room, but it is fine for outdoor use!

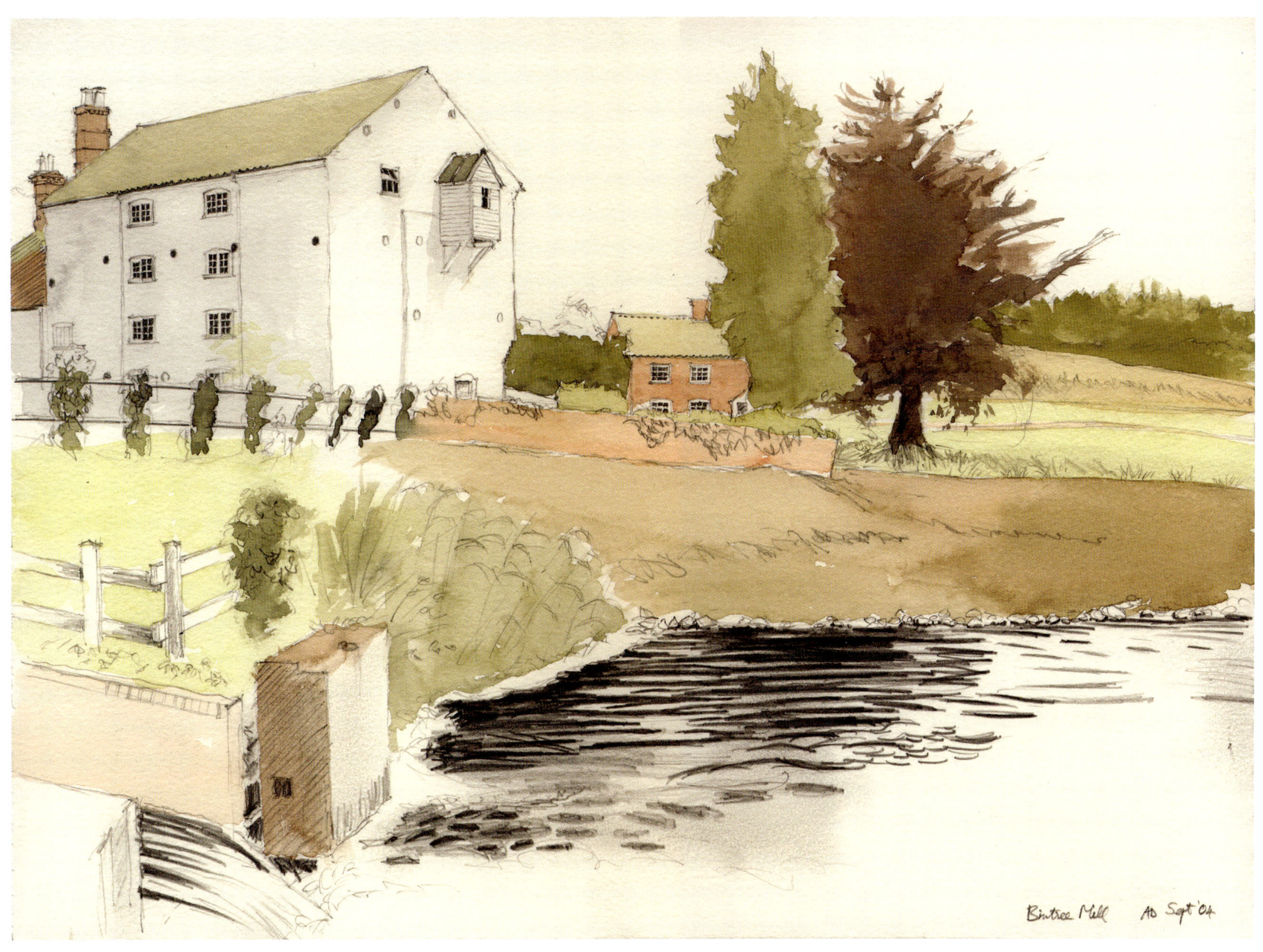

Bintree Mill (Pencil and Wash from sketchbook) 14½" x 11" 2004

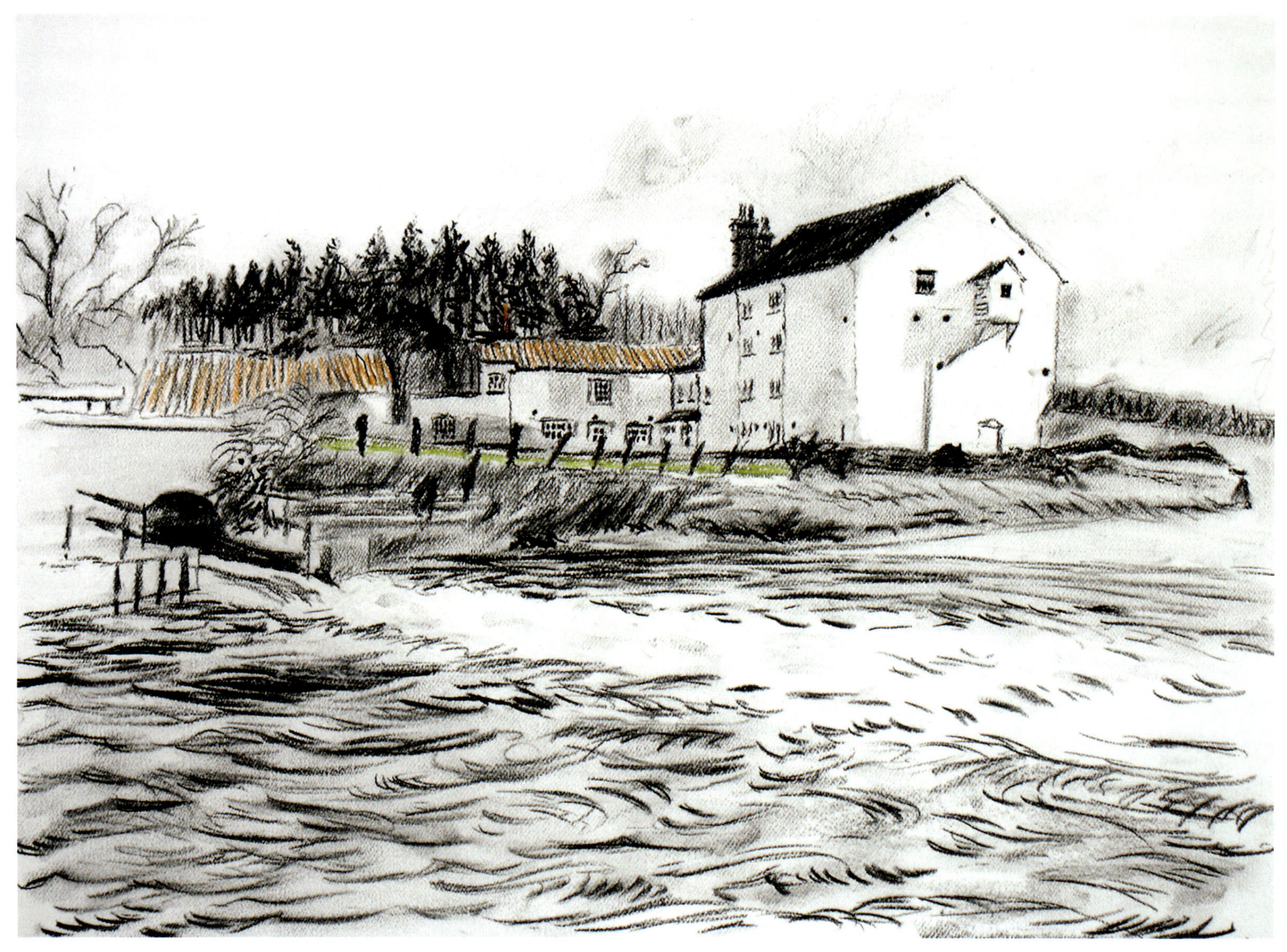

Bintree Mill (Charcoal and Pastel) 26" x 19" 2005

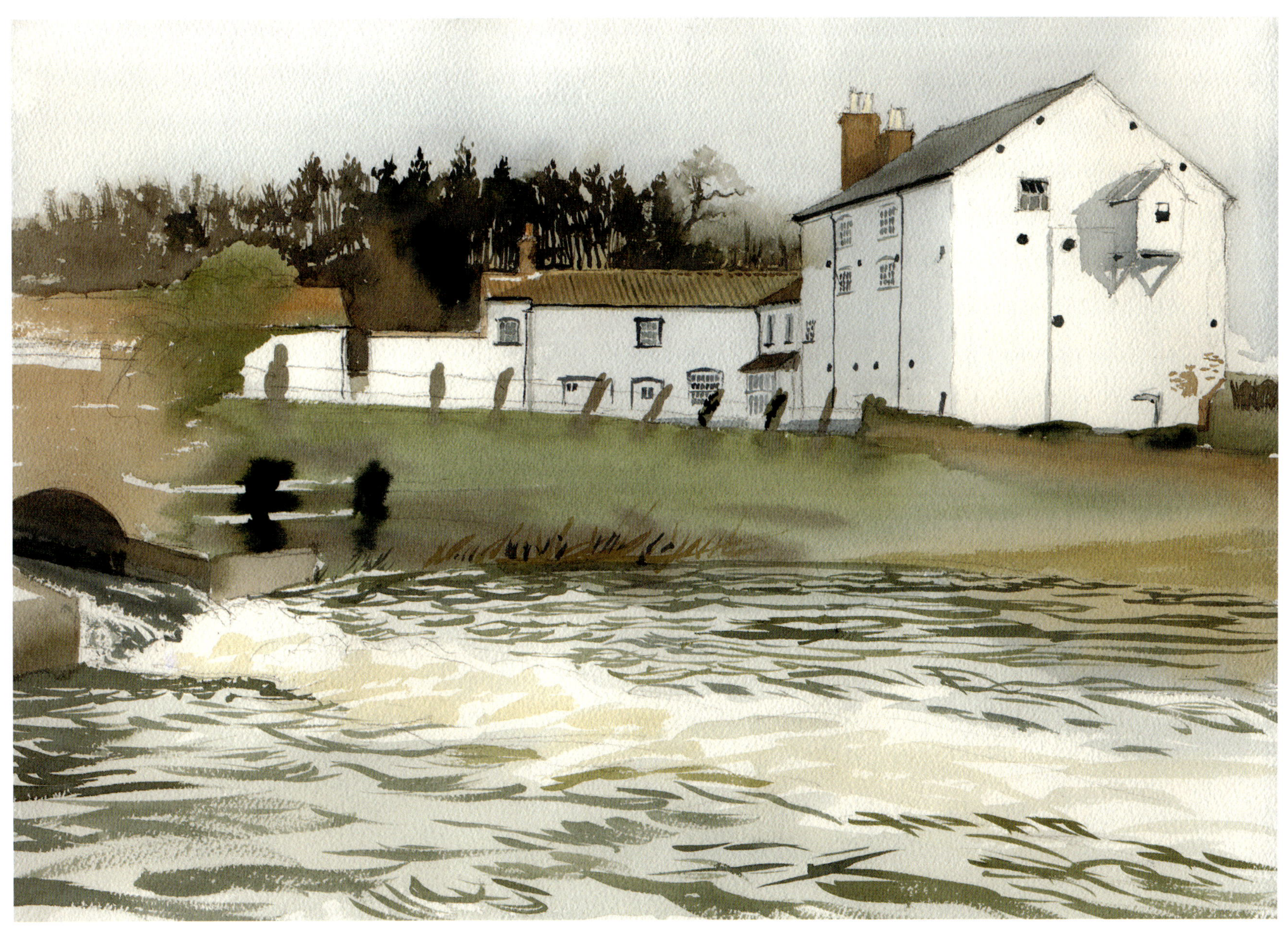

Bintree Mill II Watercolour 14" x 20" 2005

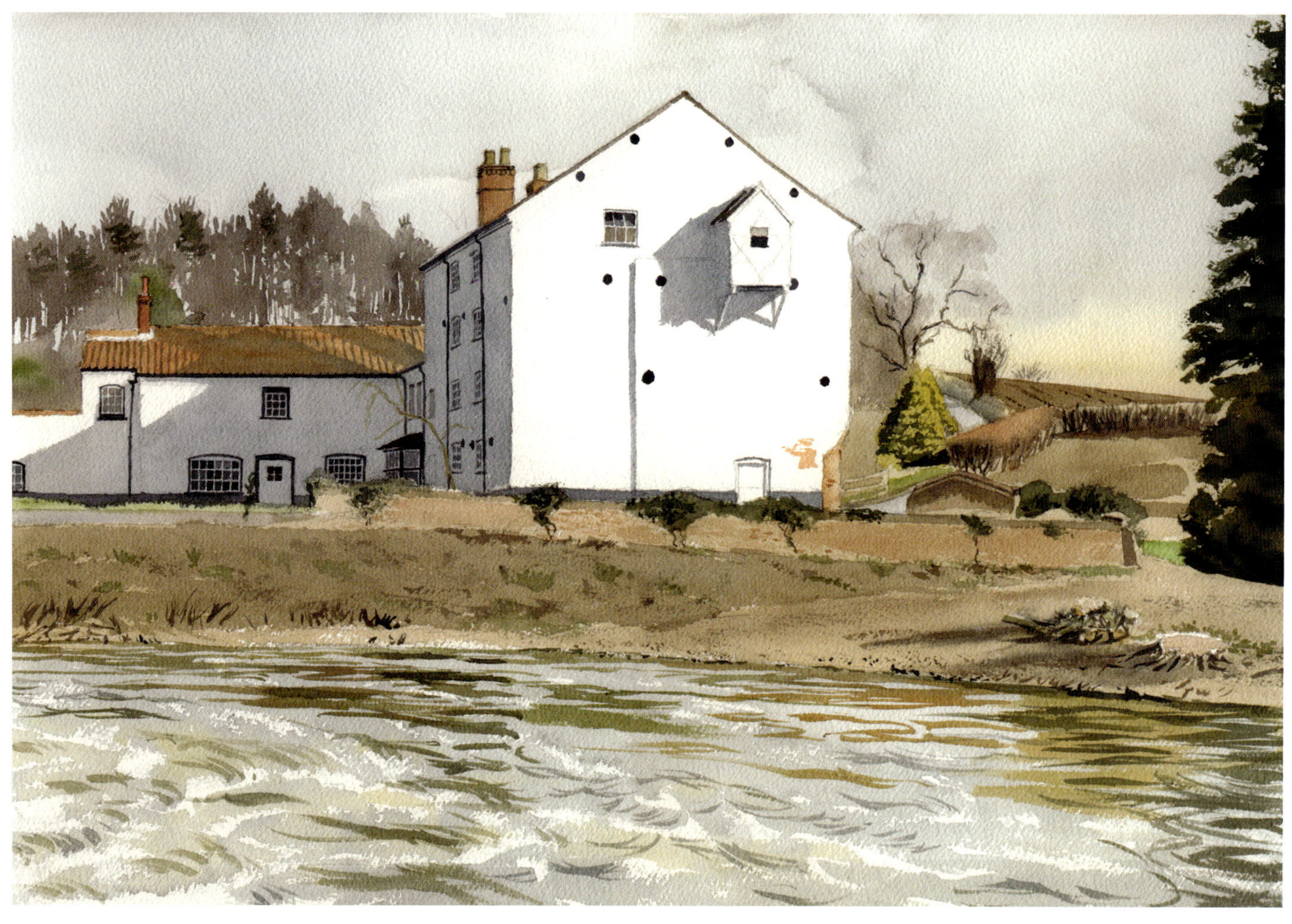

Bintree Mill III Watercolour 14" x 20" 2005

Opposite: *Bintree Mill IV* Charcoal Drawing 33" x 23½" 2005

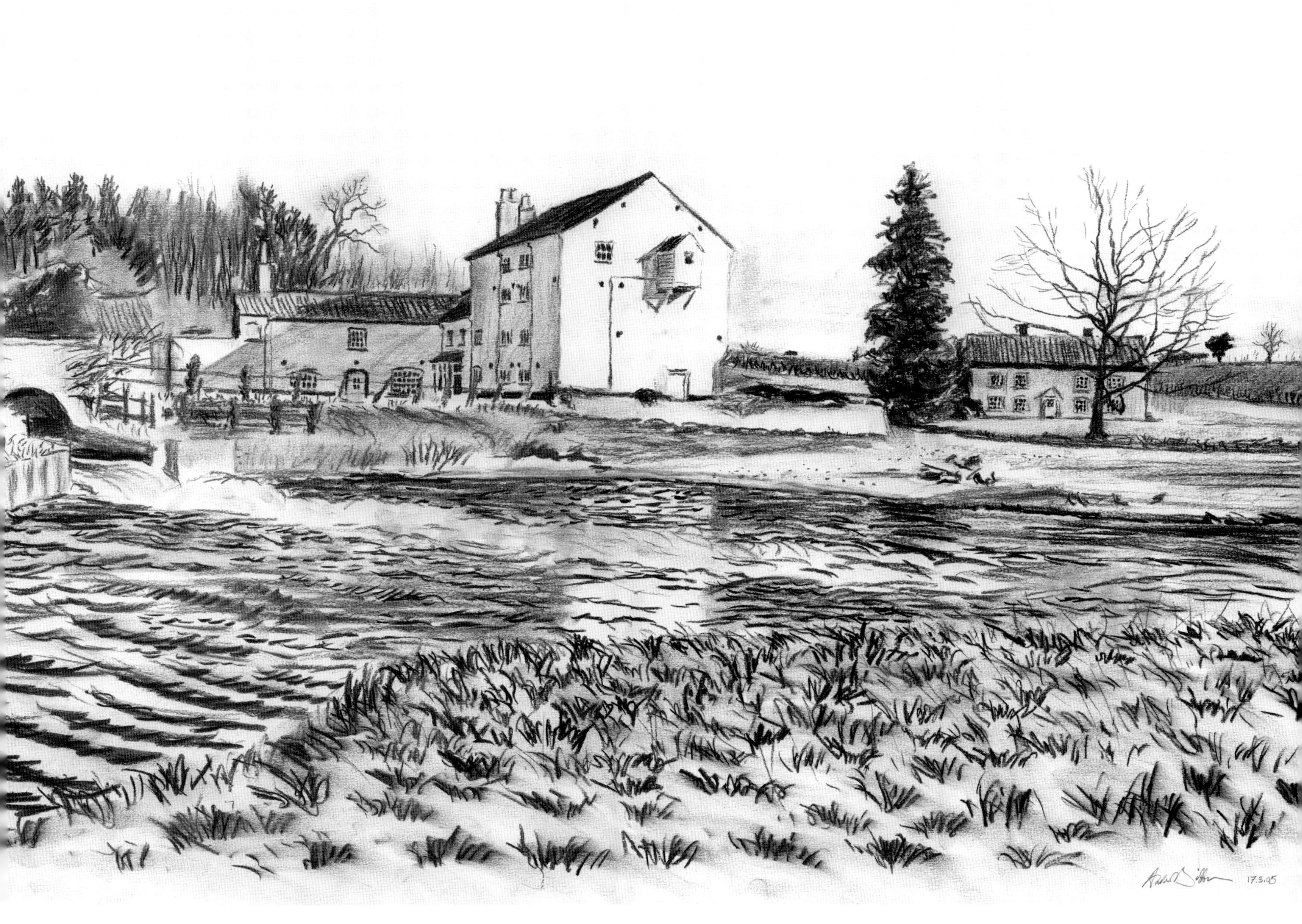

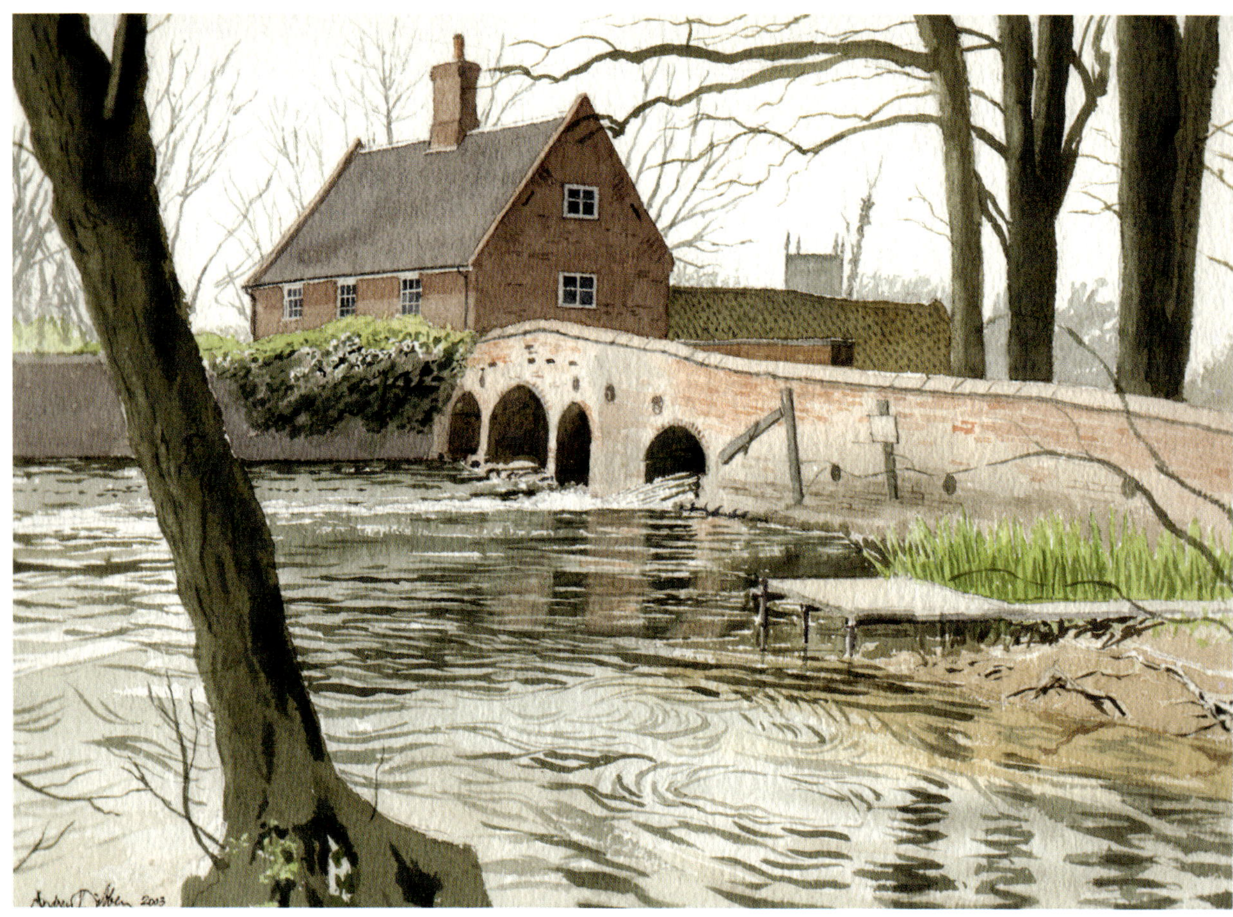

Lyng Mill Watercolour 9" x 12" 2003

The Wensum rises north-west of Fakenham, flowing under a number of very fine watermills on its way to Norwich, where it joins the rather smaller Yare. At this point, the river bears the ignominy of having to take on the name of the smaller watercourse, becoming the Yare for the 40-odd remaining miles of the journey to Great Yarmouth. I have often wondered how this came to be, but I suppose that 'Great Wensum-mouth' would have been a bit tricky to pronounce! I sat under the trees by the water's edge to paint the little picture above, on a warm day in early spring 2003. A group of children came to frolic in the water, diving in from the little landing stage. The water was still very cold, which caused some squealing! As I packed up to leave, the eldest girl in the party came to ask anxiously if I was leaving because of the noise they were making! Who says that young people nowadays are inconsiderate?

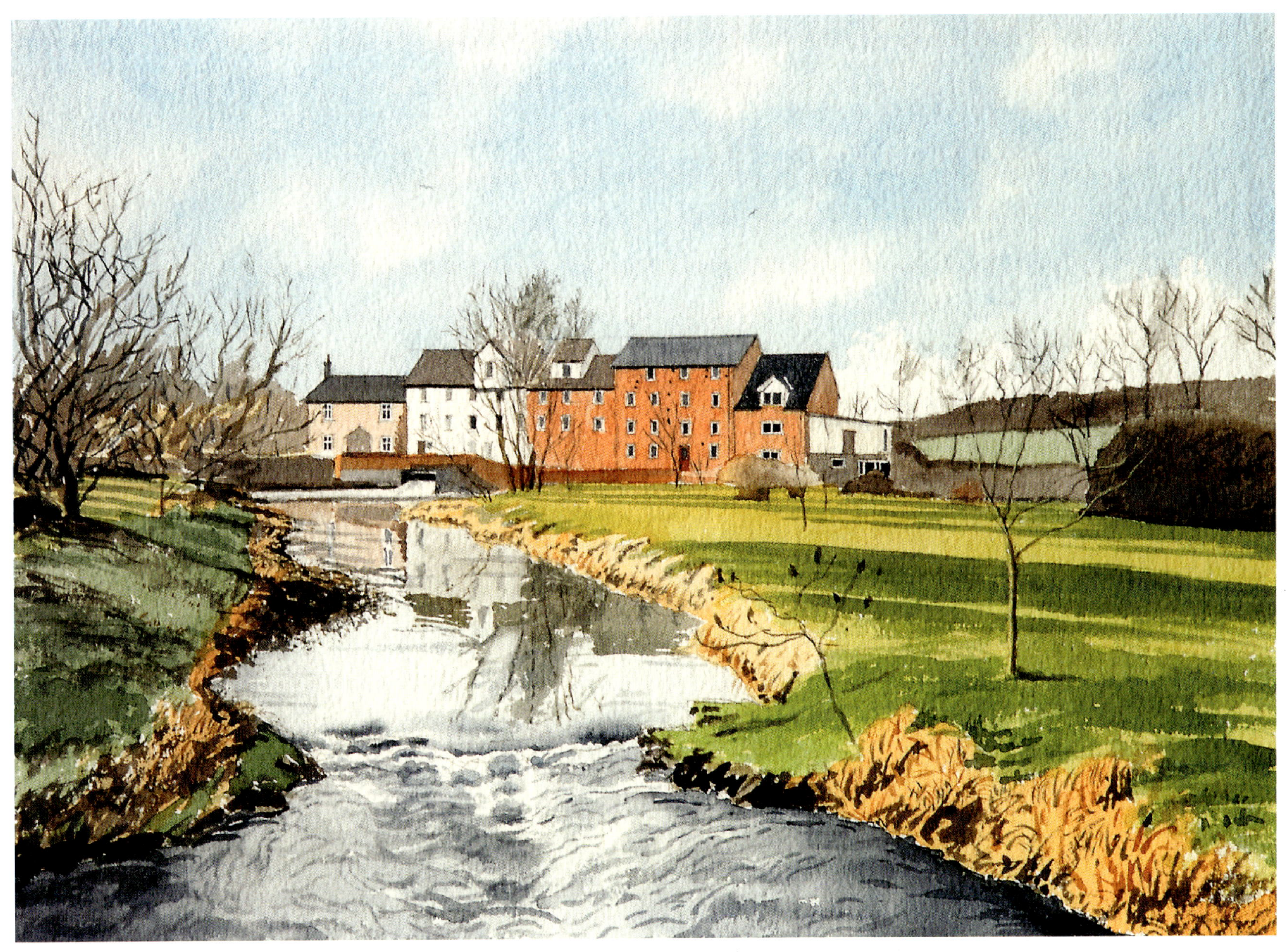

Above: **Elmham Mill** (River Wensum) 9" x 12" 2003

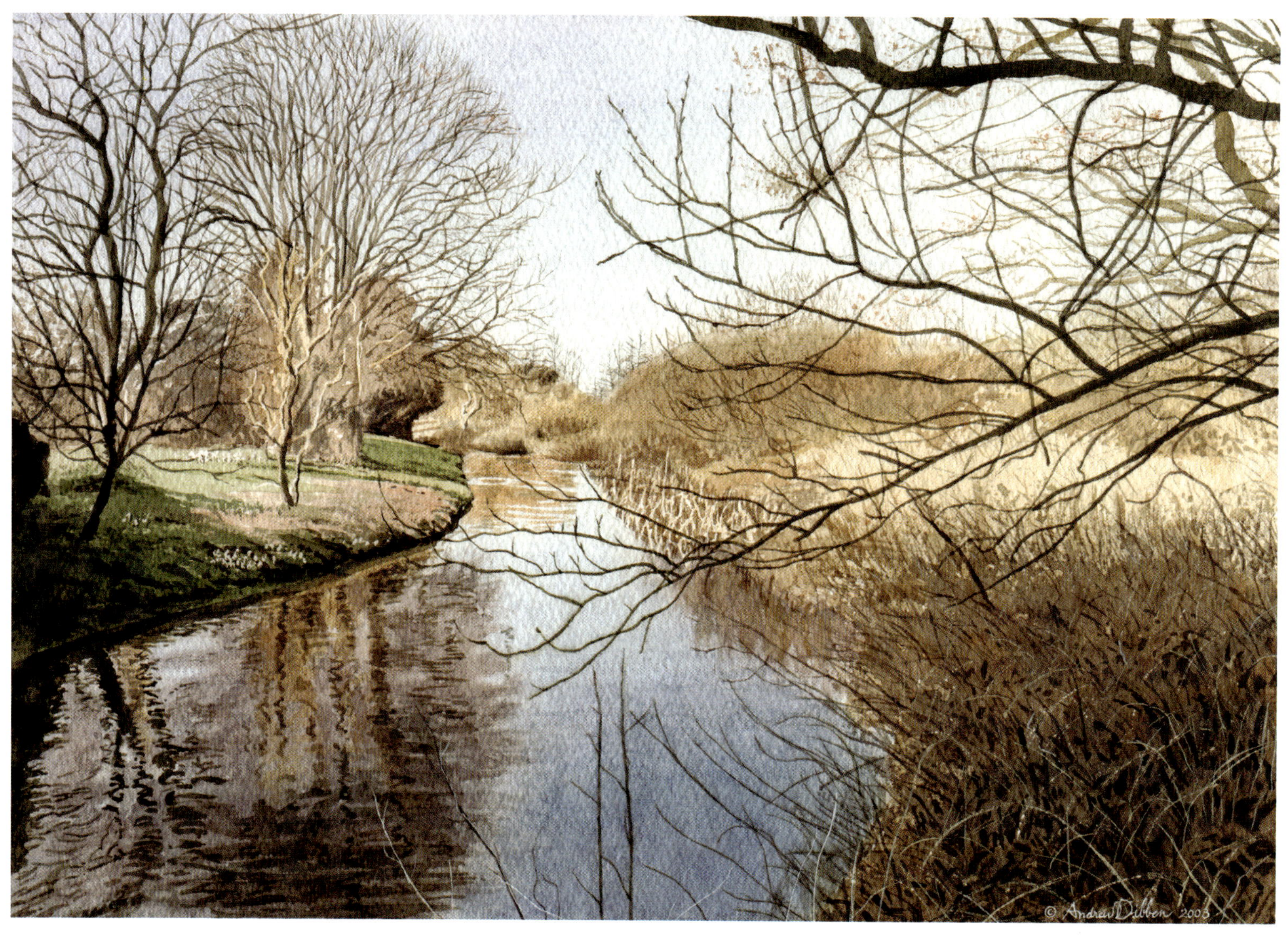

Upper Reaches of the Bure at Corpusty 14½” x 10½” 2003

I enjoyed the most wonderful weather one day in late April while painting this watercolour of Tharston Mill, on the River Tas. I was very pleased with the progress I was making, and came away fairly satisfied with my work. Strangely though, I always find that the acid test is when I get back home with something produced in the field, and look again at what I have achieved! I was rather disappointed with this one, but cannot quite work out why it somehow fails to meet the mark. Some of the windows are at slightly strange angles, which may be a bit disconcerting to the eye when looking at a picture, but then, that is how they appeared in reality. Nevertheless, I felt that it would be interesting to include the picture in my set of watermill studies.

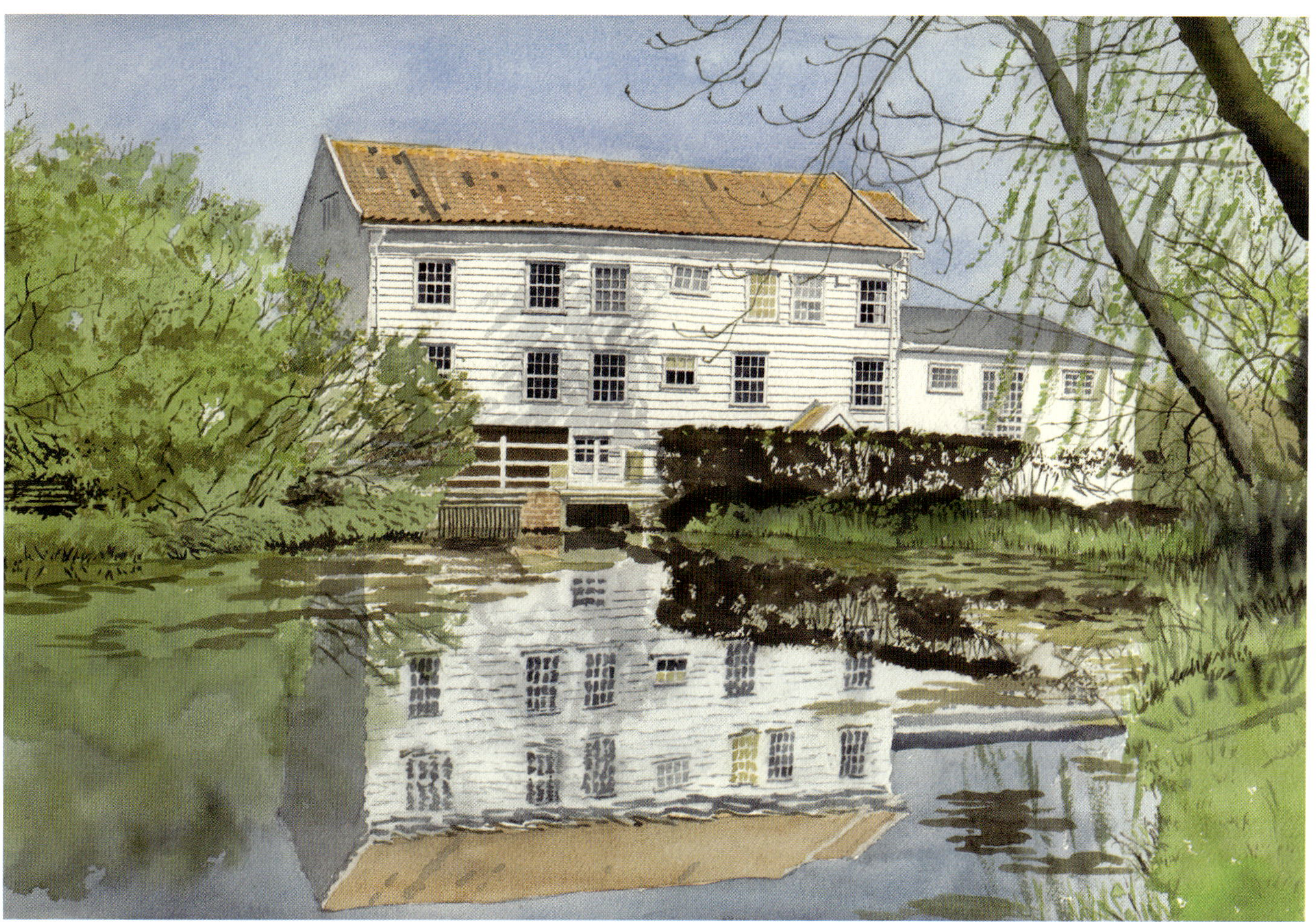

Tharston Mill Watercolour study 14" x 20" 2005

Ellingham Mill

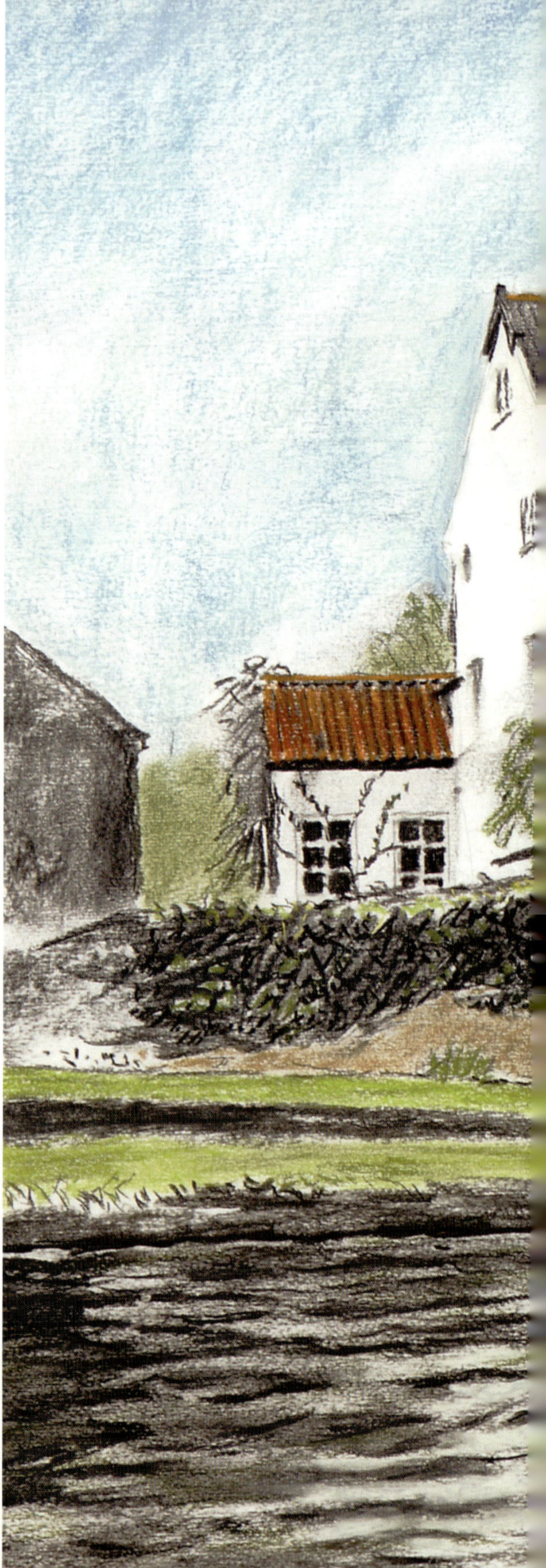

When my wife and I were first married (33 years ago), we lived for a couple of years within a few miles of Ellingham Mill, and would occasionally go and admire it, and also visit the art gallery that it contained in those days. The owner of the mill then was an American artist by the name of Chester Williams; I recall some very fine, slightly abstract watercolours he had done, inspired by all the running water around the building.

The watermill straddles a little tributary of the Waveney, among a small cluster of buildings that were all originally related to the activity of the mill itself, at a spot where the river valley slopes gently down to the banks of this major watercourse. Walking along the lane here, there seems to be water coming from all directions, and a number of little tree-covered islands has been formed by the various streams diverted to supply the motive force of the mill. It is all so pretty that a more idyllic location is hard to imagine. Further along, a road bridge crosses the Waveney on top of a weir, over which the river hurls itself to a level some four or five feet lower. Looking at the surrounding flood plain, it is difficult to understand how there can be this sudden change in level, for it seems to be flat as far as the eye can see along the river. The raison d'être of the whole hamlet is the substantial mill building itself, wonderful in its asymmetry, with seemingly random different roof heights, and portions that are weather-boarded, while others are rendered. At the northern end, the Miller's Cottage nestles against the main building, its façade charmingly enriched by a lovely set of gothic-arched windows. The present owner of the mill is another artist, Miss Margaret Thomas, and another wonderful character; approaching her ninetieth year, she is still working, and still drives her four-wheel-drive vehicle into central London to call on her galleries.

Having worked out that the best spot from which to sketch the mill was in someone's garden, I pleaded with the owners for permission to spend a few hours at the water's edge in order to produce this drawing. They could not have been more helpful, and led me over stepping-stones in yet another stream to the perfect viewpoint. I decided to use charcoal once again, but then experimented by adding a few touches of colour with pastels. It is a slightly curious mixture perhaps, but I feel that the colour does help to explain some of the areas.

Ellingham Mill Charcoal and Pastel 33" x 23½" 2005

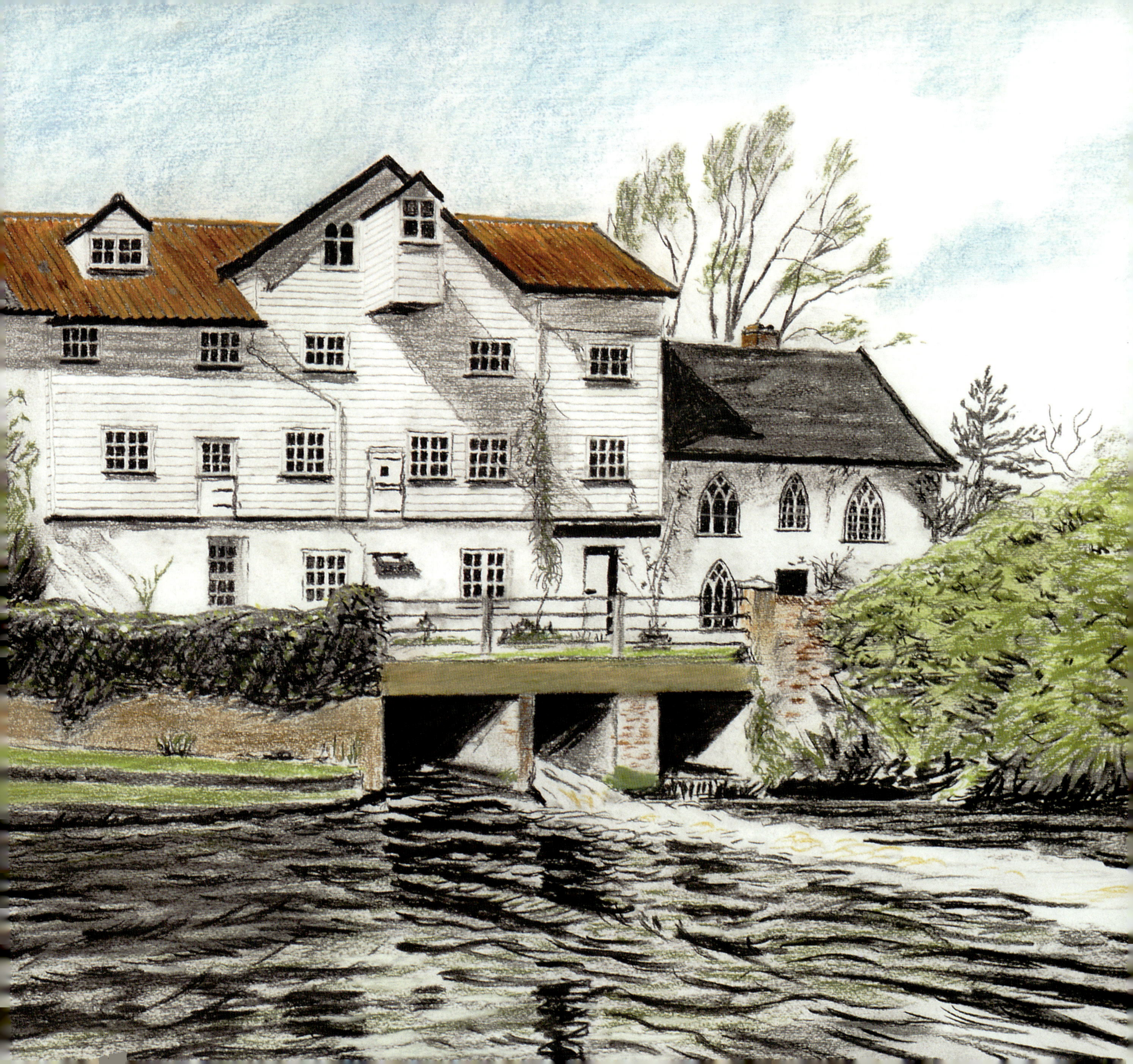

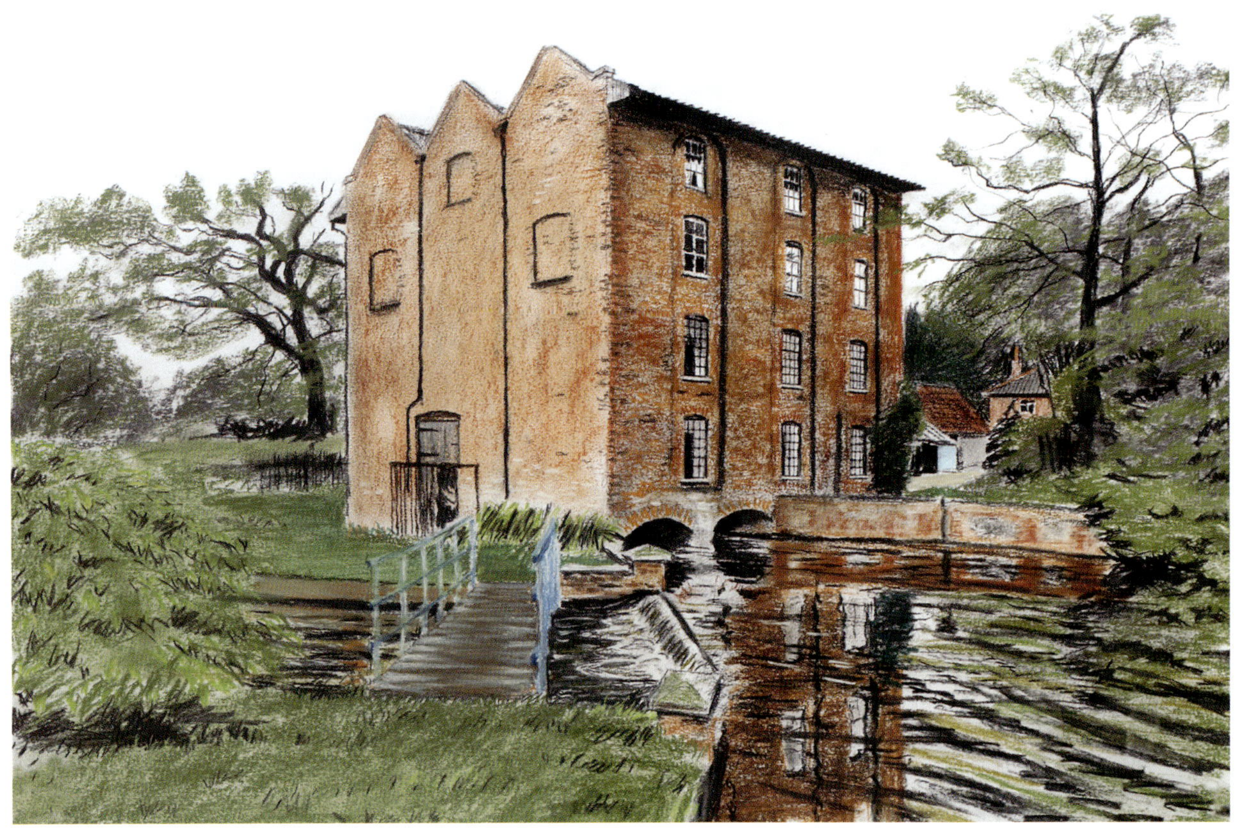

Letheringsett Mill Charcoal and Pastel 33" x 23½" 2005

Letheringsett Mill, as mentioned earlier, is now the only working watermill remaining in Norfolk, and yet it is possible to visit the building, and witness the rumble of machinery as wheat is ground into flour. Voted the county's most popular attraction (by visitors) for some eleven years, the mill site is charming in the extreme, with its delightful grounds, and resident population of rescued chickens and ducks. When I arrived to ask permission to work in the mill grounds, I was somewhat surprised to find the garden absolutely full of artists! It seems that the local art group often come here from the village hall, as the subject matter is so plentiful; I just happened to pick their day! I didn't get too far with my picture however, as it soon began pouring with rain, and I had to finish working on it at home, with slightly mixed results. Letheringsett is a little unusual in being all red brick construction, and with the roof built of three spans along the length of the building. By contrast, Keswick Mill, just south of Norwich on the River Yare, is a classic white weather-boarded mill astride a lovely brick bridge.

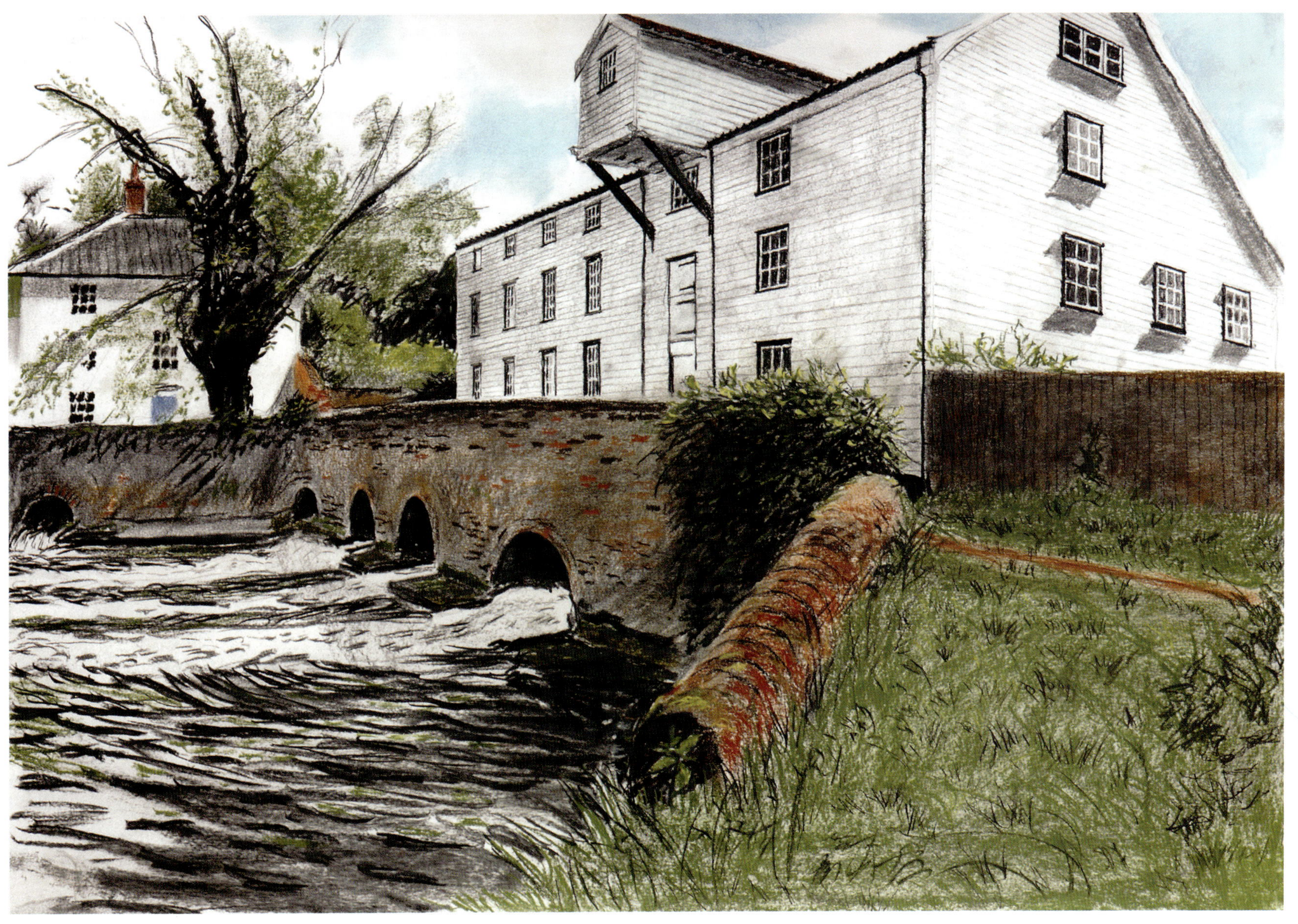

Keswick Mill Charcoal and Pastel 33" x 23½" 2005

Burgh-Next-Aylsham Mill

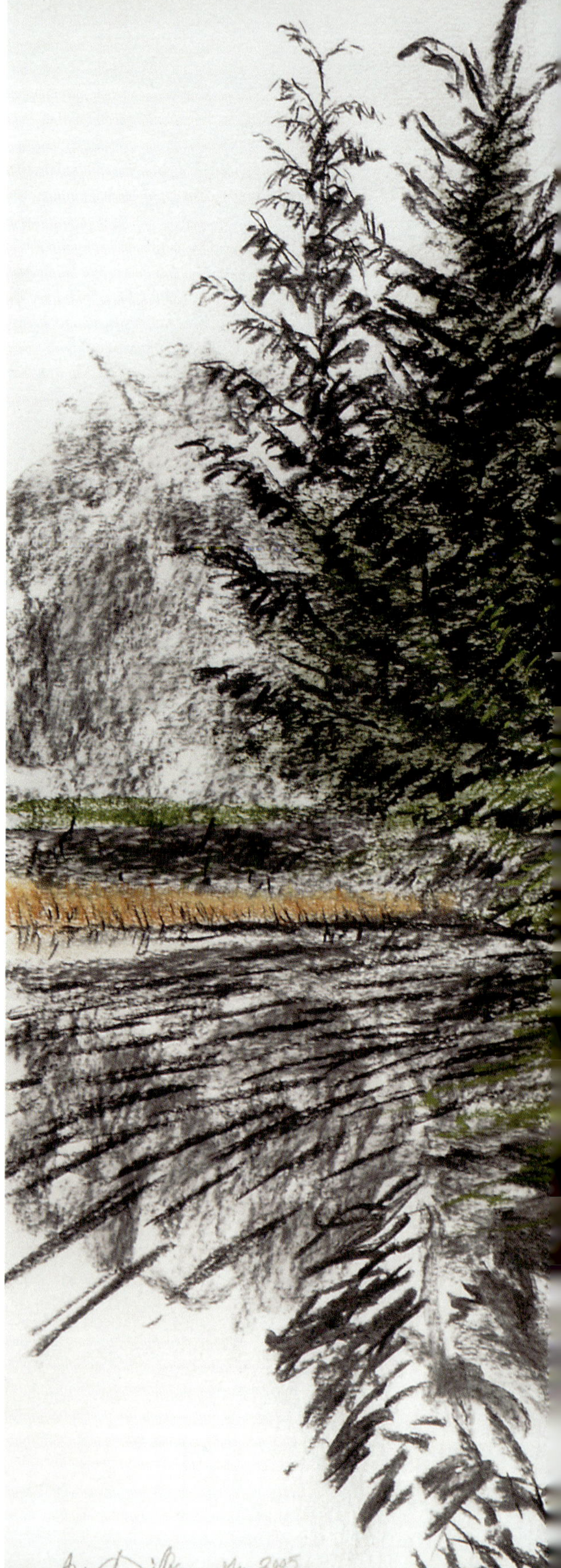

The charming owners of this mill, Mr and Mrs Grix, very kindly allowed me to set up my easel at the water's edge in their grounds so that I could produce this picture. Michael Grix was in fact the miller when this was still a working watermill, up until 1980, and he took over from his father, Mr James Grix. Burgh Mill was mentioned in the Domesday Book in 1085, and the present structure dates from about 1700. The building was used for interior shots in the BBC series of Hardy's *The Mill on the Floss*. It is an extraordinary structure, and quite an exuberant piece of timber architecture for this country. Mr Grix pointed out to me the strange fact that there are six gables on this side of the building, but only five on the other! The fabric of the mill is in a rather sorry state now, but one imagines it would require a huge investment to restore it; Mr Grix hopes that its listing status may be upgraded, so that it could then qualify for a grant towards restoration. I do hope that this happens, because Burgh mill is a truly magnificent piece of our heritage.

As with one or two of the other mills depicted here, the setting is glorious; mind you, I was fortunate with the weather, which stayed dry, though cool and windy, with occasional sunny intervals. The lovely reflections only revealed themselves from time to time, when the wind dropped. But as I worked feverishly on the mass of detail, I could hear cuckoos calling, as well as various water fowl. A swan sat on her nest behind the large trees on the left, and hissed loudly at me when I had to pass near her to cross the footbridge on the far side of the building. Like Ellingham, there seems to be water everywhere, with various sections of the Bure diverted to control the flow to the mill, and a low weir providing a background sound of rushing water.

Burgh-Next-Aylsham Mill Charcoal, Pencil and Pastel 33" x 23½" 2005

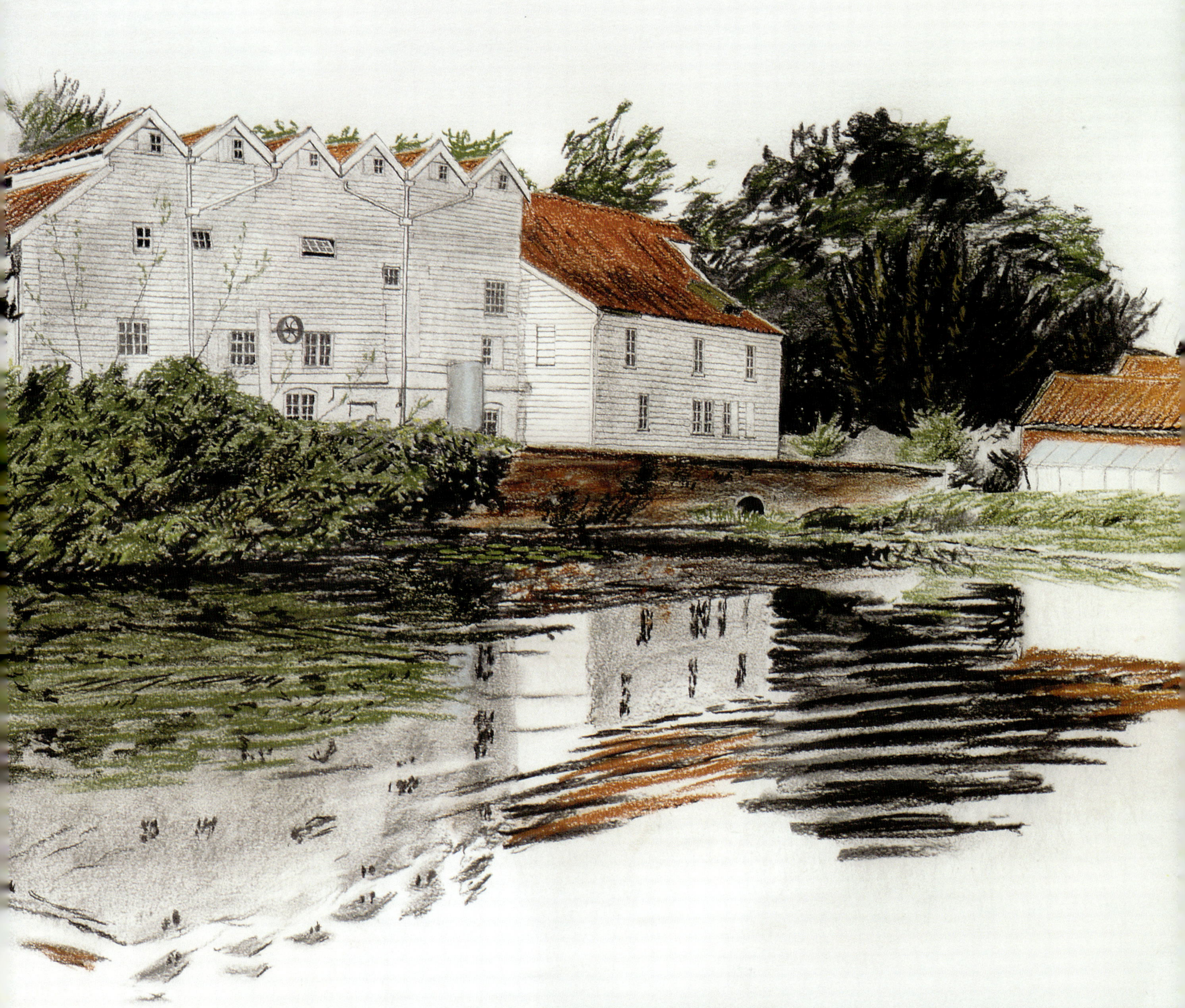

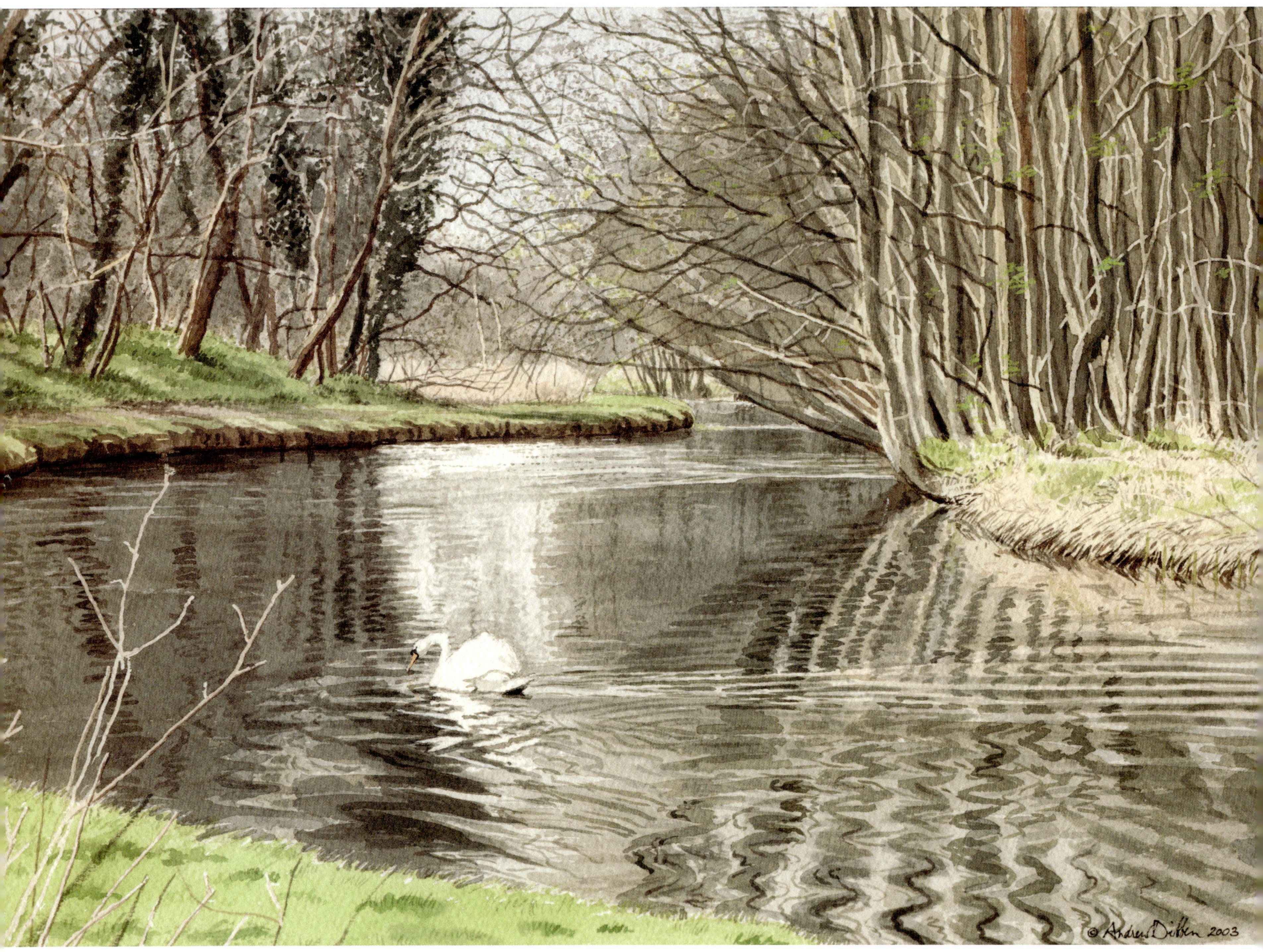

COMMERCIAL REACHES

The Norwich Riverfront

I had great hopes for the Norwich river frontage after the old Boulton and Paul industrial site was cleared in the early 1990s. The result is disappointing however, with rather cheap and temporary looking commercial buildings, some with metal-clad roofs, creating a new leisure complex on this very large brownfield site, as well as a number of rather unnecessary retail outlets duplicating much of the city centre. The area is certainly popular with the younger generation; it is positively heaving with people late at night on Fridays and Saturdays; but none of them have come to admire the architecture, that's for sure! The river is slowly being tidied up nevertheless; the new houses downstream from the leisure area are quite attractive; the concrete silos of Reed's flour mill, Just upstream of Carrow Bridge, have just been demolished as I write, to be replaced with apartments, and the older buildings on the site are being converted. Quayside, just downstream of Fye Bridge, is also being redeveloped currently. I sat on the opposite bank in 1989 and painted this slightly industrial scene, which has recently vanished after years of neglect. If all goes well, this stretch of the Wensum should soon look quite prosperous and trendy.

All this is a far cry from the times when ships would come up as far as Reed's, Carrow Bridge lifting to let them through, and they would discharge cargoes of timber on Riverside, or load scrap metal at Archie King's site next to the flour mill. All that ended in September 1989, and finished for good with the building of the new road bridge for the southern bypass, a couple of miles downriver.

Downstream from Carrow Bridge, and on the northern bank, is the extensive Colman's industrial complex. A large portion of this stands derelict since the parting of the ways of the Reckitt & Colman businesses, the latter remaining in Norwich while Reckitt's operations were moved to Hull and elsewhere. Many of these industrial buildings, particularly the Victorian ones, are quite magnificent pieces of architecture, and a far cry from the very utilitarian metal-clad buildings being erected these days. Their future is rather uncertain, but there is no doubt that they could be converted into superb apartment blocks, should the site be sold off.

Opposite: ***The Wensum Near Great Witchingham*** 11½" x 14½" 2003

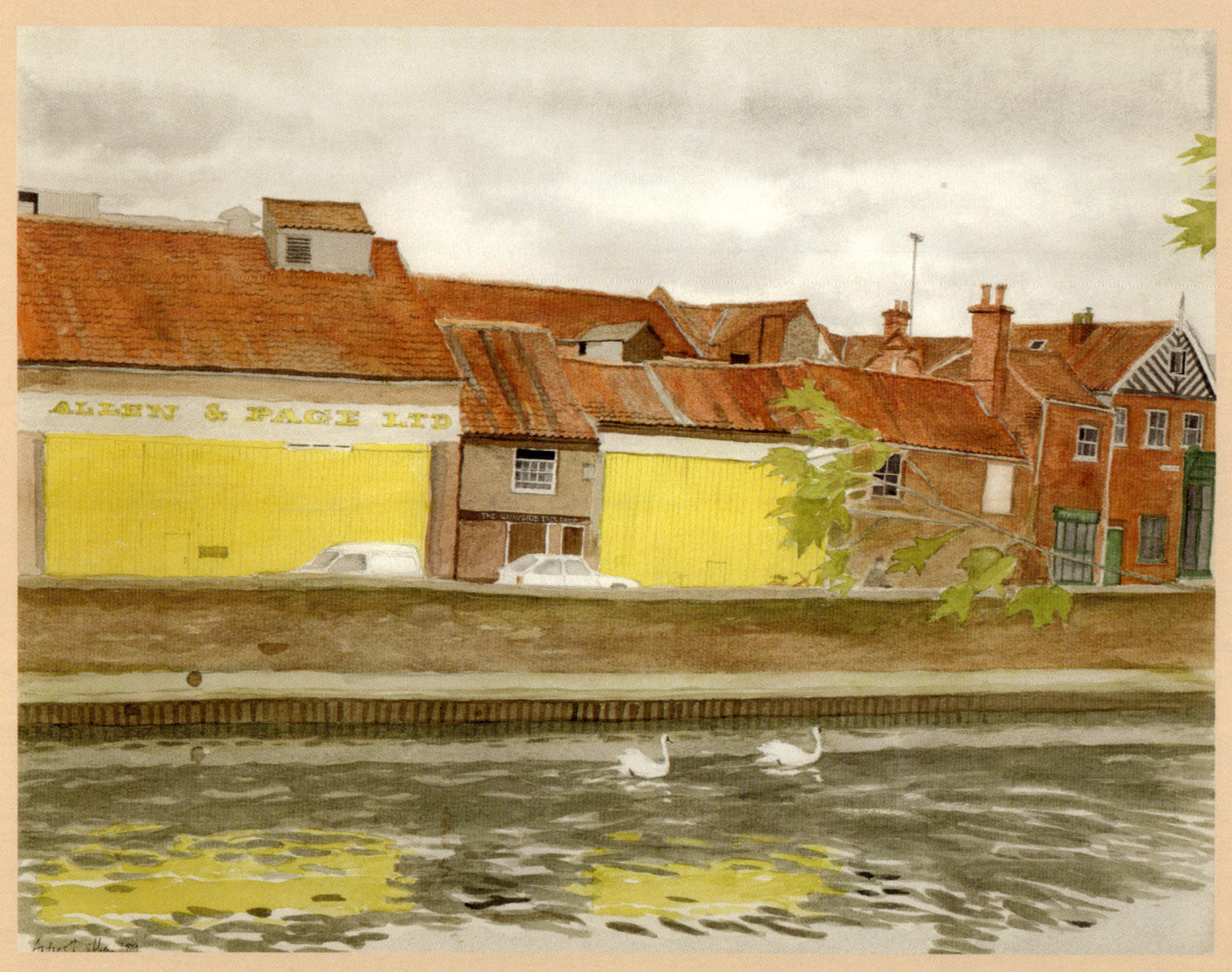

ALLEN & PAGE LTD

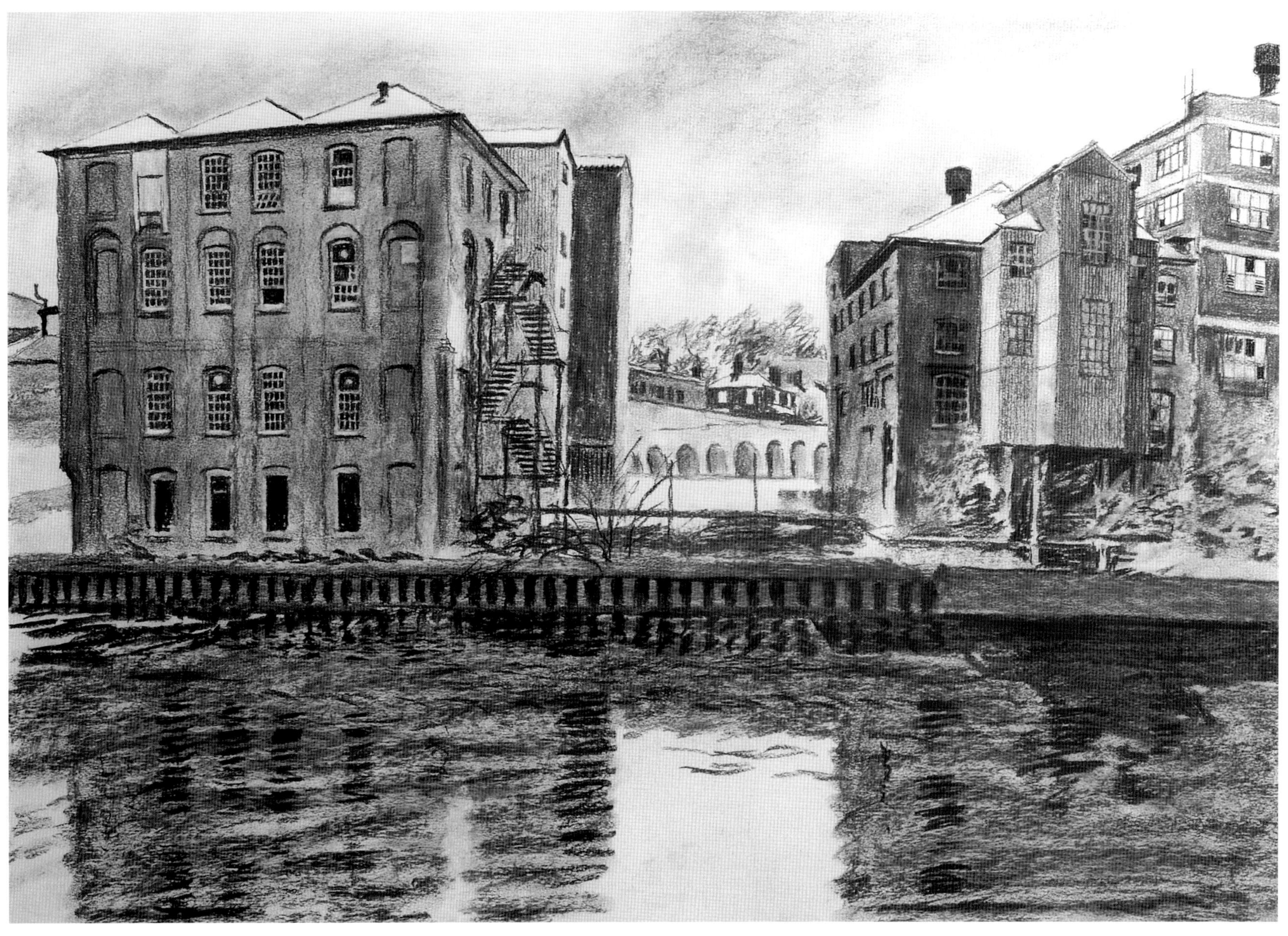

Colman's Works, Carrow, Norwich Charcoal 33" x 23½" 2005

Opposite: ***Quayside, Norwich*** 20" x 15" 1989

King's Lynn

King's Lynn possesses a wealth of wonderful architecture along its historic streets and squares, as well as on the waterfront. I visited the town in May 2005, intending to do a picture of the Customs House and Purfleet, only to find the building shrouded in scaffolding! From the opposite quay, I turned round and instead drew this view of King's Staithe Square and its very fine buildings. Just left of centre can be seen one of a number of towers which wealthy merchants had built on top of their houses, so that they could look down the Great Ouse and over the Wash. They would then scan the horizon to spot a ship arriving, so that they could rush down to the quays, and be the first to negotiate a deal for the cargo on board!

Another day, I did a large charcoal drawing of some of the shrimp boats in the Fisher Fleet, adjacent to the docks area. Sadly, I had not studied the tide times that morning; I suddenly noticed that the tide was beginning to come back in, and soon, the boats were starting to rise as if in a slow lift, and also, drift around in the strong breeze! The sun decided to go in too, and so the scene changed quite dramatically, but I persevered as long as I could! There is a fascinating variety of craft moored down here; one or two are state-of-the-art steel boats, but there are still a few very old wooden boats, some of which are in working order, while others lie abandoned, with flowers and weeds growing out of their decks.

King's Staithe Square Charcoal and Pastel 33" x 23½" 2005

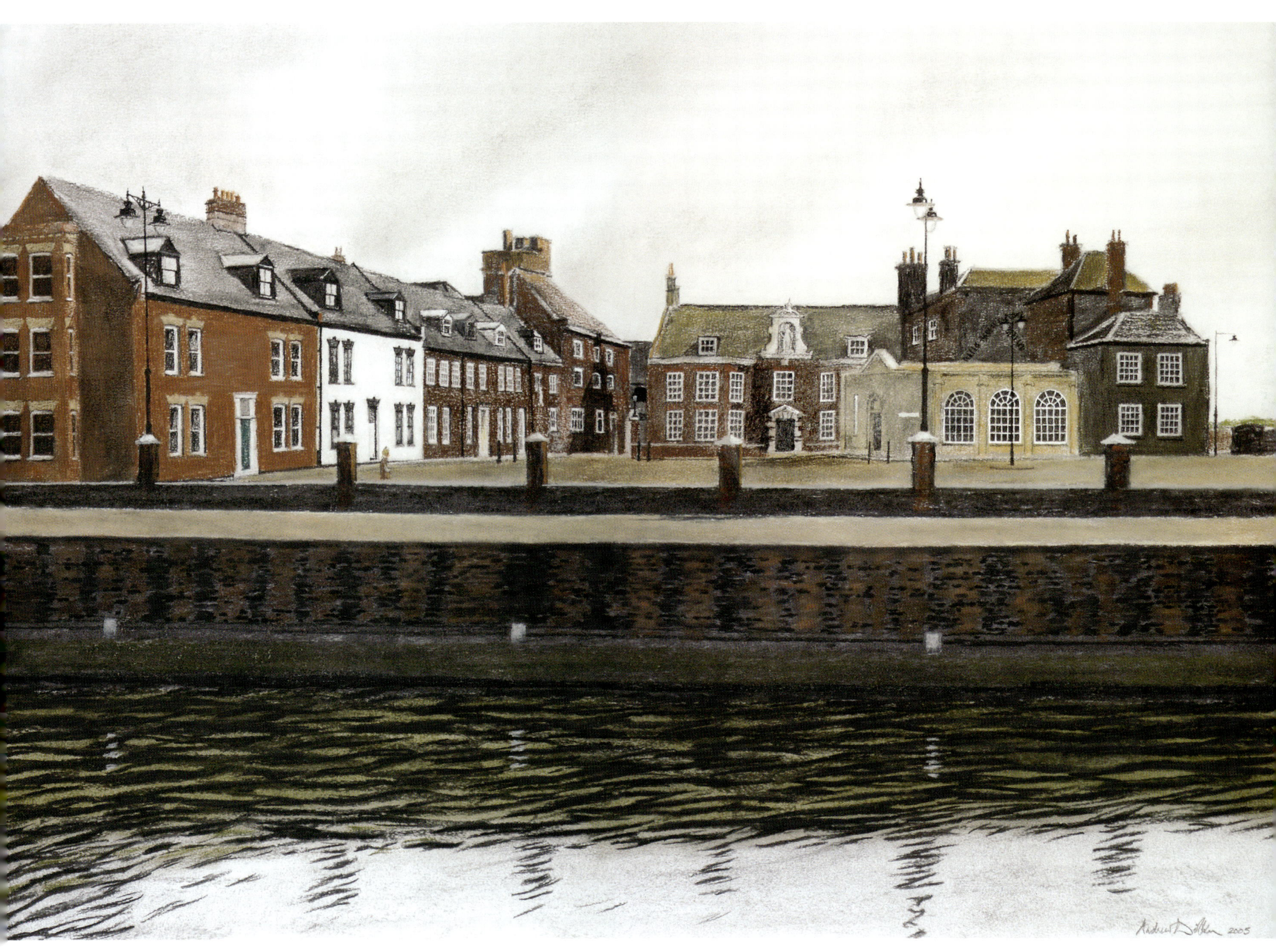

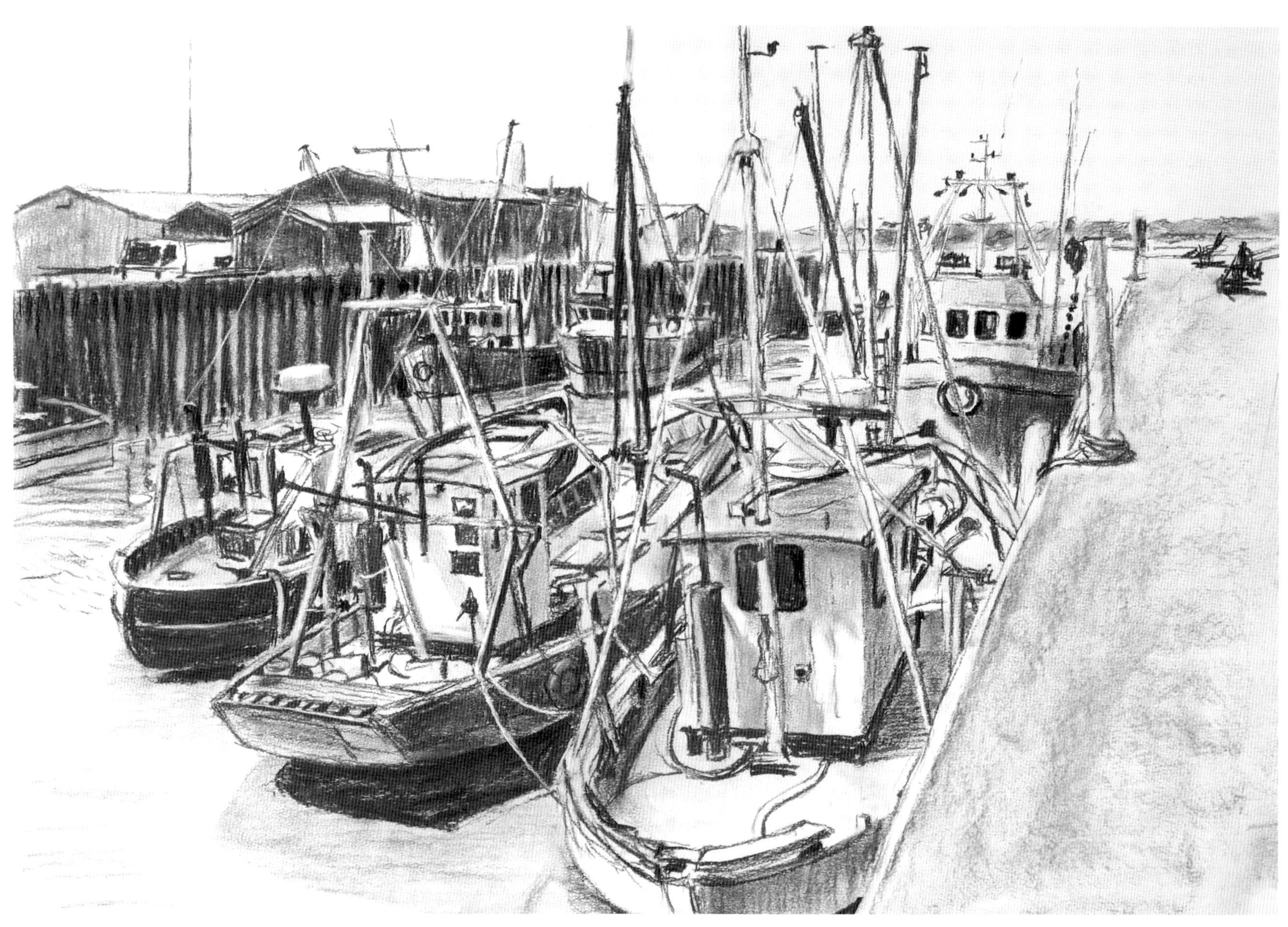

The Fisher Fleet, King's Lynn Charcoal 33" x 23½" 2005

SALT WATER

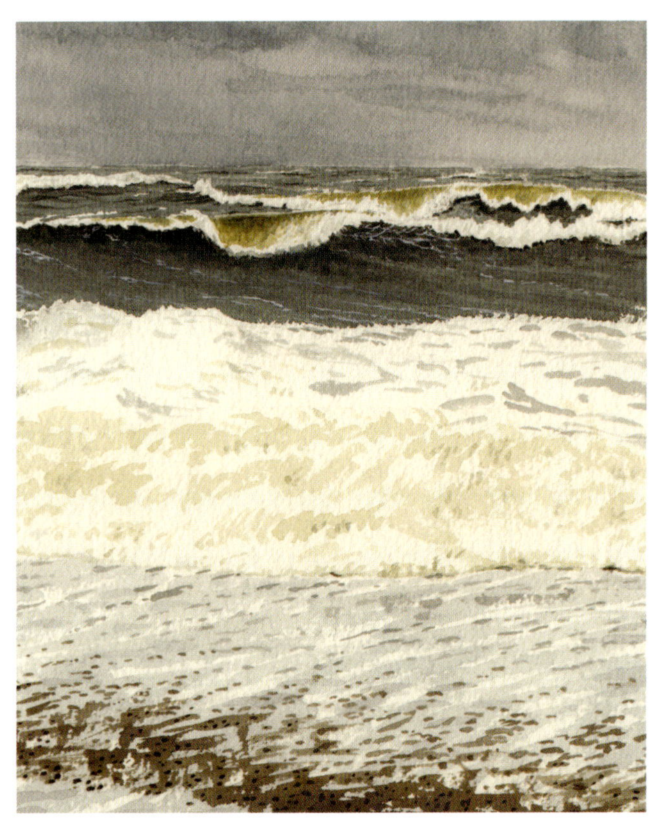

ON THE BEACH

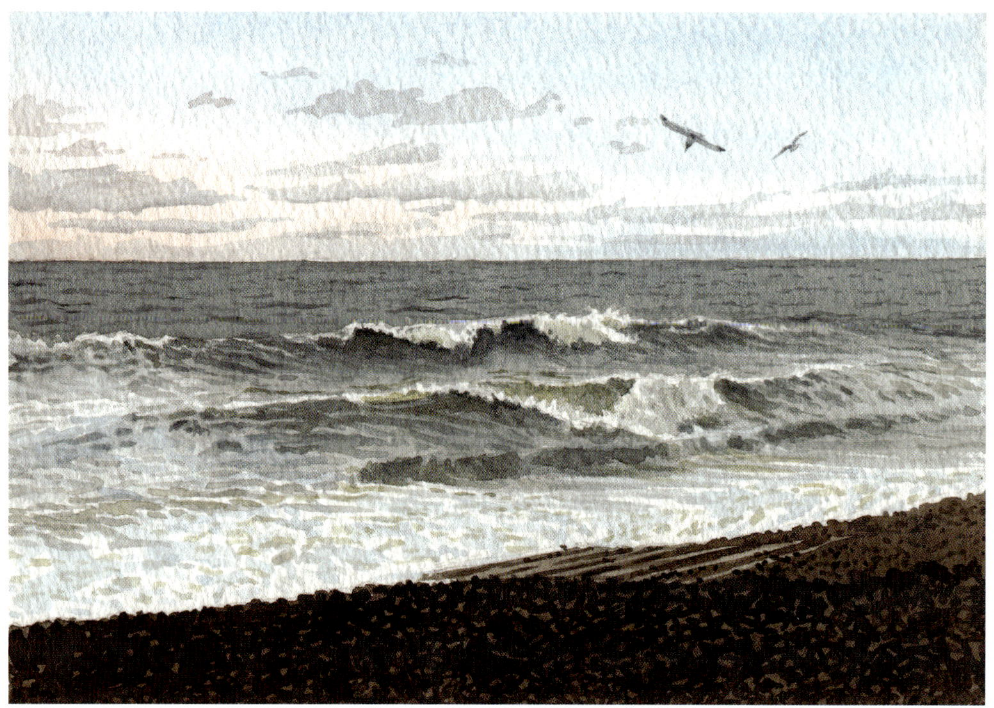

Sheringham Slip, Rough Sea 7" x 5" 2004

Around Norfolk's long coastline, there are some wonderful beaches. It is surprising how varied they can be; when I studied navigation, many years ago, I was fascinated by the diversity of material that makes up the seabed, even in a relatively small area. Charts are marked with abbreviated notes giving this information so that mariners can know how well an anchor will hold, or what kind to use, or even to help find their position in zero visibility. A totally awe-inspiring number of wrecks is also marked. On this coast, beaches are comprised mostly of sand, but some areas can have scattered shingle, or even be wholly made up of shingle. The section between Sheringham and Blakeney Point is all shingle (excepting the large dunes at the end of the spit), with the raised bank from Weybourne westwards resembling Chesil Bank in Dorset. The sandy beaches can be backed by salt marsh, or by extensive sand dunes, or by cliffs. West Runton has the unique combination of a bed of chalk liberally strewn with very large flints, which creates lovely rock pools at low tide. Old Hunstanton's beach is sandy, at the foot of rock cliffs that have occasionally shed large boulders on to the sand below. Most of the sandy beaches shelve very gradually, but Weybourne's shingle shelves steeply, and there is a surprising depth of water close inshore. This led to greater work on defences here during the Second World War, as there were fears that an invasion might take place at this point.

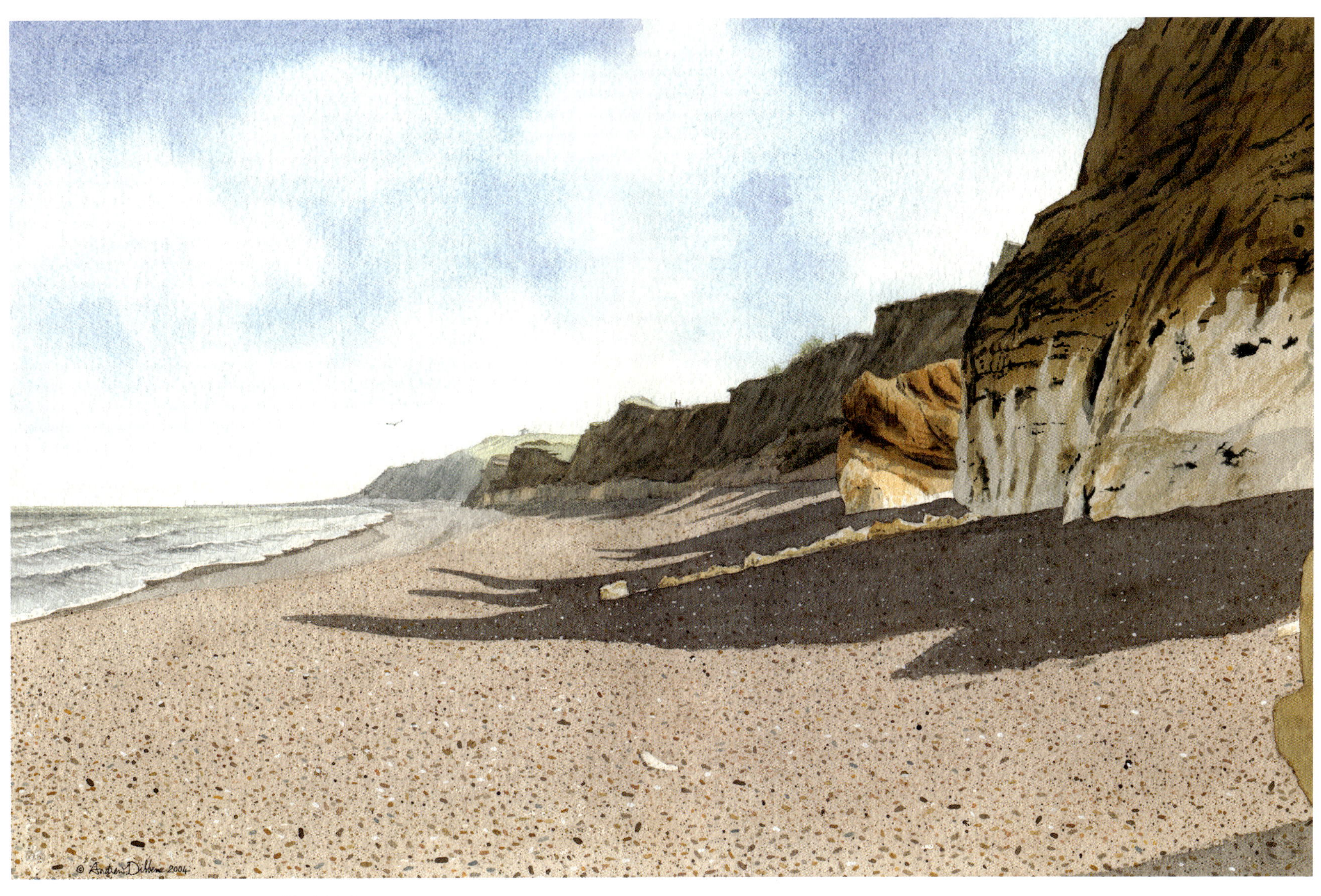

Weybourne Beach 21½ x 14" 2004

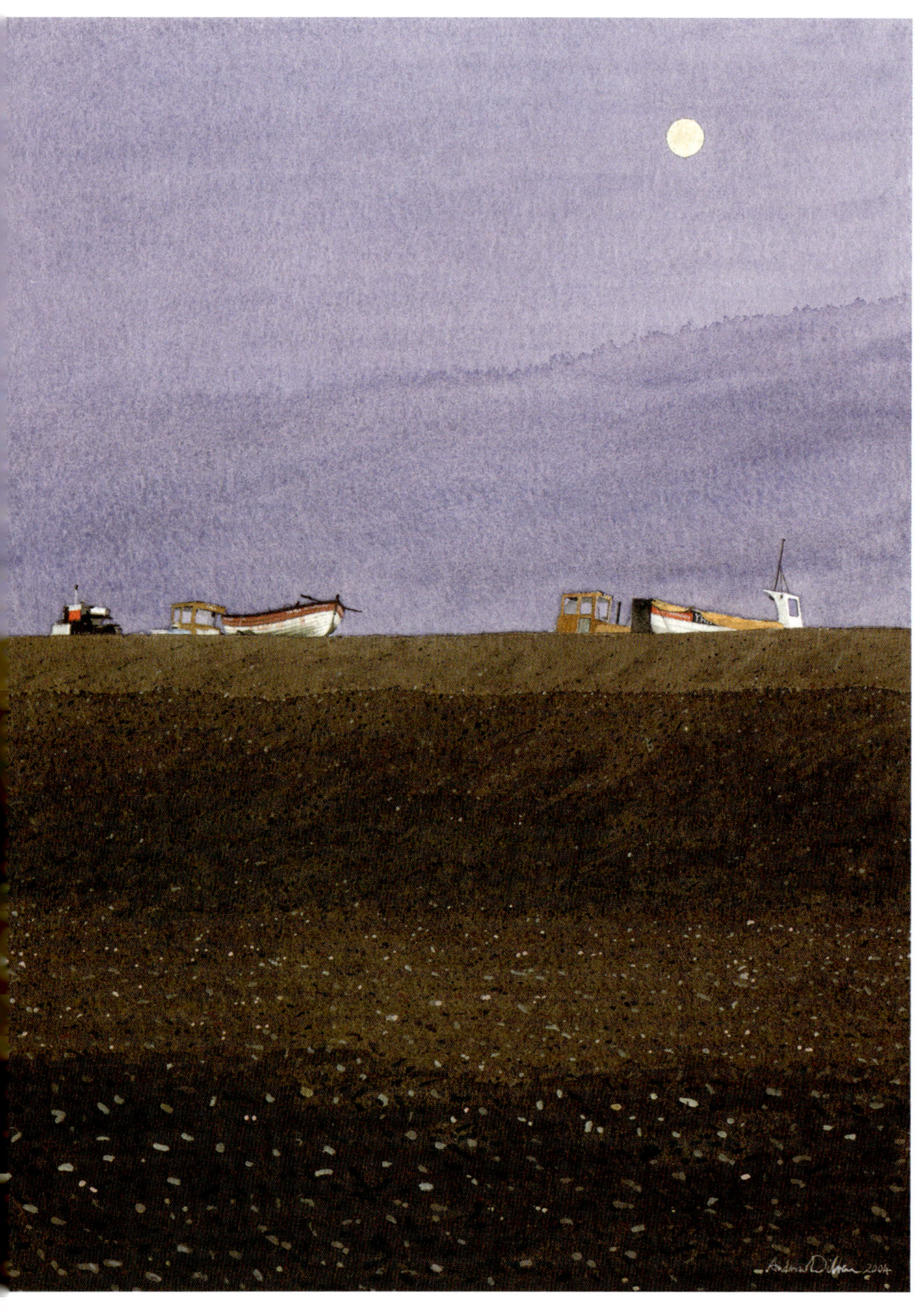

Climbing up on to Weybourne shingle bank, early one evening, I found that it was low tide. It wasn't one of the lowest tides of the year, but nevertheless the water was a long way down. I scrambled down to the water's edge and looked back, to notice the moon overlooking the scene. The little fishing boats and their attendant tractors perched just over the crest of the bank, well out of reach of the sea. Looking up the stepped slope of the bank, the distance to the ridge was so great that it seemed inconceivable that the sea could really break over the top at times, and yet it happens; I have seen it happen.

The tidal range in the southern North Sea is really not very great compared to other parts of the world, such as the Channel Isles, or Nova Scotia's Bay of Fundy. Here we have a rise and fall of six to eight feet, depending on the time of the lunar month and the time of year, while the Bay of Fundy's range is some sixty feet! The problem here is that because we rarely see extreme conditions, we are ill prepared for them. But every so often an exceptionally high tide will occur during a severe northerly storm, and the North Sea's water is pushed south by the wind. The shallow nature of the North Sea reduces its ability to absorb the additional water, and the result is a flood.

On this particular evening however, conditions were balmy, and the scene was quite serene.

Full Moon Over Weybourne Shingle Bank
10½" x 14½" 2004

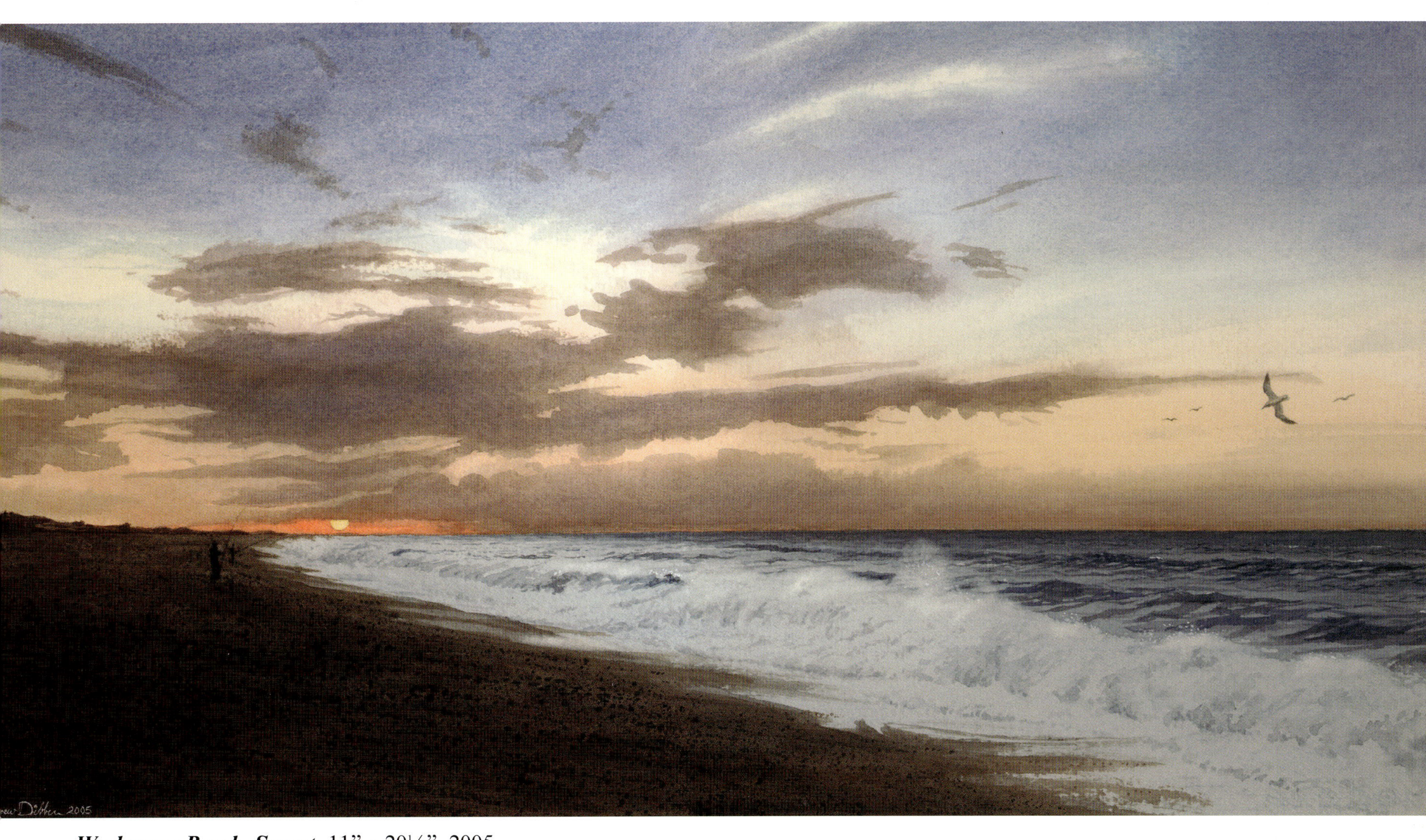

Weybourne Beach, Sunset 11" x 20½" 2005

A WINTER STORM – WEYBOURNE BEACH

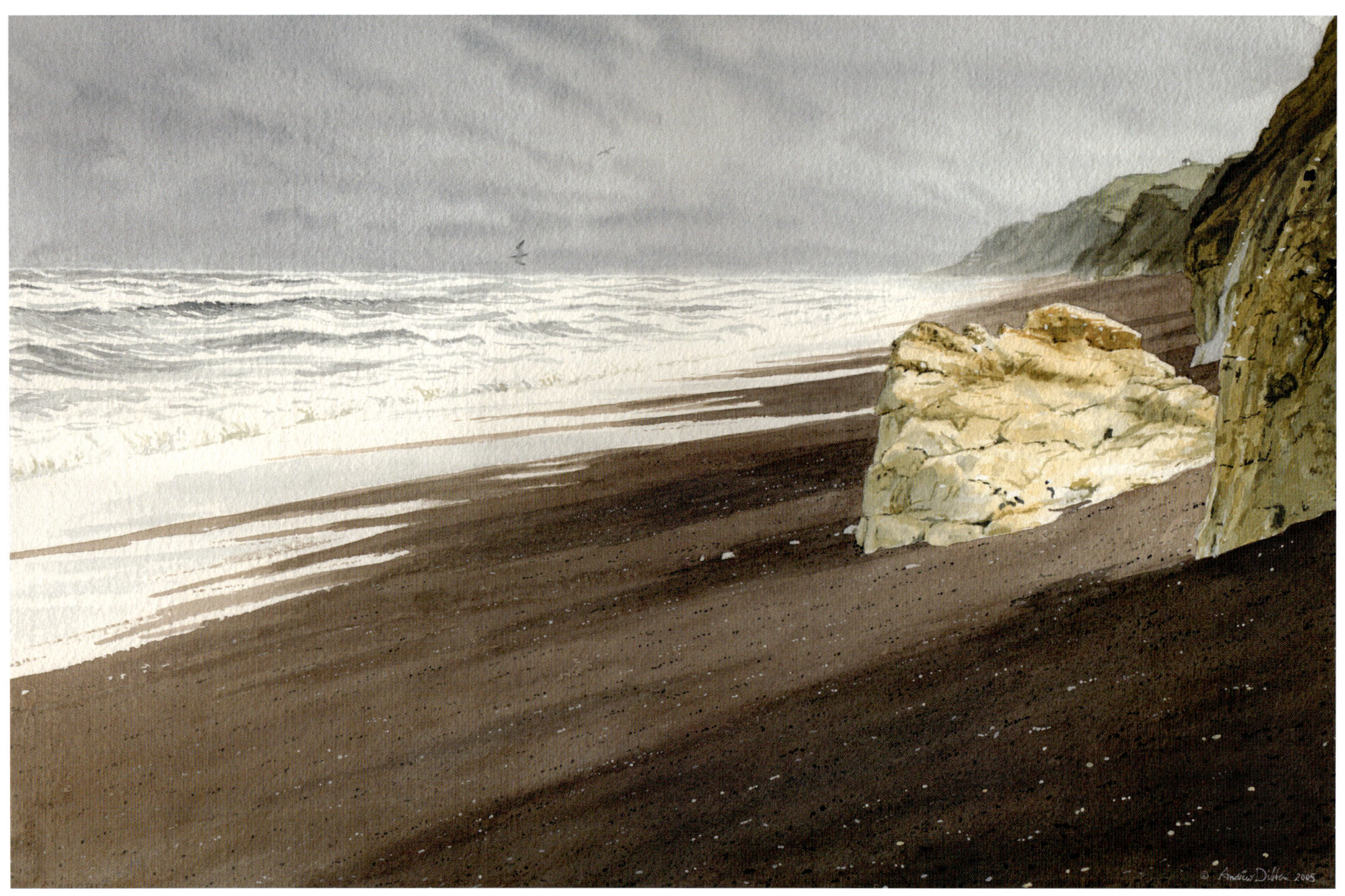

Weybourne Beach & Cliffs, Winter Storm 14½" x 21½" 2005

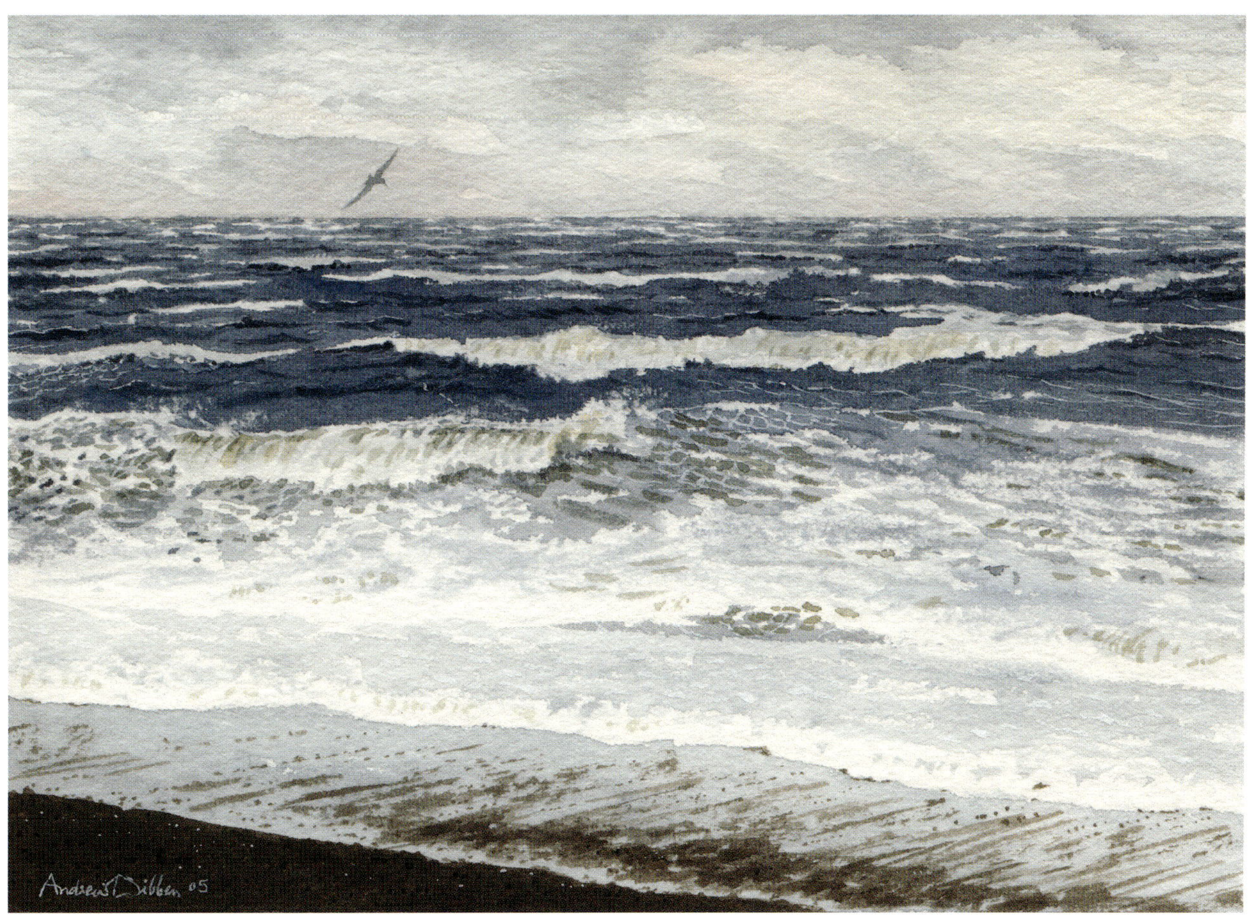

Weybourne Sea, February 5" x 7" 2005

I have become very fond of the Weybourne locality; the village is lovely, with some beautiful flint cottages, a very fine church, with the ruins of an earlier one in the churchyard, a wonderful windmill, and some fine hilly landscape for a backdrop. Then there is the beach, strangely also known as Weybourne Hope; it is an extraordinary conglomeration of billions of small pebbles, which shift with the tides and storms, and batter the rather fragile cliffs mercilessly. The cliffs are an interesting layer-cake of sand deposited on a rather soft chalk base. Water and frosts work at the sand from the top, causing large chunks to tumble on to the beach. In places, harder outcrops of chalk resist the weather, and stand like little islands in the shingle, glowing a beautiful golden colour in the sunlight, studded with black and grey flints of all sizes. These rocks have become a favourite subject in recent months. The beach is also an excellent spot from which to observe a wild sea in the winter months.

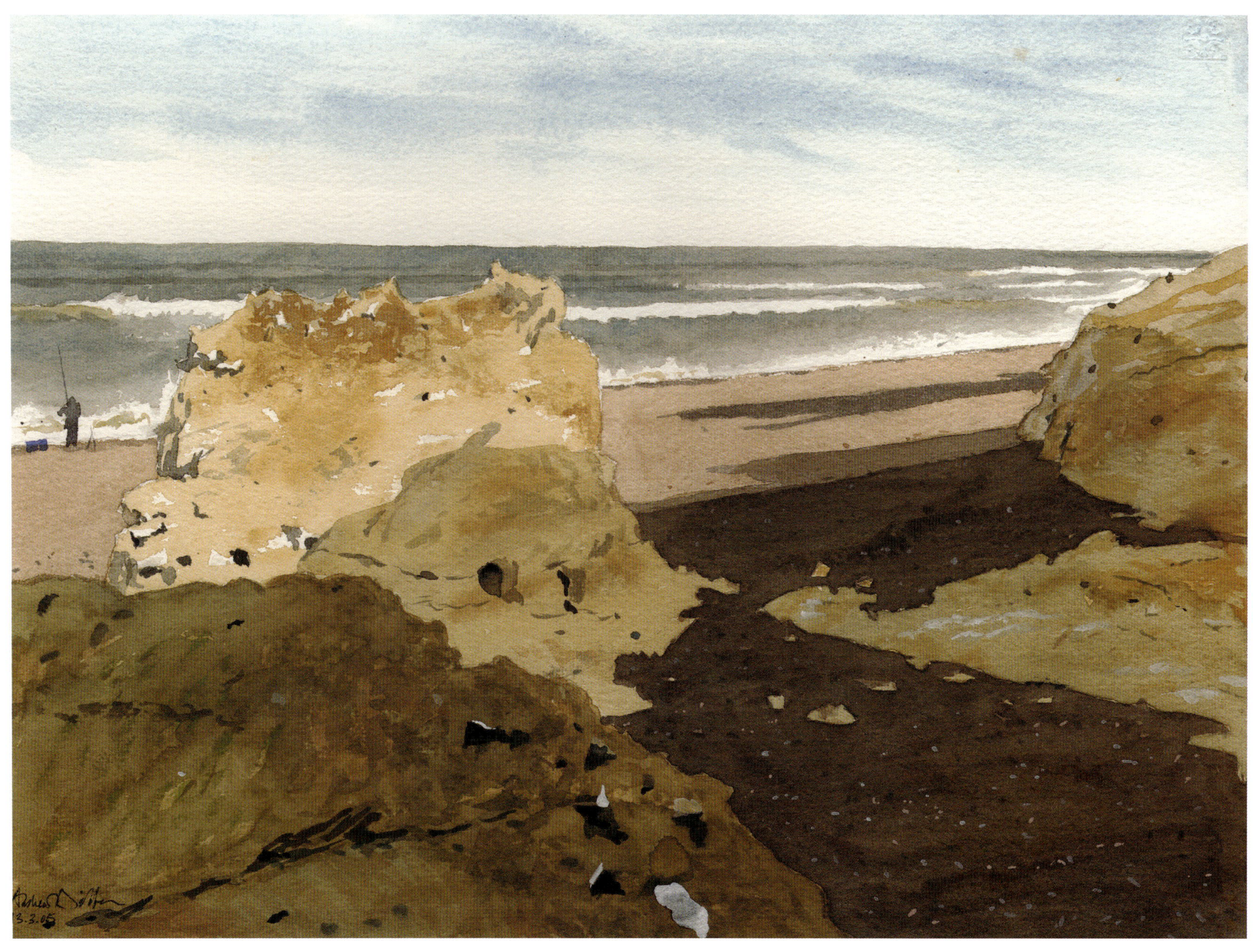

Weybourne Rocks (From Sketchbook) 11" x 14" 2005

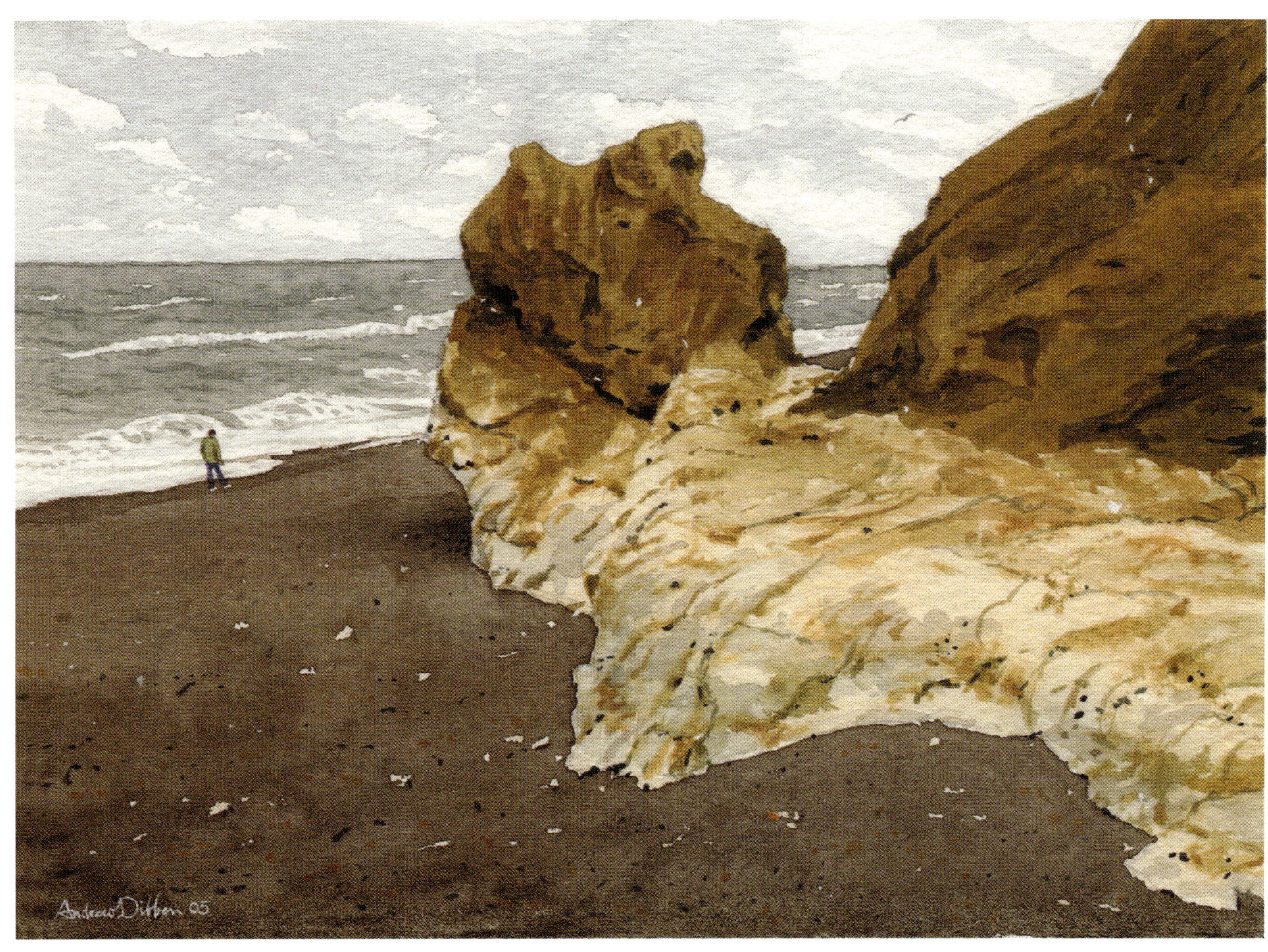

Weybourne Rocks 7" x 5" 2005

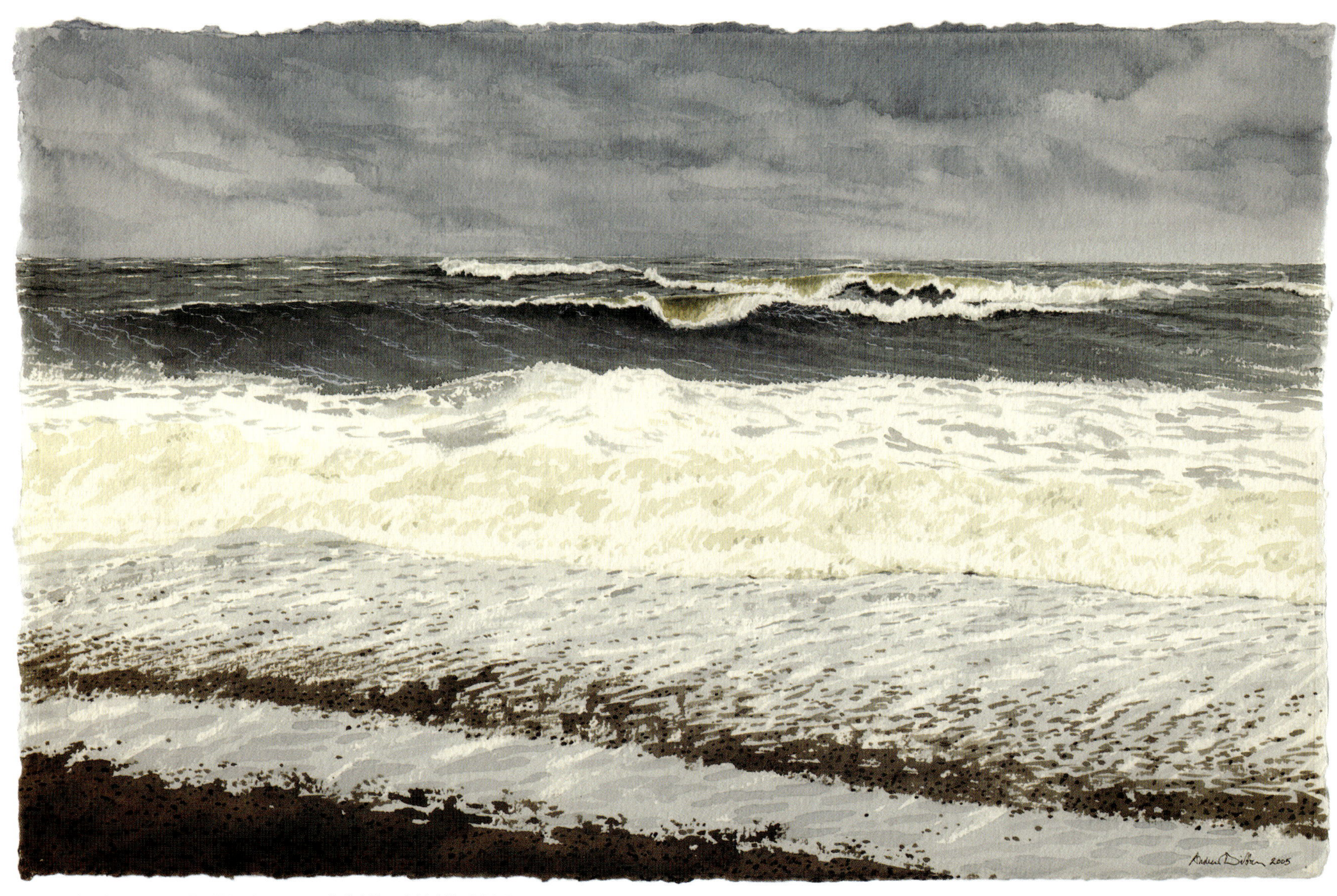

Northerly Force 7, Weybourne 14½" x 21½" 2005

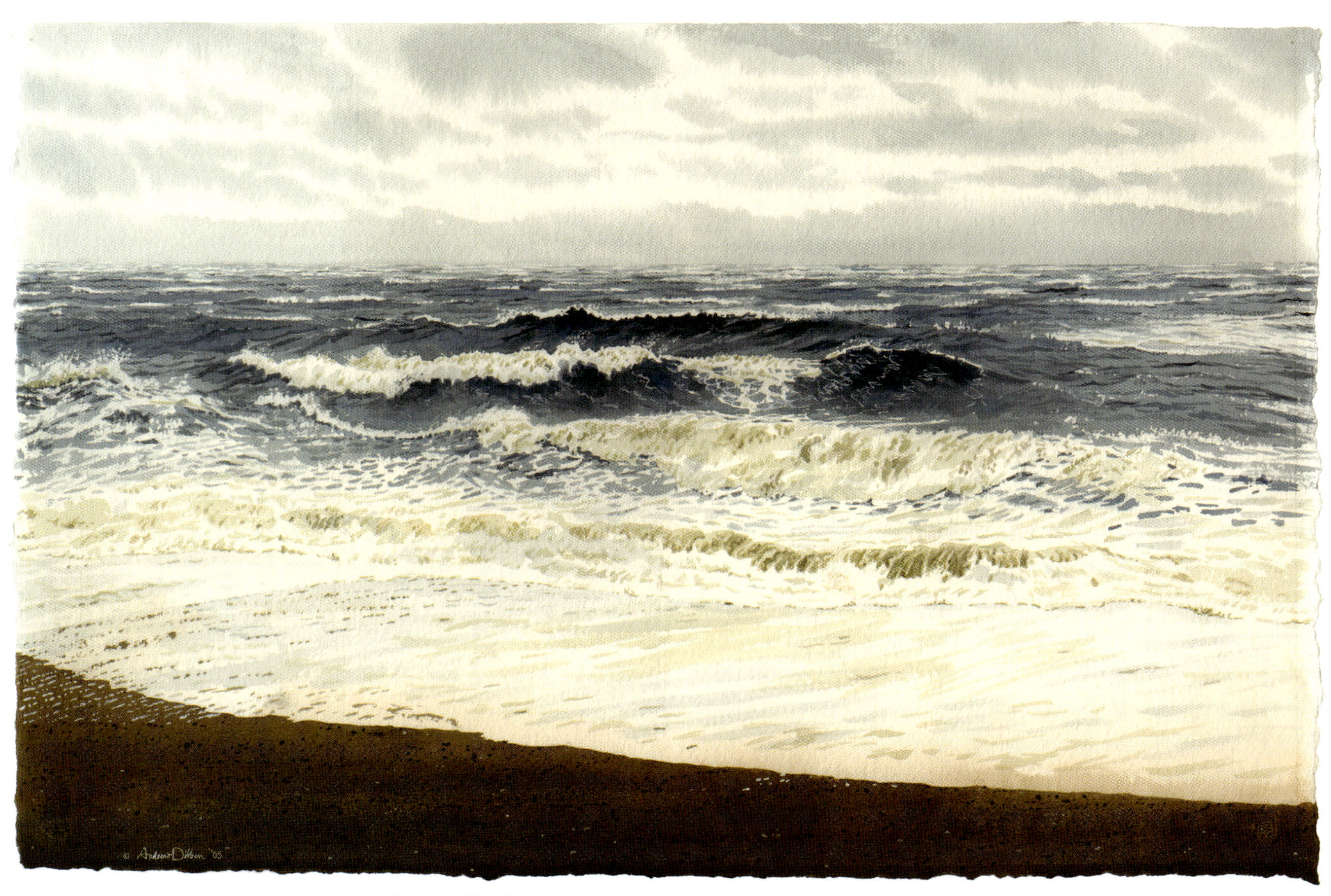

Northerly Force 7, Weybourne II 14½" x 21½" 2005

I very much enjoy painting the sea; there are endless variables in its depiction, since the subject itself changes constantly, and the way one approaches a picture can also be varied. This pair of paintings is a case in point. Based on observation of a fairly rough sea at Sheringham, working afterwards in the studio, I produced two paintings of the same frozen moment, using different colours to observe the different atmosphere each might convey. I did change the scale quite radically too; the greener version was worked at twice the size of the other, and I also gave the second picture a different, softer sky. Together with the colour change, this gives the feel of an earlier time of day.

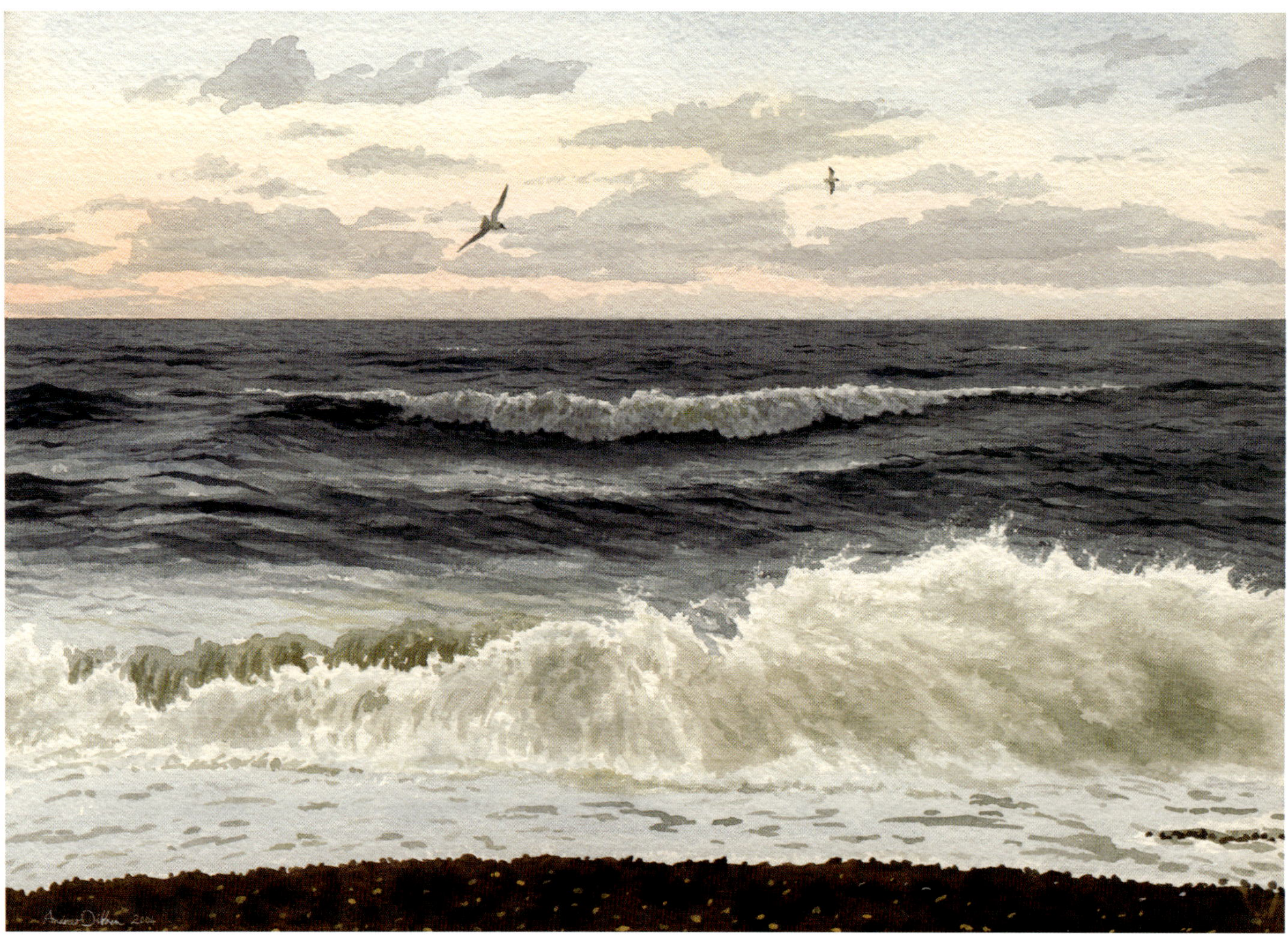

Breaking Wave, Sheringham Beach 21½ x 14" 2004

Opposite: *Breaking Wave, Sheringham Beach* 29" x 21½" 2004

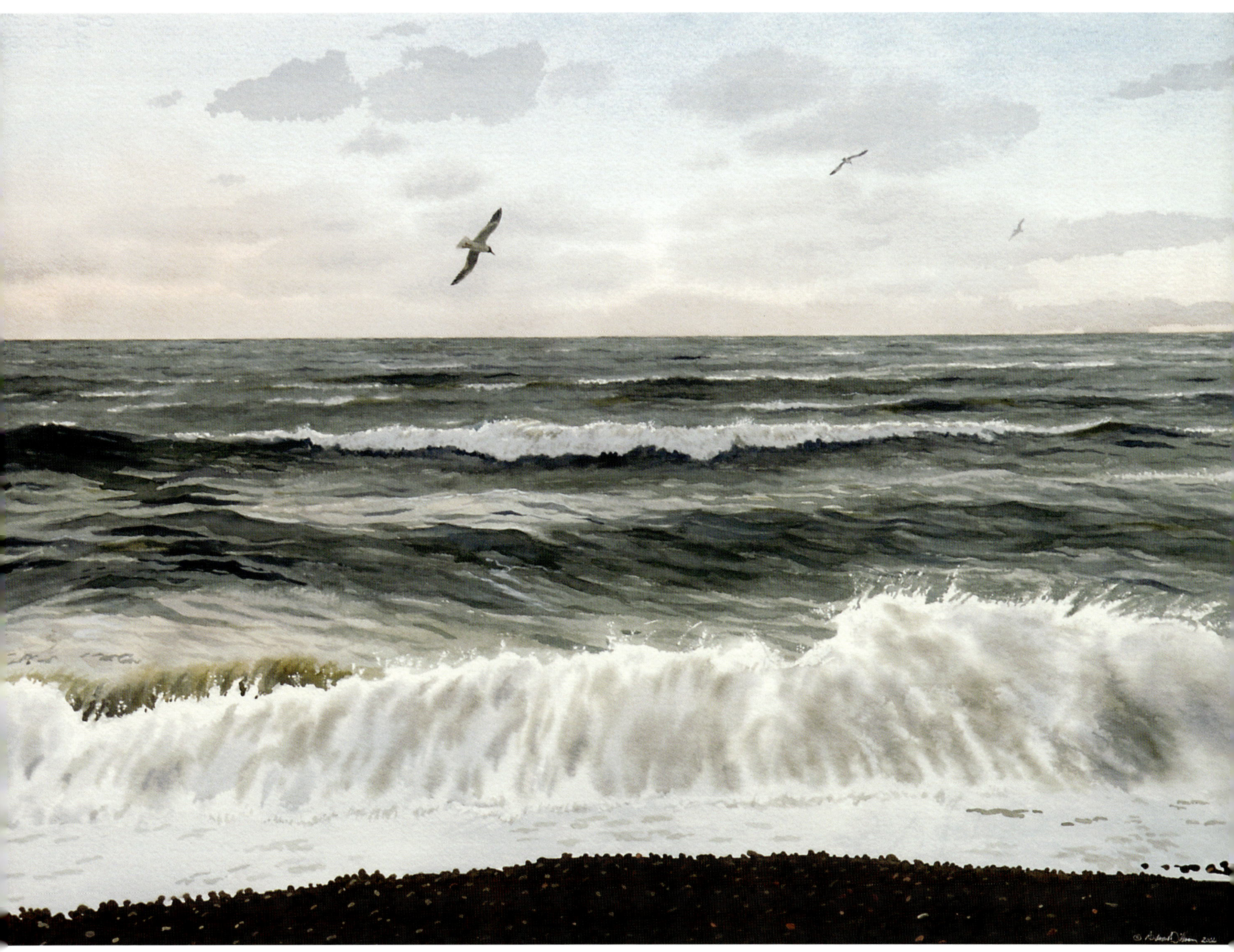

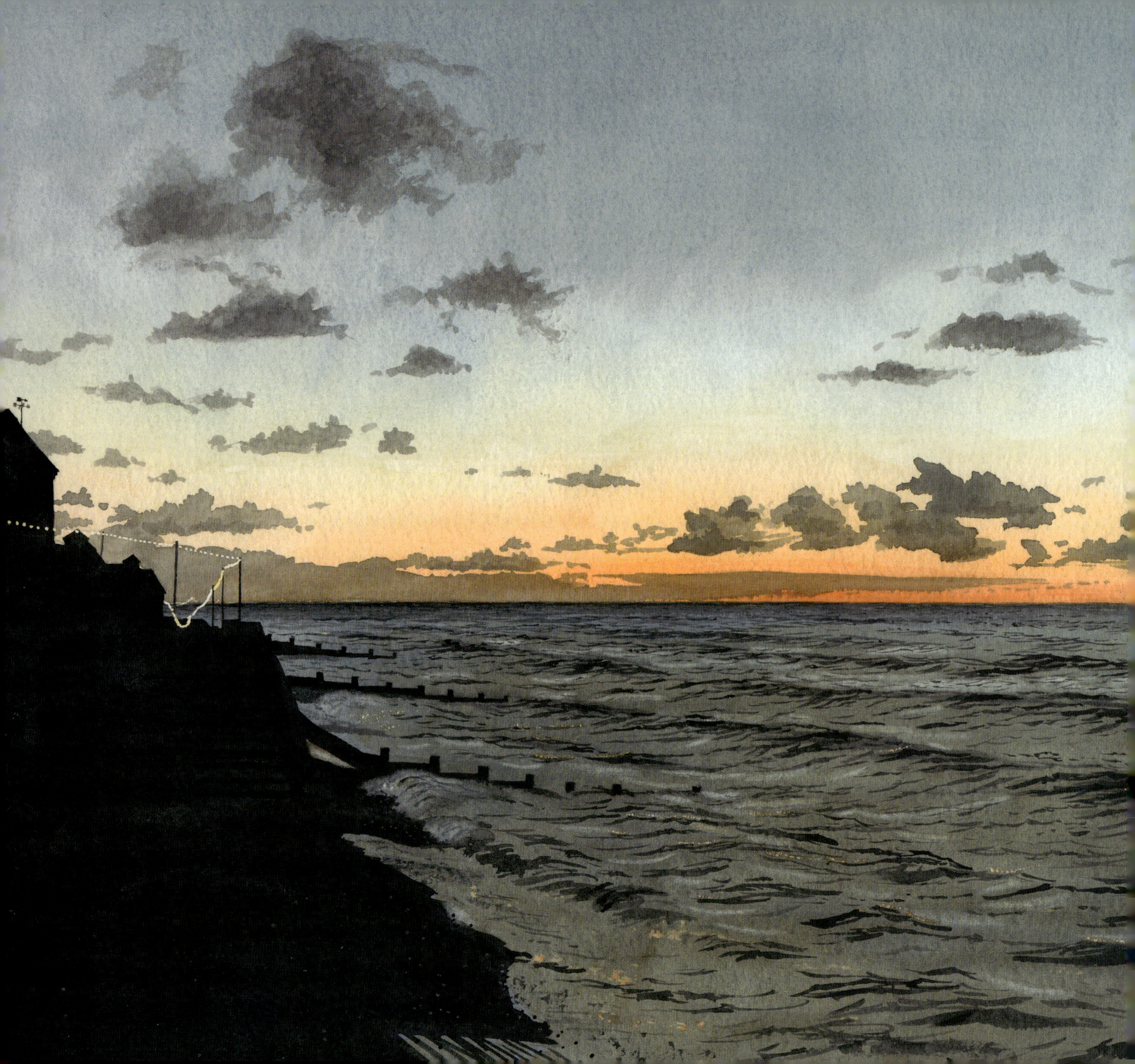

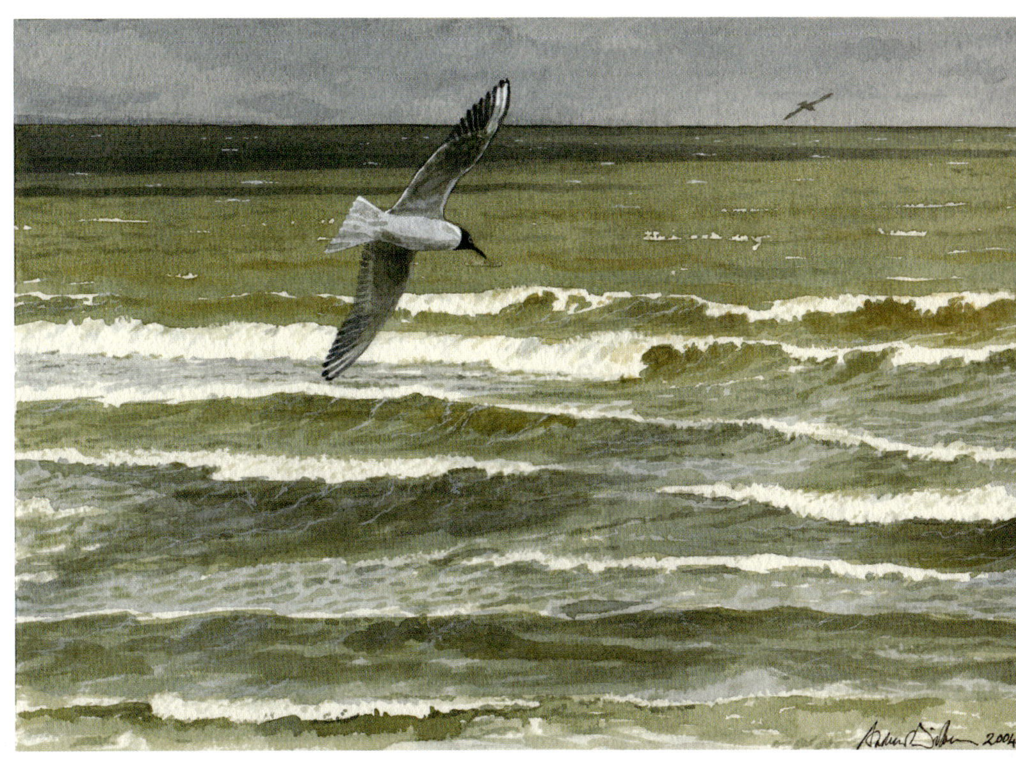

Wheeling 7" x 10" 2004

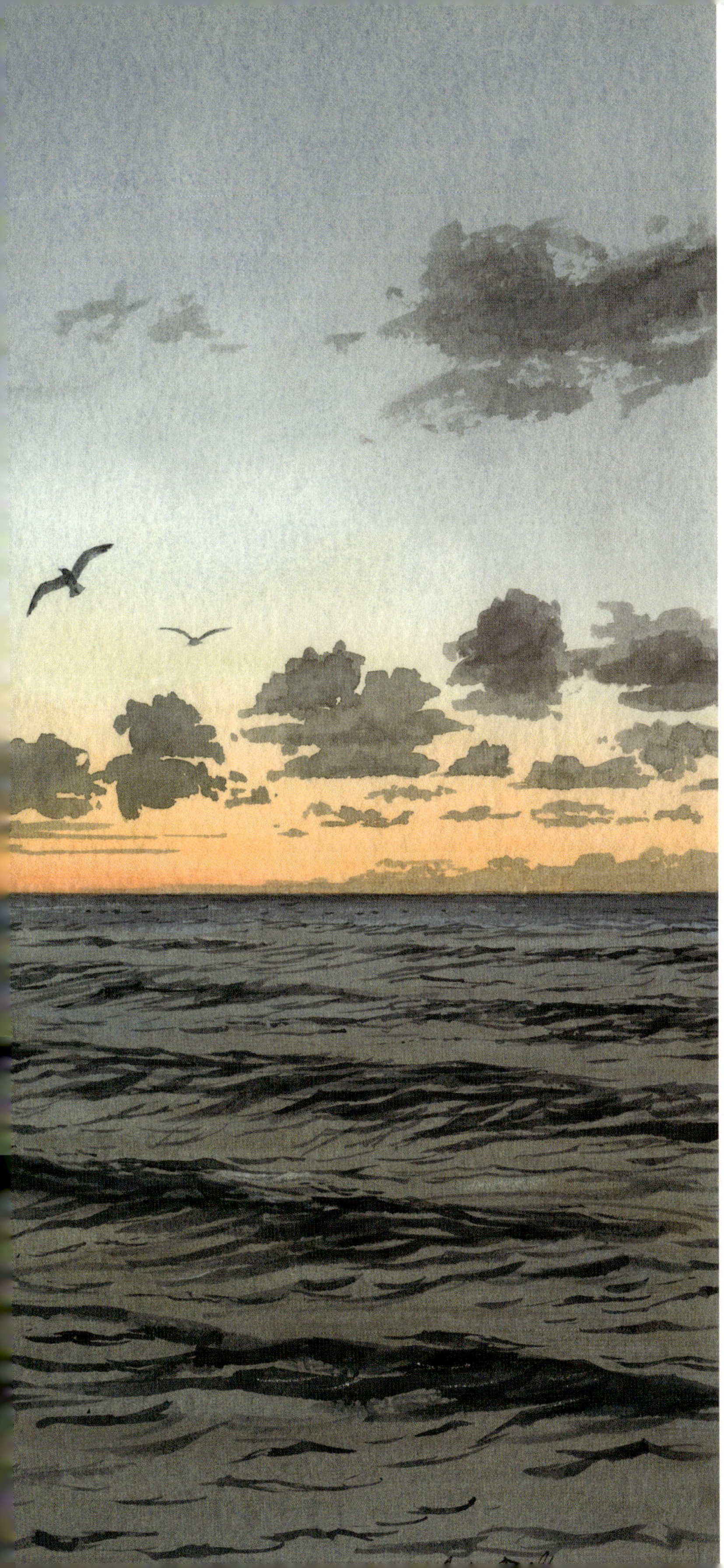

Sheringham Beach, Sunset 21½ x 14" 2005

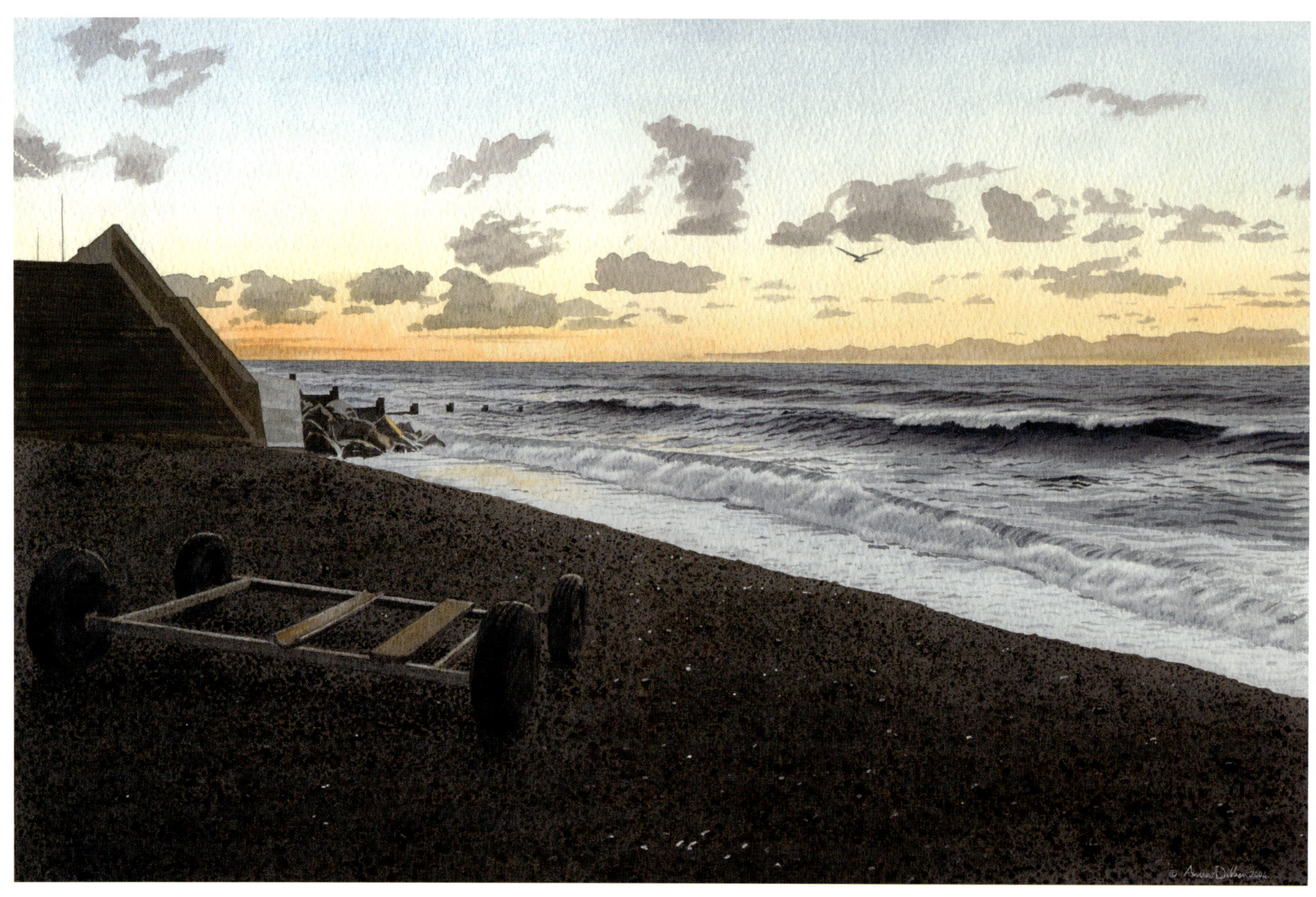

Launching Trolley, Sheringham Beach 21½ x 14” 2004

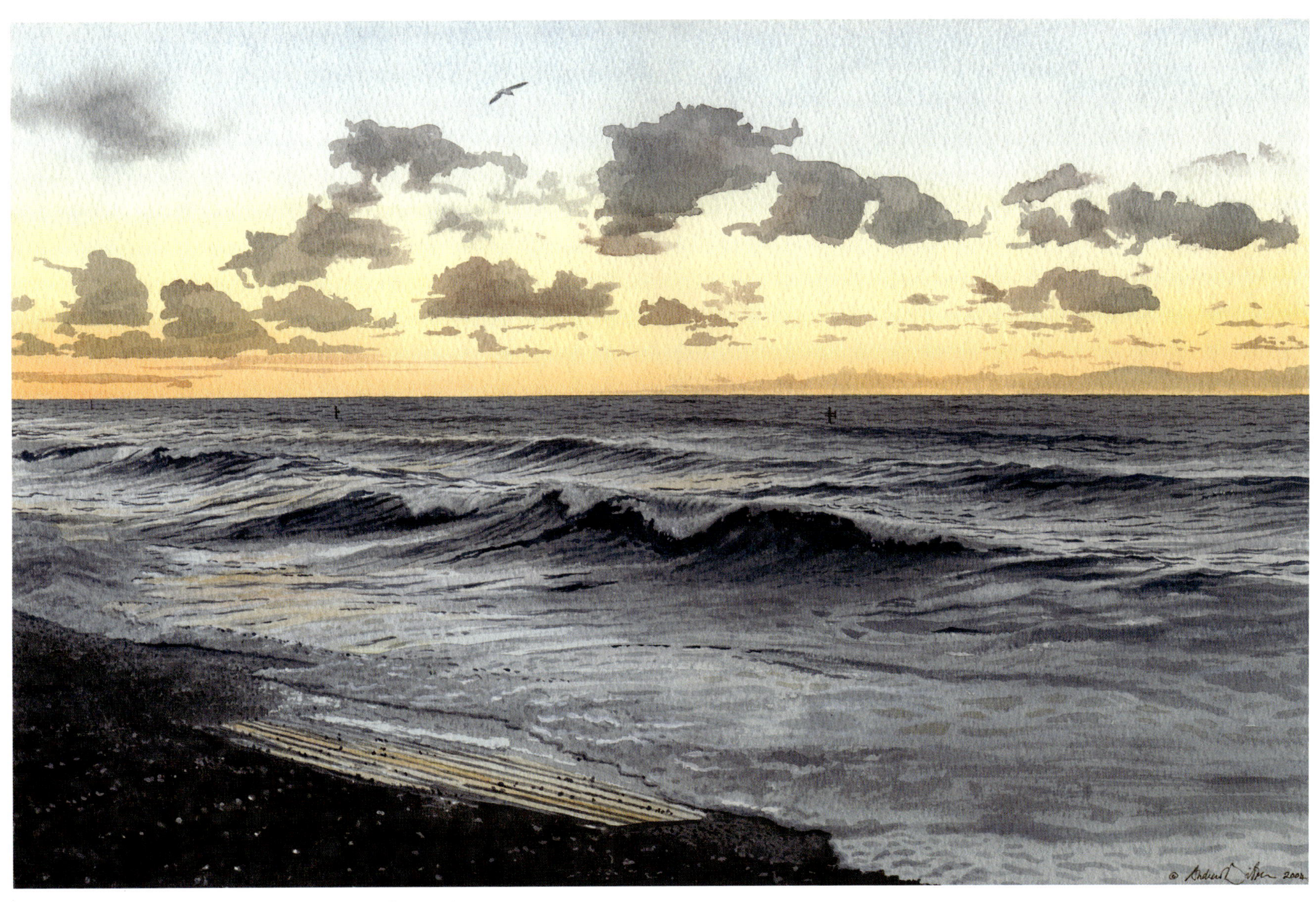

Sheringham Slipway, Sunset 21½ x 14" 2004

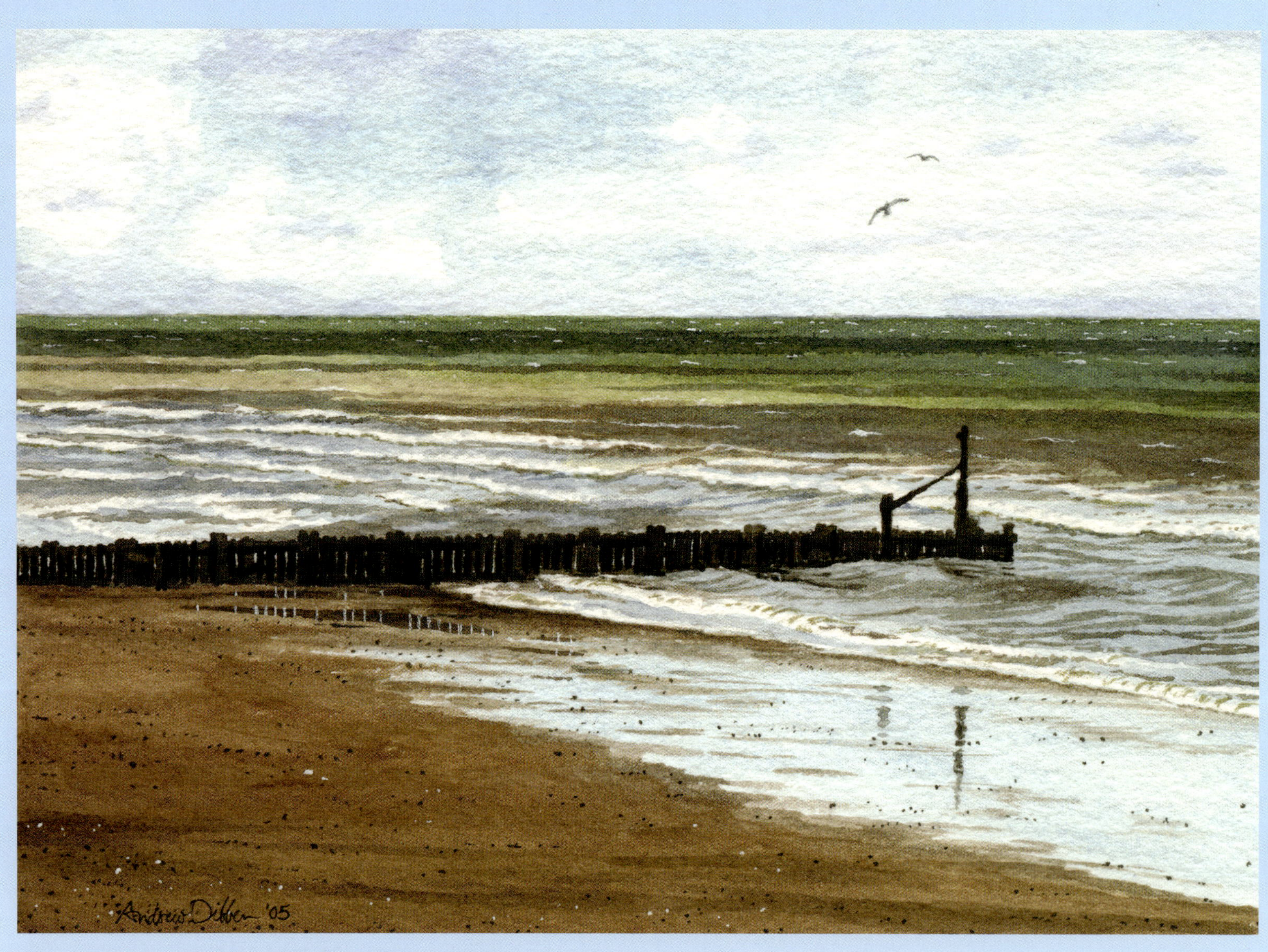

Overstrand Beach, Cloud Shadows 7" x 5" 2005

For many people the most wonderful beach in this area is the stretch between Holkham and Wells-next-the-Sea. Backed by lovely pinewoods, the beach is vast, and at low tide the sea recedes an amazing distance, rather like Moses' parting of the Red Sea. Large dunes have built up towards the seaward side, and these make a perfect sunbathing perch. If in summer you become too hot, aside from the water, you can retreat to the shade of the pinewoods. The ability of this beach to take large numbers of people and yet still appear uncrowded is uncanny. I have been here on a summer's day and found hundreds of cars parked in Lady Ann's Drive, but then wondered where all their occupants have vanished to once arriving on the sands. Holkham Beach has been mentioned more than once in newspaper surveys of the country's finest beaches, and rightly so.

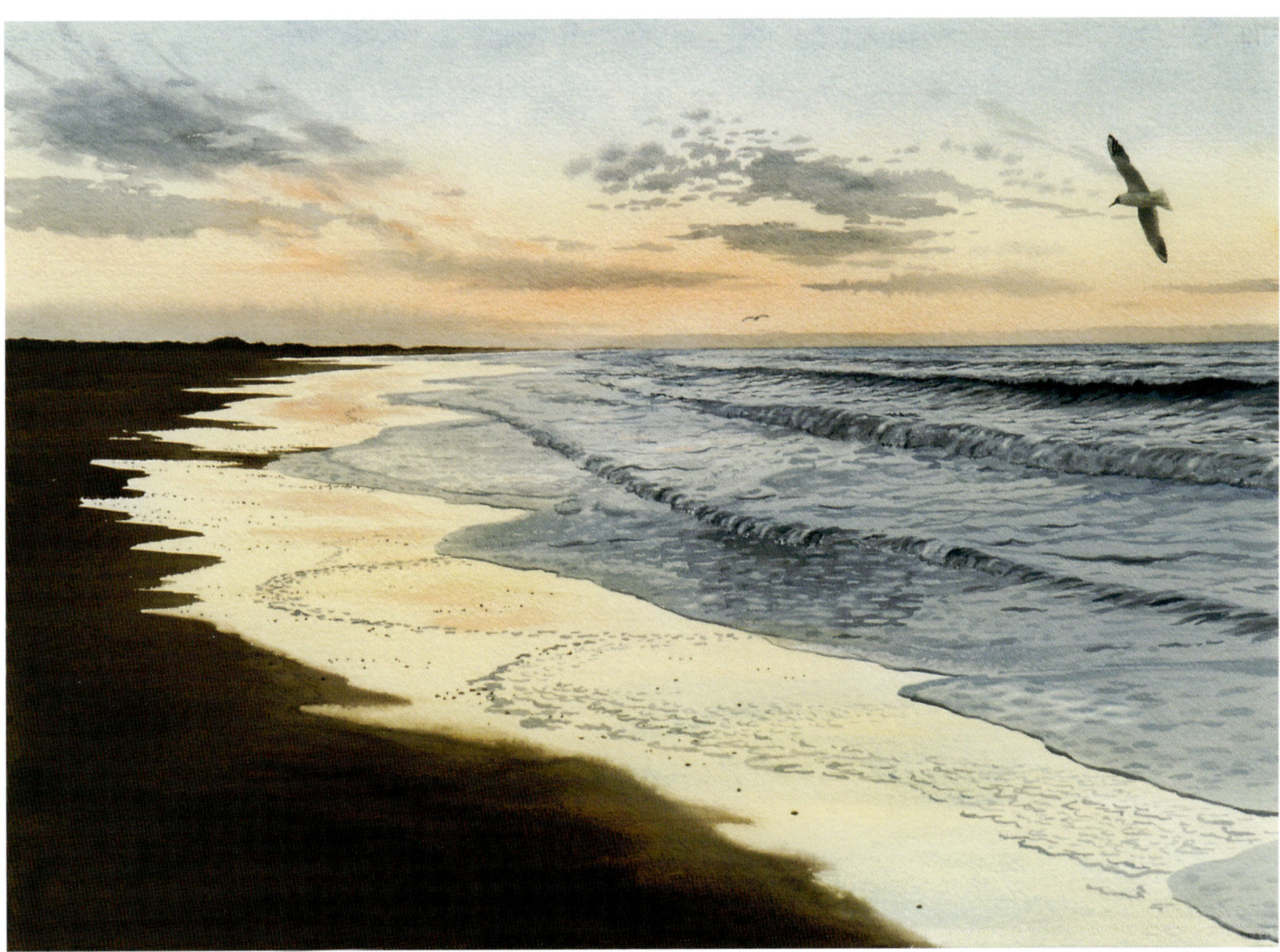

Holkham Beach Sunset 29" x 21½ 2004

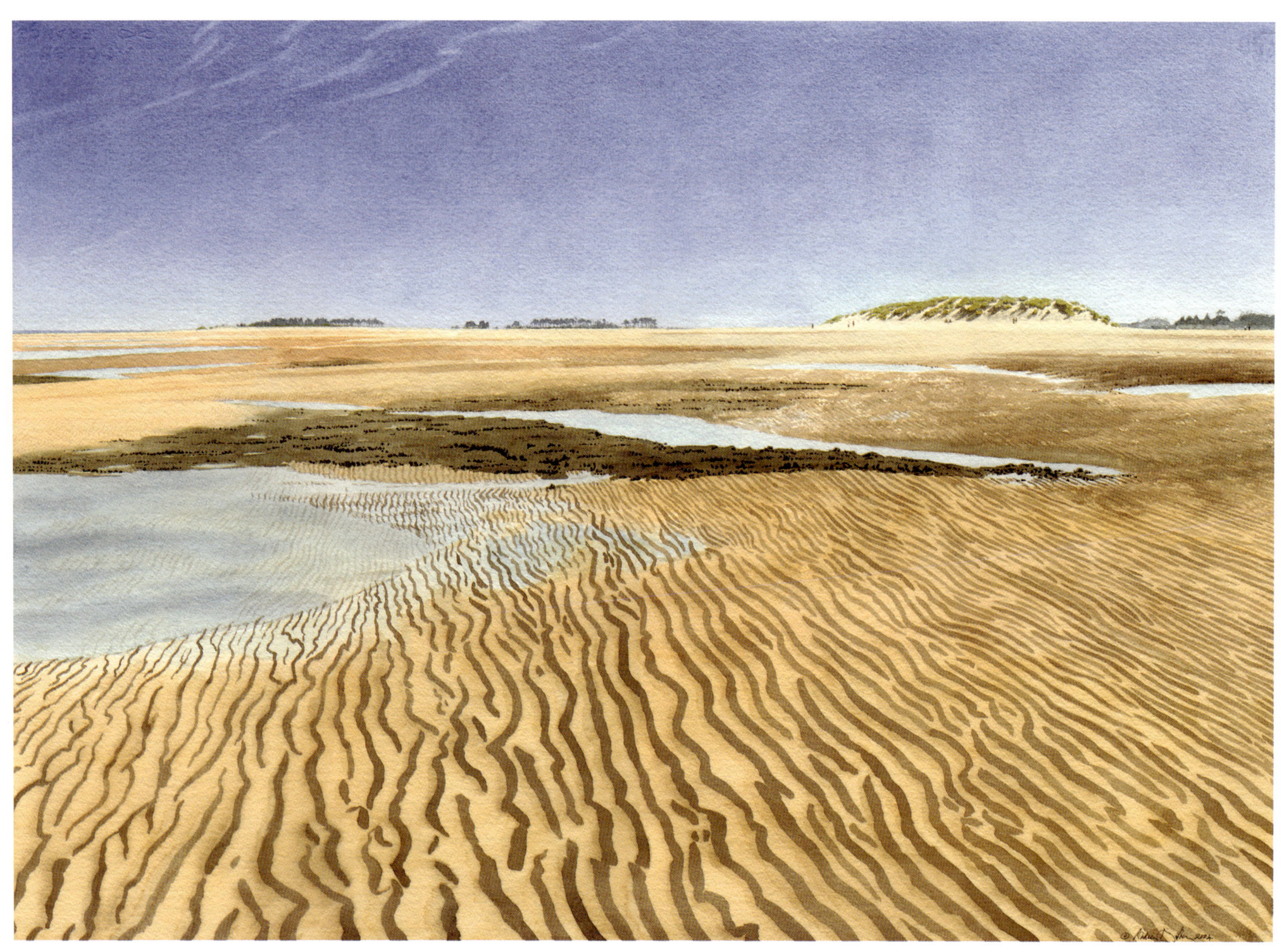

Holkham Beach, Sand & Mud 29" x 21½ 2003

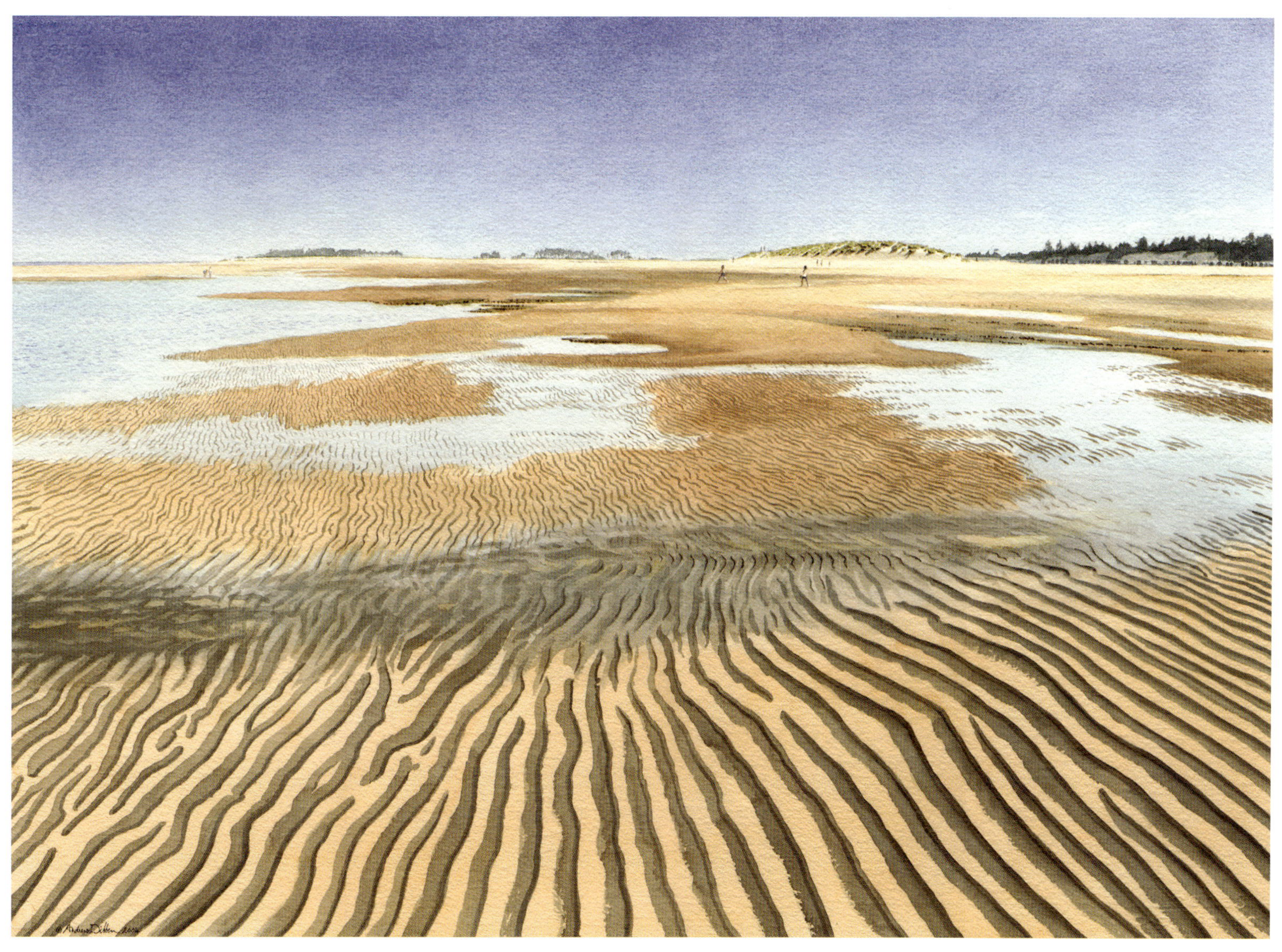

Holkham Beach, Towards Wells 29" x 21½" 2004

At Holkham beach one is very aware of the sky; there is nothing to impede one's view of it, and no shelter from the weather. If it rains, a mad dash for the woods becomes necessary.

OVERY STAITHE BEACH AT SUNSET

I have painted a number of pictures of dusk and night scenes recently; the light and colours at these times are particularly evocative, atmospheric, and romantic. I came across this scene after the long walk on the raised bank alongside the salt marsh and the creek at Overy Staithe, and the climb over the sand dunes. The light was quite bewitching, the cloud-scape very striking, and there was a sensation of enormous endless open space, enhanced by the complete absence of any living thing.

Though the sky in itself was vast and arresting, the feeling of space was magnified when it was reflected in the flat pools left at low tide. I chose to include areas of ridged sand scoured by the tide, as these give perspective, which helps define the depth in the scene. The strong contrast between areas of sand and water were very satisfying. These paintings are virtually abstracts, and as such they live or die by whether the simple shapes formed by the sky, water and land are appealing to the eye.

Overy Beach Sunset 2 21" x 14" 2003

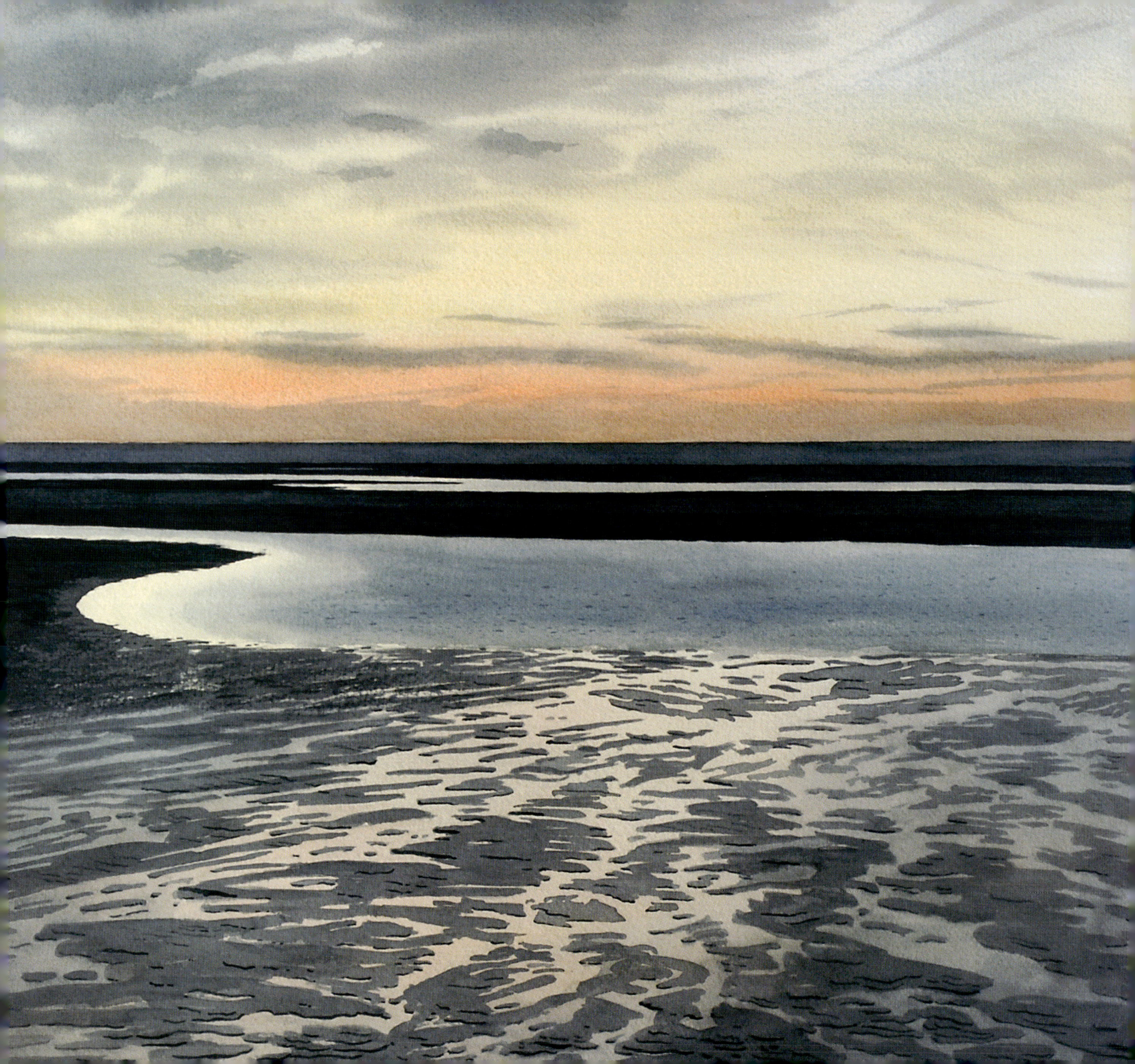

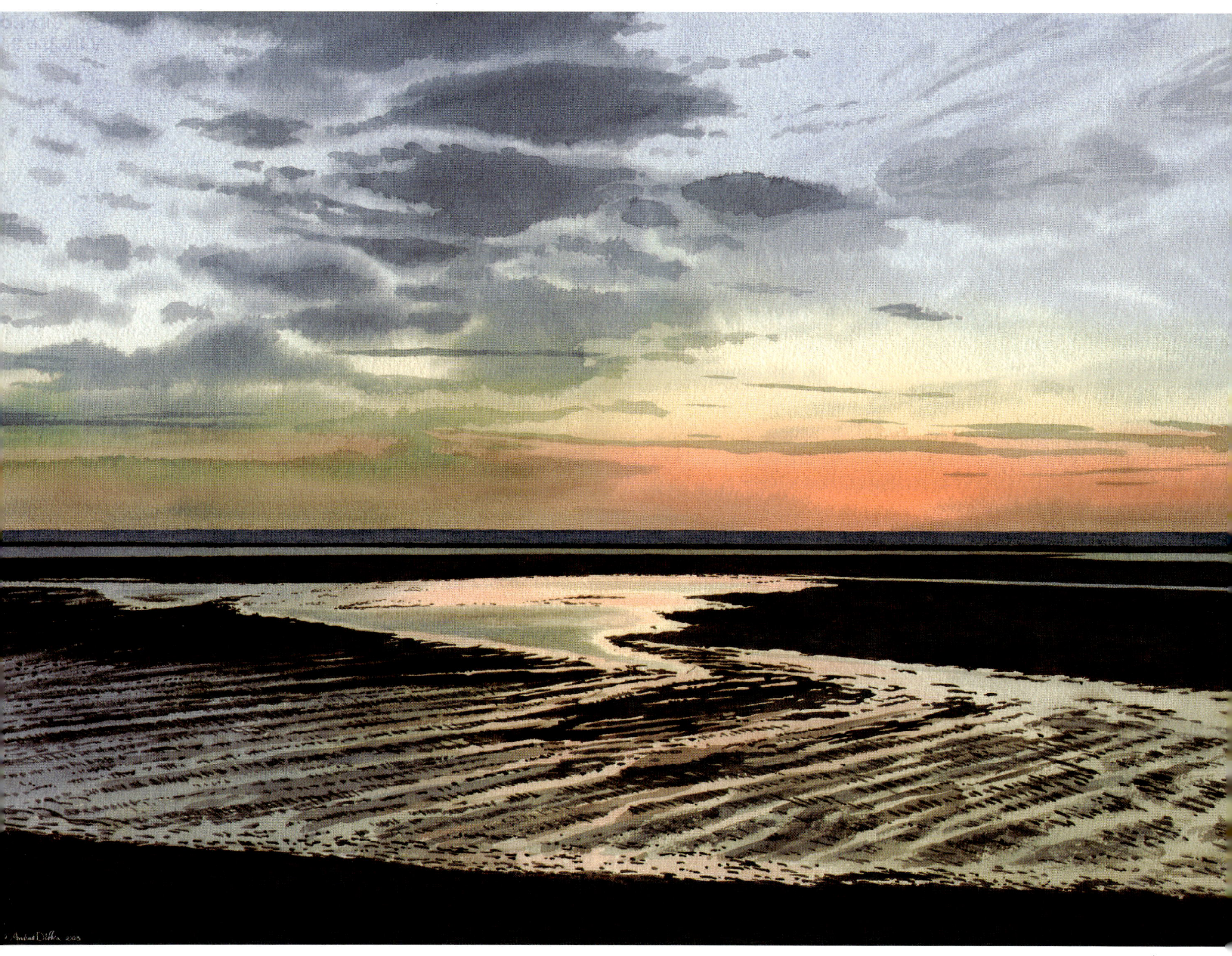

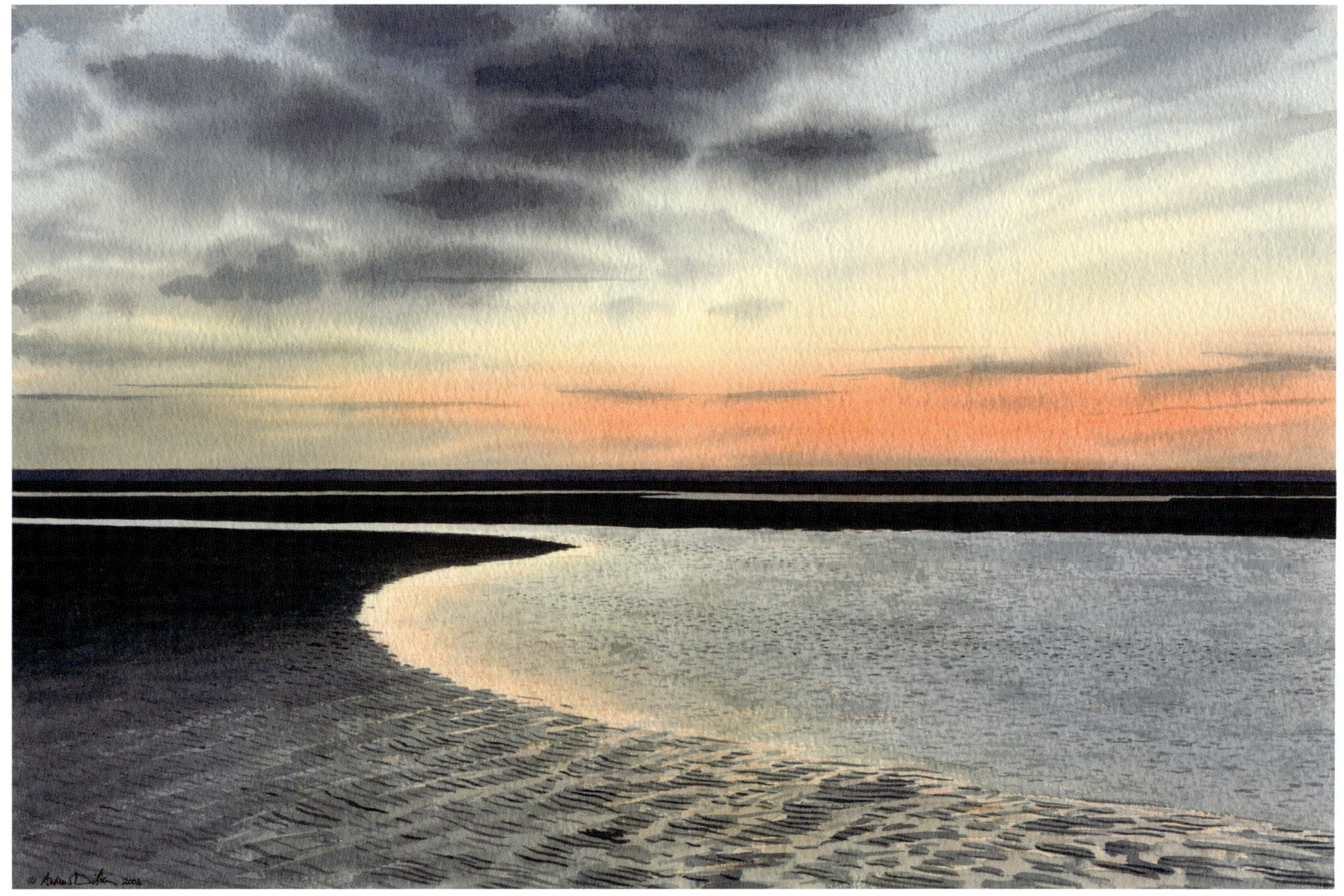

Overy Beach Sunset III 21" x 14" 2004

Opposite: *Overy Beach Sunset* 29" x 21" 2003

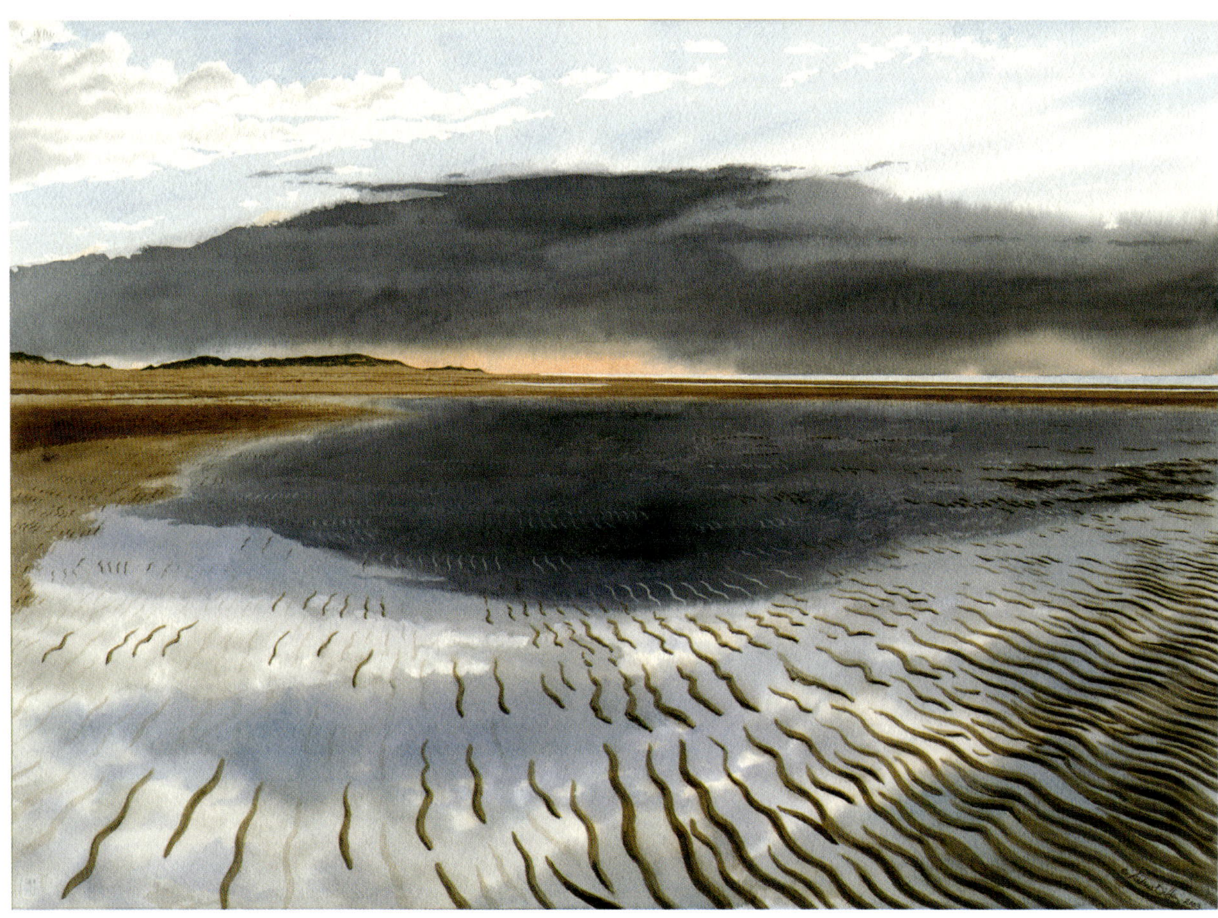

Storm Clouds Over Scolt Head 29" x 21" 2003

On another occasion on Overy Staithe beach, storm clouds had built up to the west, over Scolt Head. Large shallow pools were still lying on the sand, still draining away slowly; ridges of sand just above and below the water appearing like a shoal of migrating eels. The cloud mass hung there, hardly moving; then, it became apparent that it was slowly moving inland, and the sun would break through again. A strange orangey-pink glow suffused the sky below the cloud mass, even though it was nowhere near sunset. Suddenly the sun broke through and lit up the sand ridges below it so brightly that it was almost painful to look at.

Opposite: *Overy Staithe Beach, Stormy Sky* 29" x 21" 2003

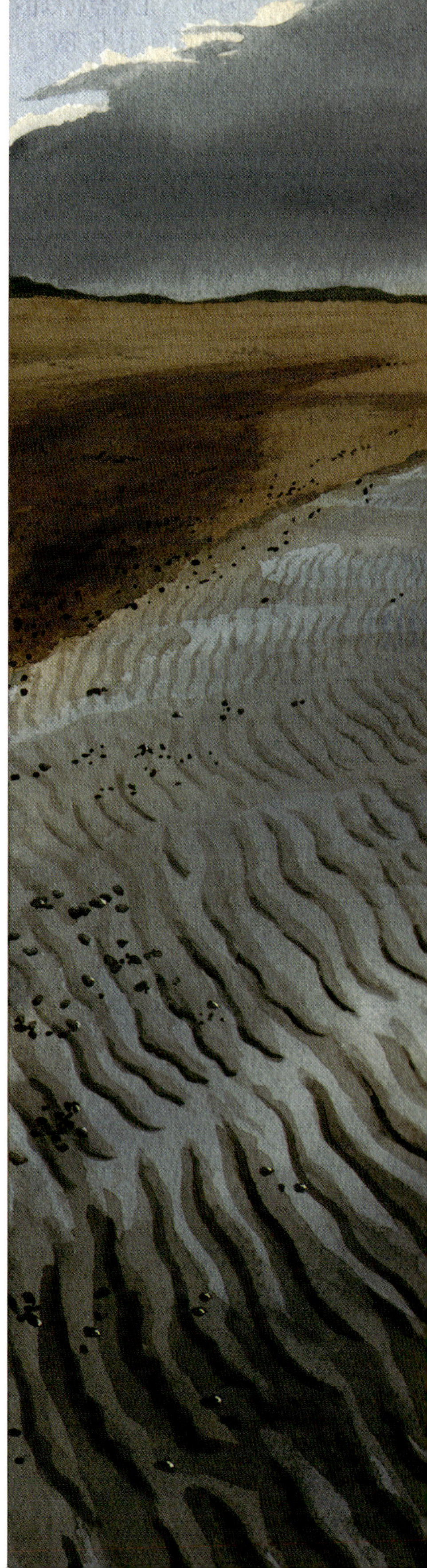

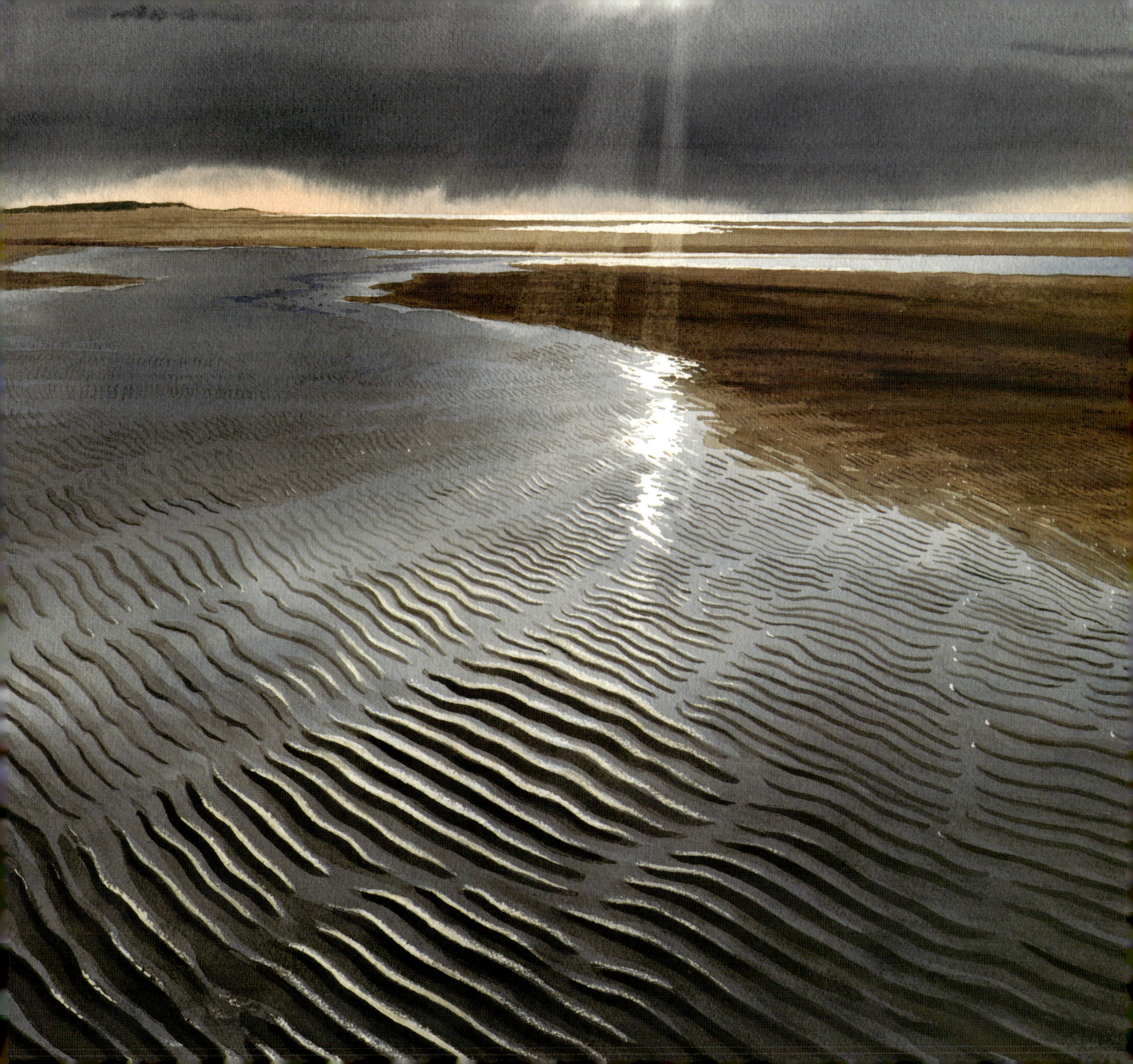

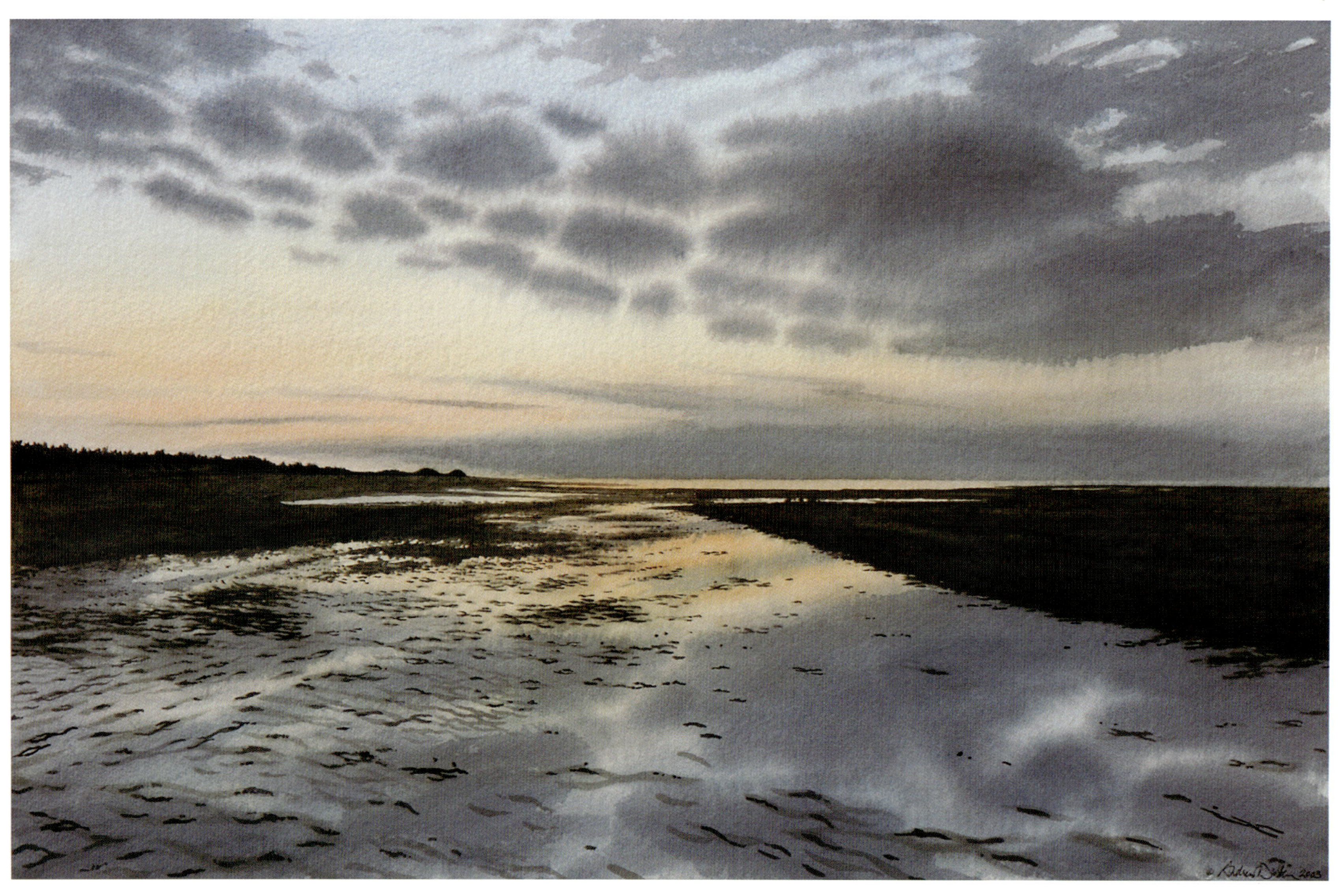

Thornham Beach, Dusk 14$\frac{1}{2}$" x 21$\frac{1}{2}$" 2003

Opposite: *Thornham Beach, Pink Sky* 14$\frac{1}{2}$" x 21$\frac{1}{2}$" 2003

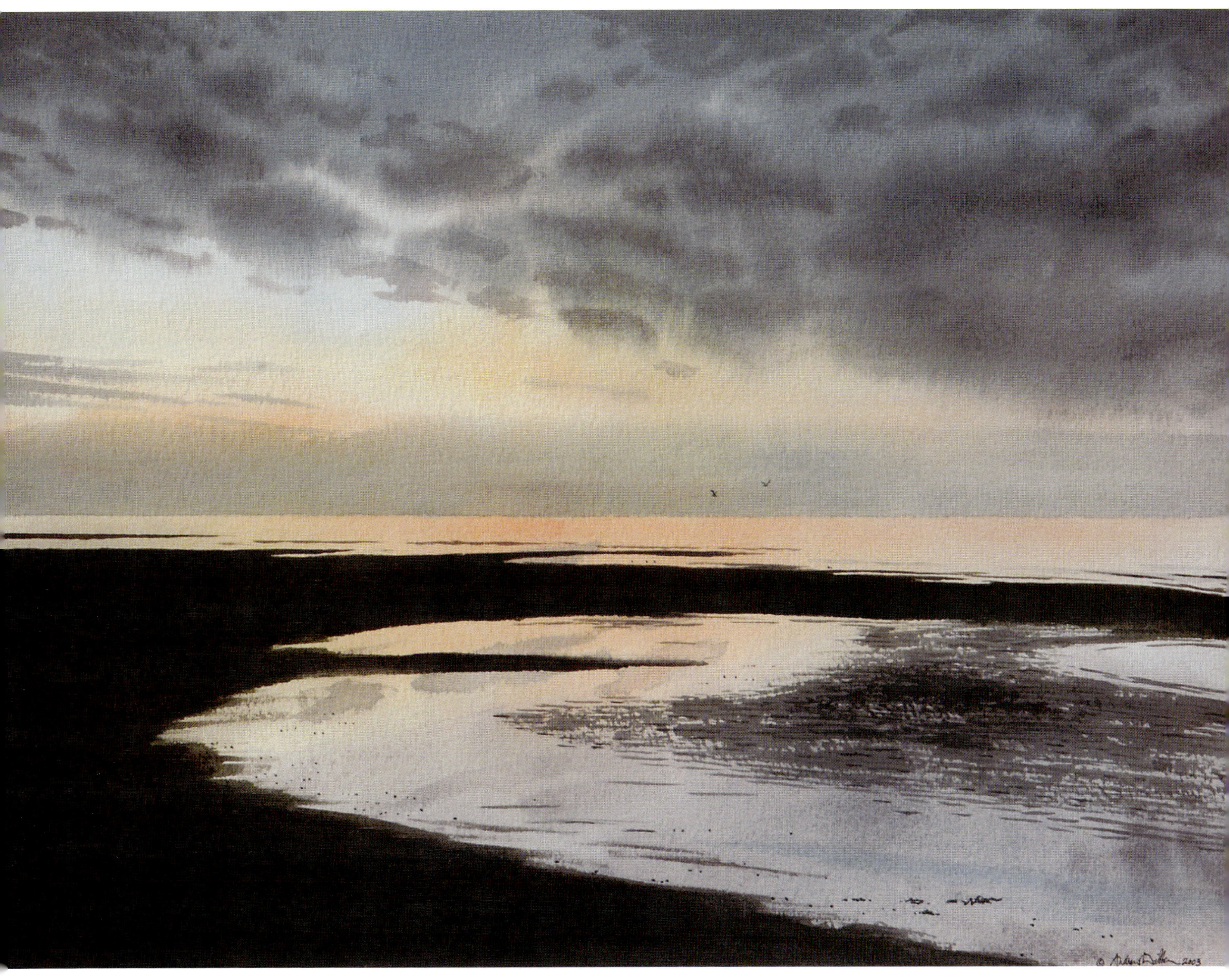

MOONLIGHT OVER THE NORTH COAST

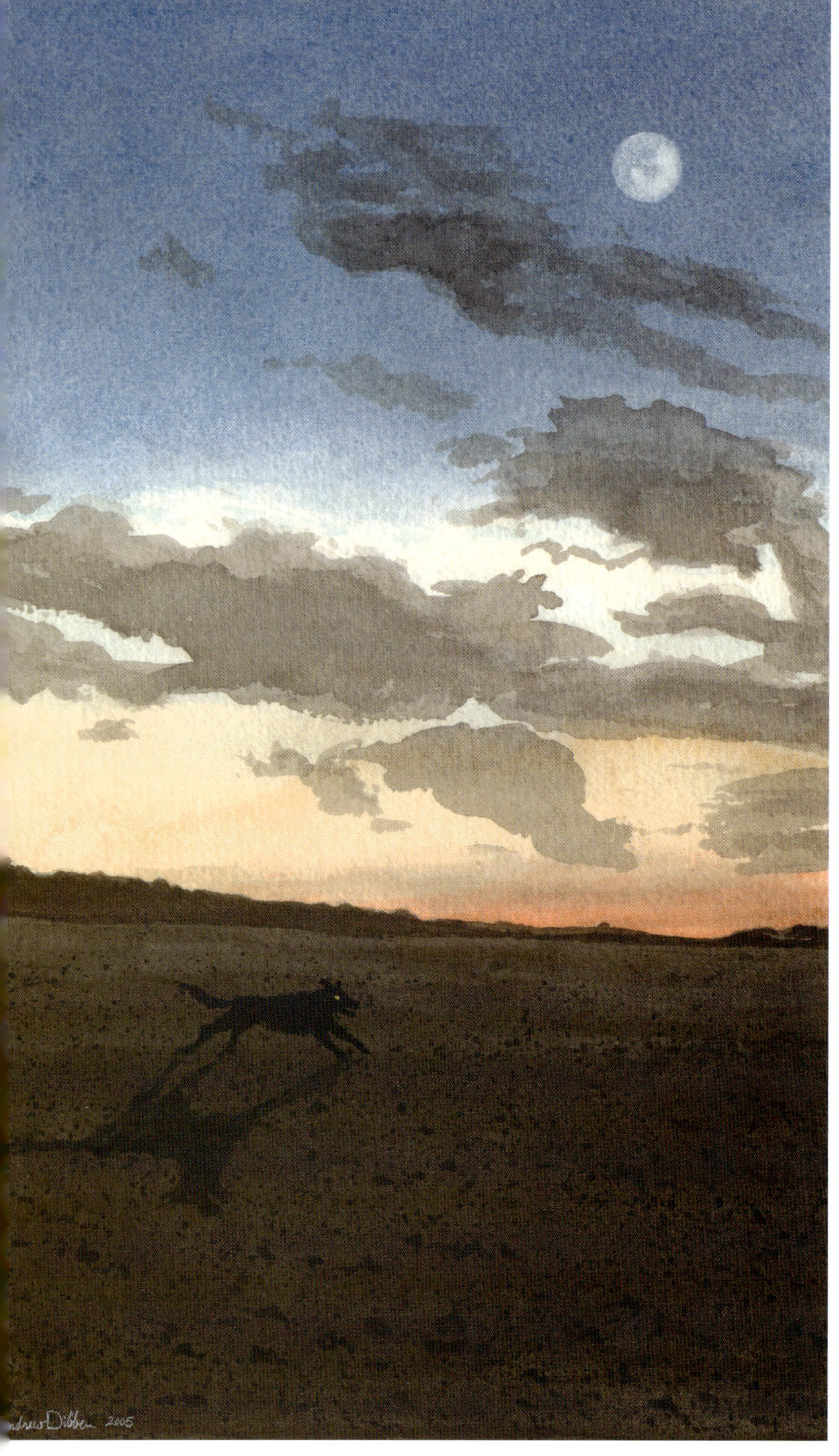

On the left is a little picture I did for fun when I had been thinking about a whole new theme for paintings of East Anglian legends, which may or may not see the light of day at some point! It began as a portion of another painting, which I had cut off to improve the composition; I try to avoid doing this kind of thing, but occasionally it works.

'Black Shuck' was the story I had been thinking about, and so I strengthened the sky to make it more dramatic, added a full moon, and painted in a running dog, and his moonlight shadow. The intention was pure whimsy; I wasn't trying to make a really scary image of a fierce dog. It is more 'Black Shuck in a happy mood!' The real Black Shuck story is sinister in the extreme, as it tells of the ghost dog breaking through a church door and killing several of the congregation, so I would prefer not to inject too much realism.

The next painting shows Blakeney on a winter's night, after the ebb of a very high tide which has left numerous puddles behind on the hard above the creek. This happens quite frequently, and in fact the water often laps across the quay, and against the foot of the Blakeney Hotel façade. On this occasion, the scene was quite enchanting, with the steel barge *Juno* moored in the creek, and a crescent moon helping to light the area.

The third picture in this little set shows the scene one rainy evening, looking from Cromer cliff-top car park towards East Runton. The sun has gone down, the lights are coming on in the Runtons, and two cyclists make their way home to Cromer under a showery looking sky.

'Black Shuck' 15½" x 8½" 2005

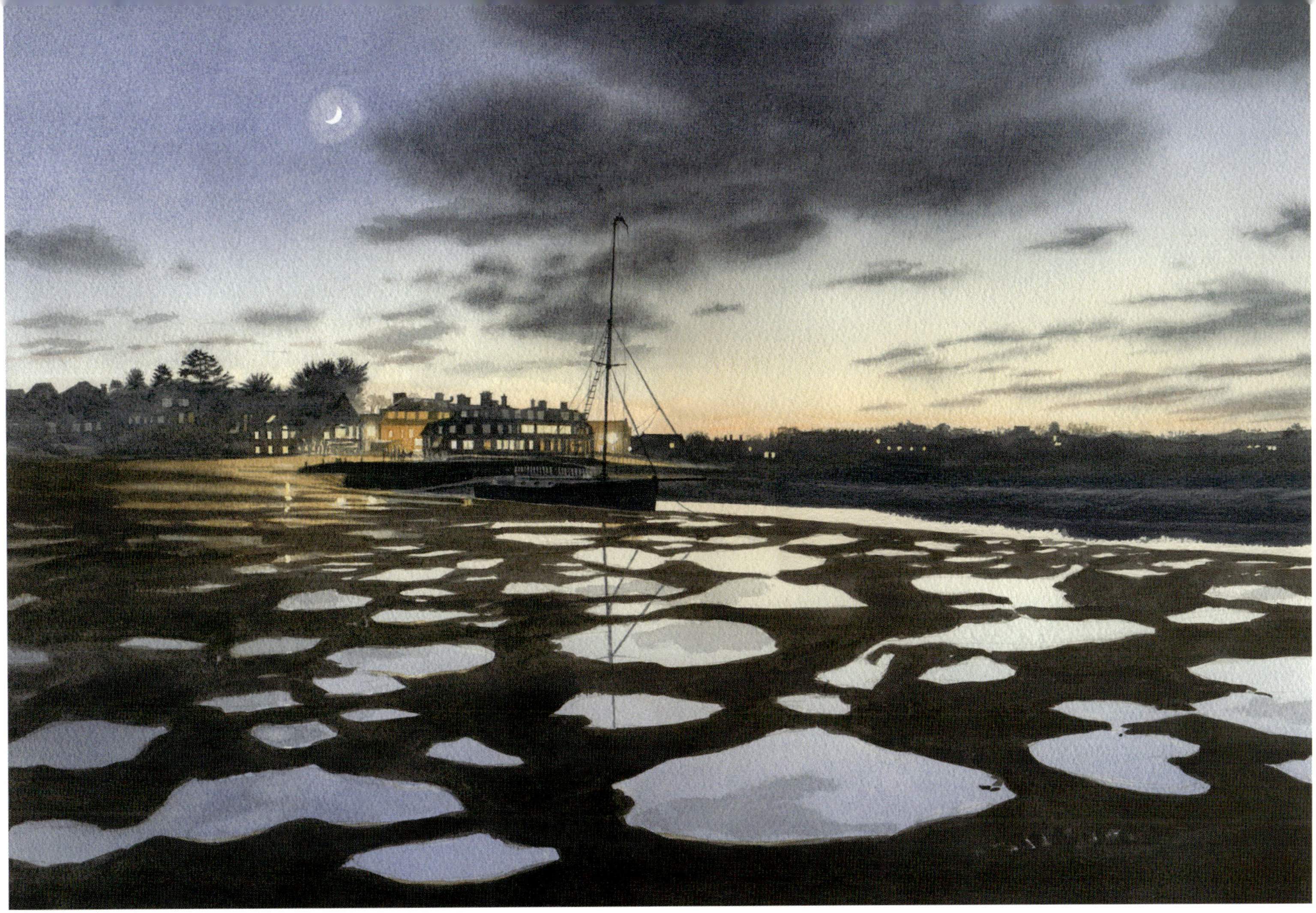

Blakeney by Moonlight
14" x 20" 2003

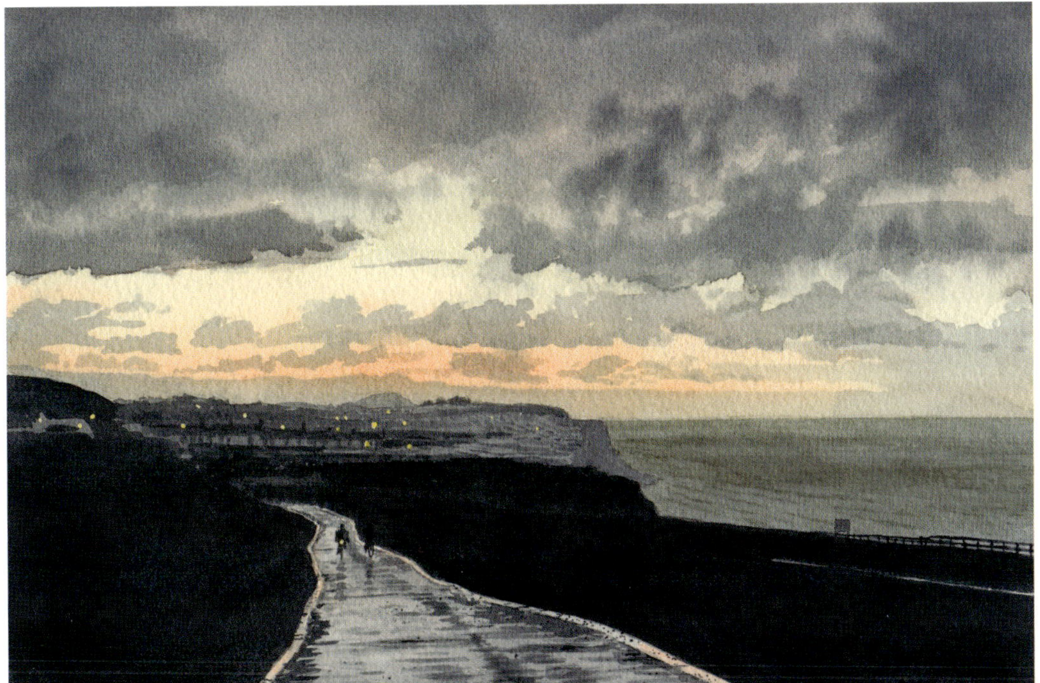

Storm Over East Runton
7" x 10" 2004

WELLS QUAY AT DUSK AND NIGHT

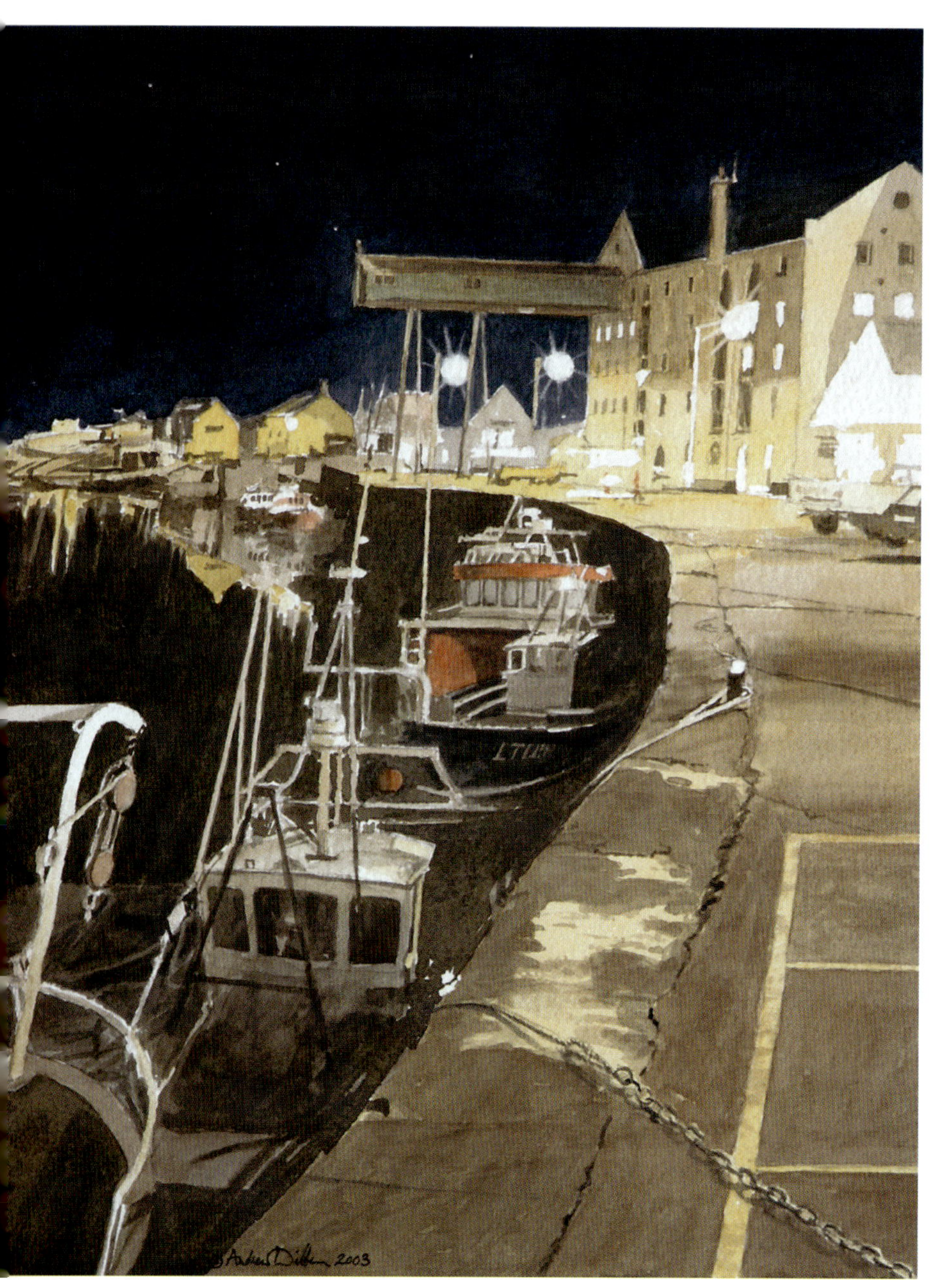

Wells Quay Night I 10" x 7" 2003

Wells-next-the-Sea has always held a great attraction for me. It is a shame that we no longer see cargo vessels tied up alongside the quay; speed being everything these days, it is more effective to take a ship to a port with easier access such as King's Lynn, Great Yarmouth or Lowestoft, and then transport the cargo by road for the last part of the journey. At Wells, ships would have to wait for the ideal moment to make the tricky journey up the sinuous channel, before being beached alongside the quay by the falling tide. It was lovely to see two or three coasters lined up at the quay, with cranes busily discharging cargoes into waiting lorries. Now the granary has been converted into luxurious apartments – very beautifully, one has to admit – and the fleet of inshore fishing vessels, the schooner *Albatros* and a handful of visiting yachts provide the only bustle.

The *Albatros*, operated by the Dutch Captain Ton Brouwer, was a former Baltic Trader, built in 1899, and holds the distinction of being the last sailing cargo vessel on the North Sea; she brought her very last cargo to Wells in September 1996. Captain Brouwer became quite attached to Wells, and so decided to base his vessel here, and run passenger trips instead to make his living. The ship makes a fine sight moored alongside, with her mass of rigging towering over the quay.

At night, the quay takes on a more mysterious appearance; everything to the north fades into blackness, apart from the regular twinkling of the channel marker buoys. The scene, with all the town's lights reflected in the black harbour waters, transports me back to the late 1950s, and late night departures of the cross-Channel ferries from Southampton or Le Havre.

I was delighted when this picture, and its companion night time one (see page 89), were selected for inclusion in the Royal Institute of Painters in Watercolours' annual exhibition, in 2004.

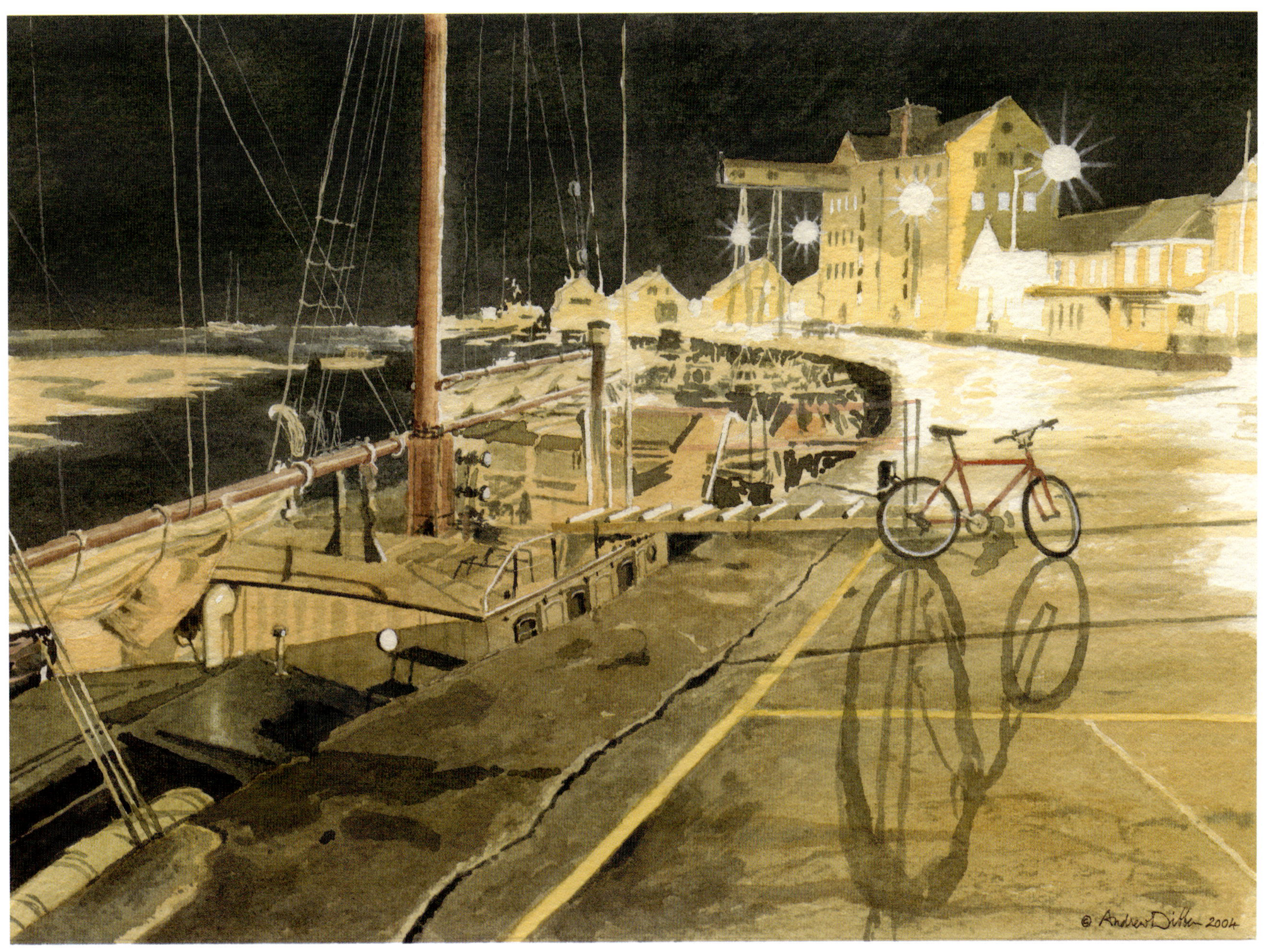

Captain Brouwer's Bike 10" x 7" 2004

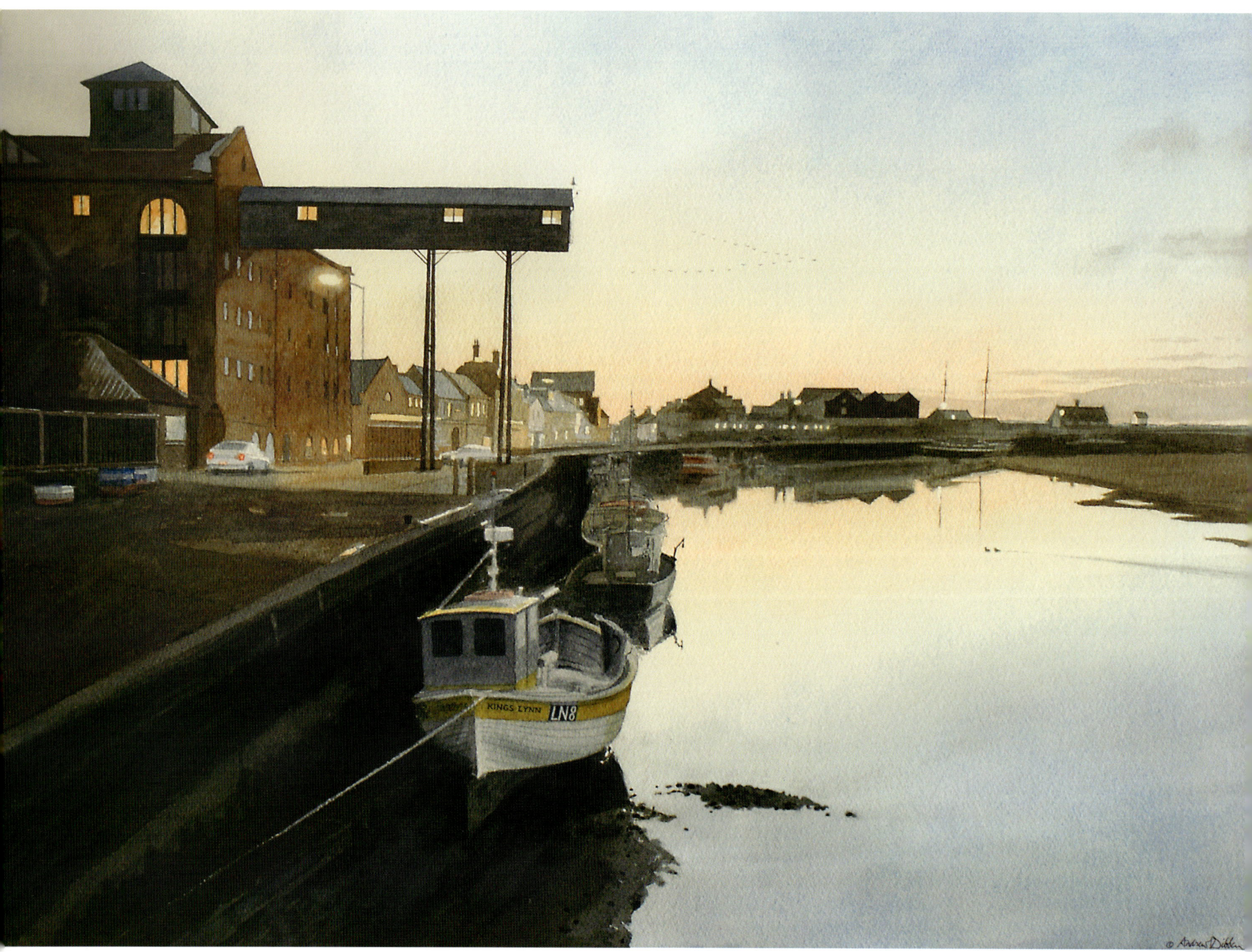
KINGS LYNN LN8

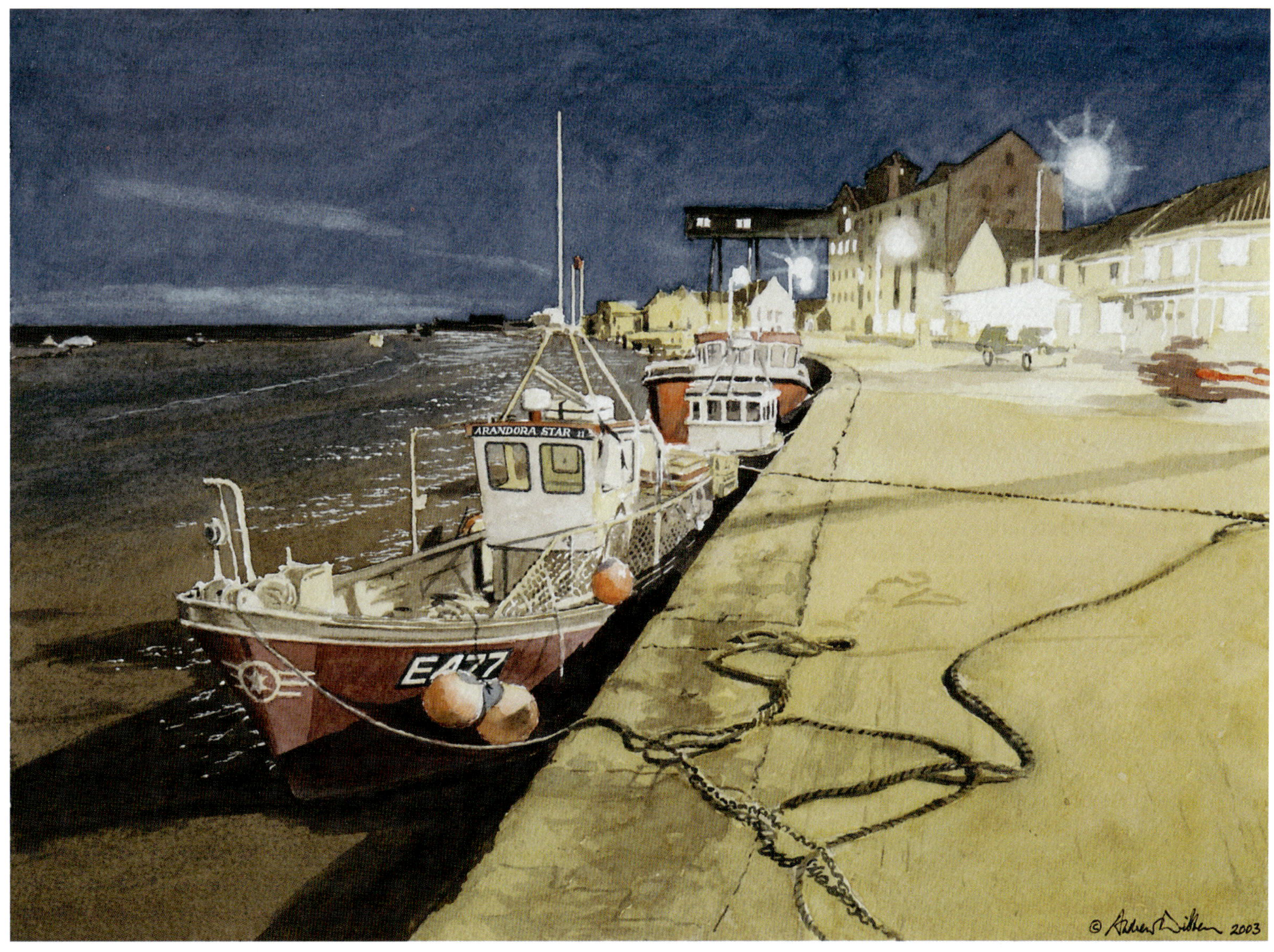

Wells Quay Night II 7" x 10" 2003

Opposite: *Wells Quay at Dusk I* 29" x 21" 2003

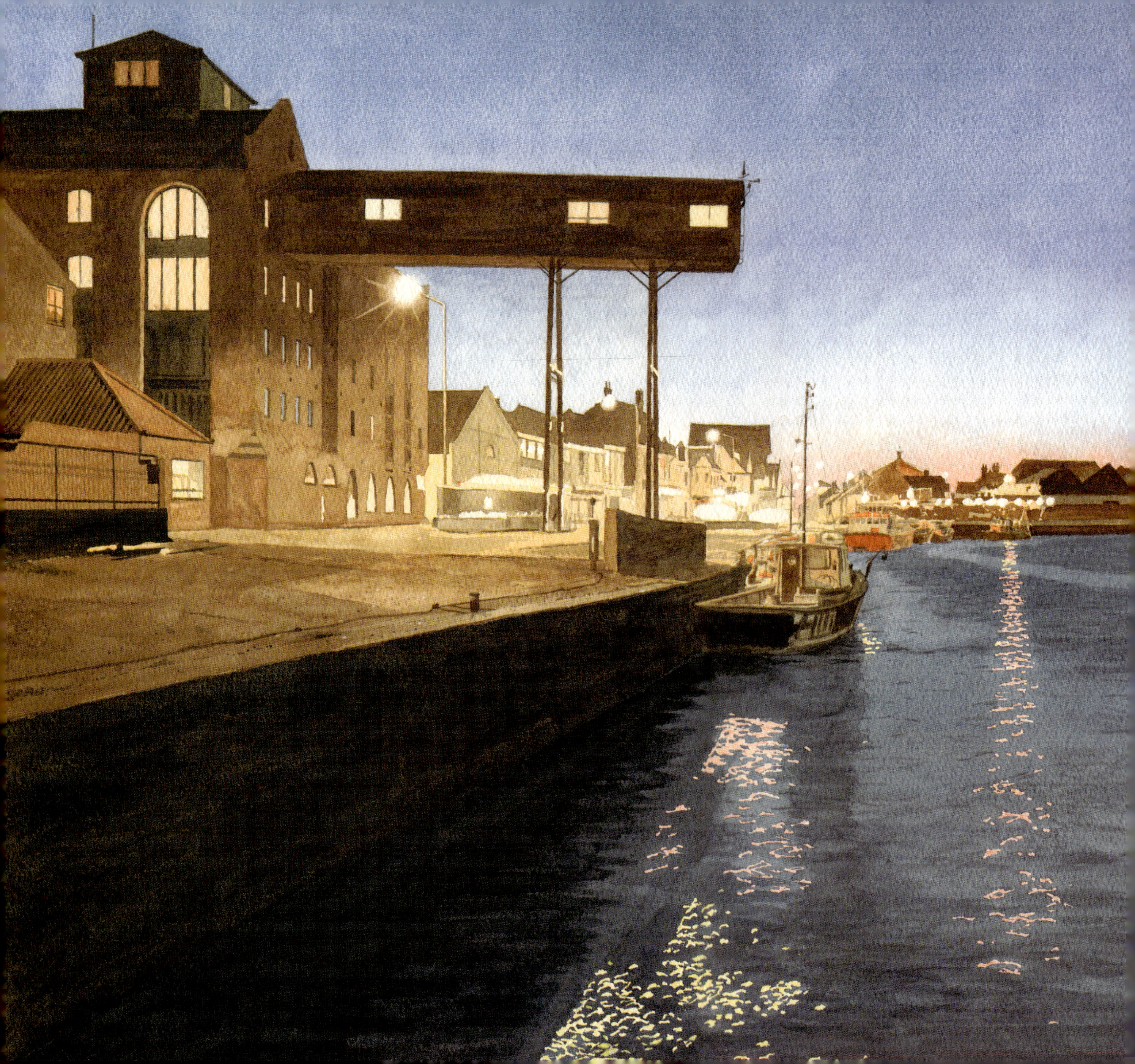

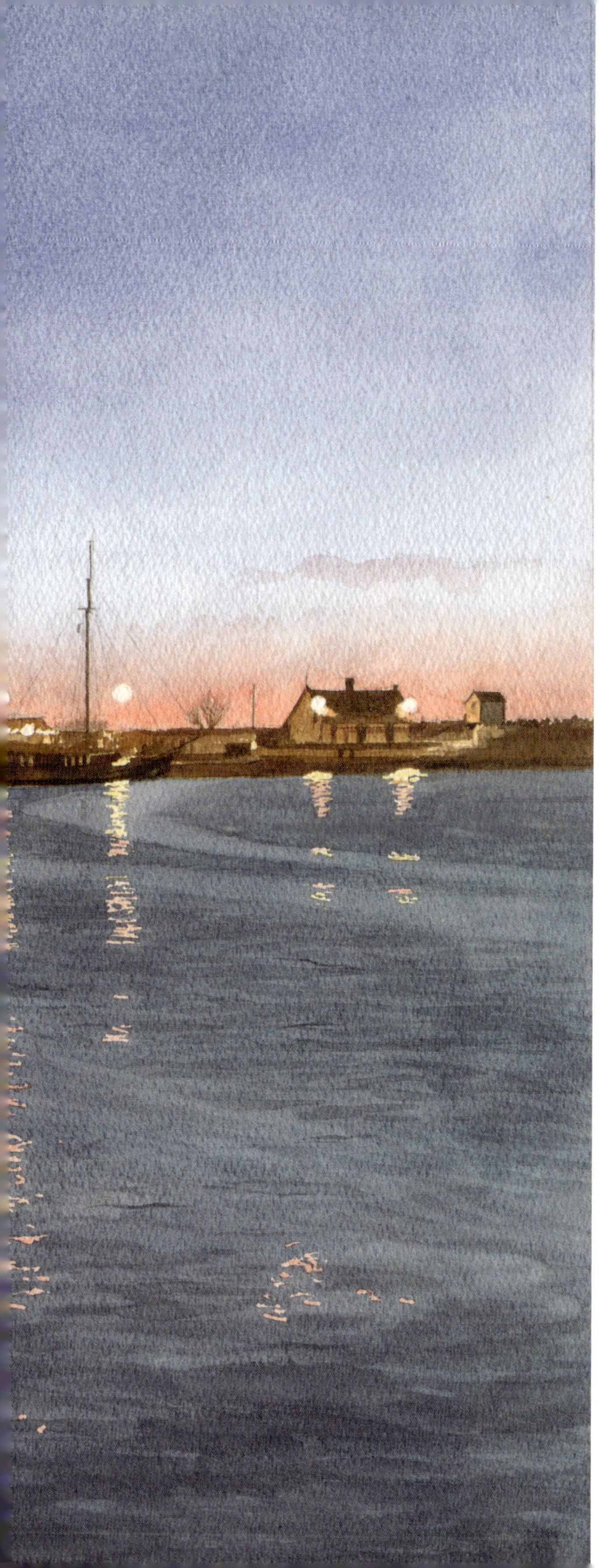

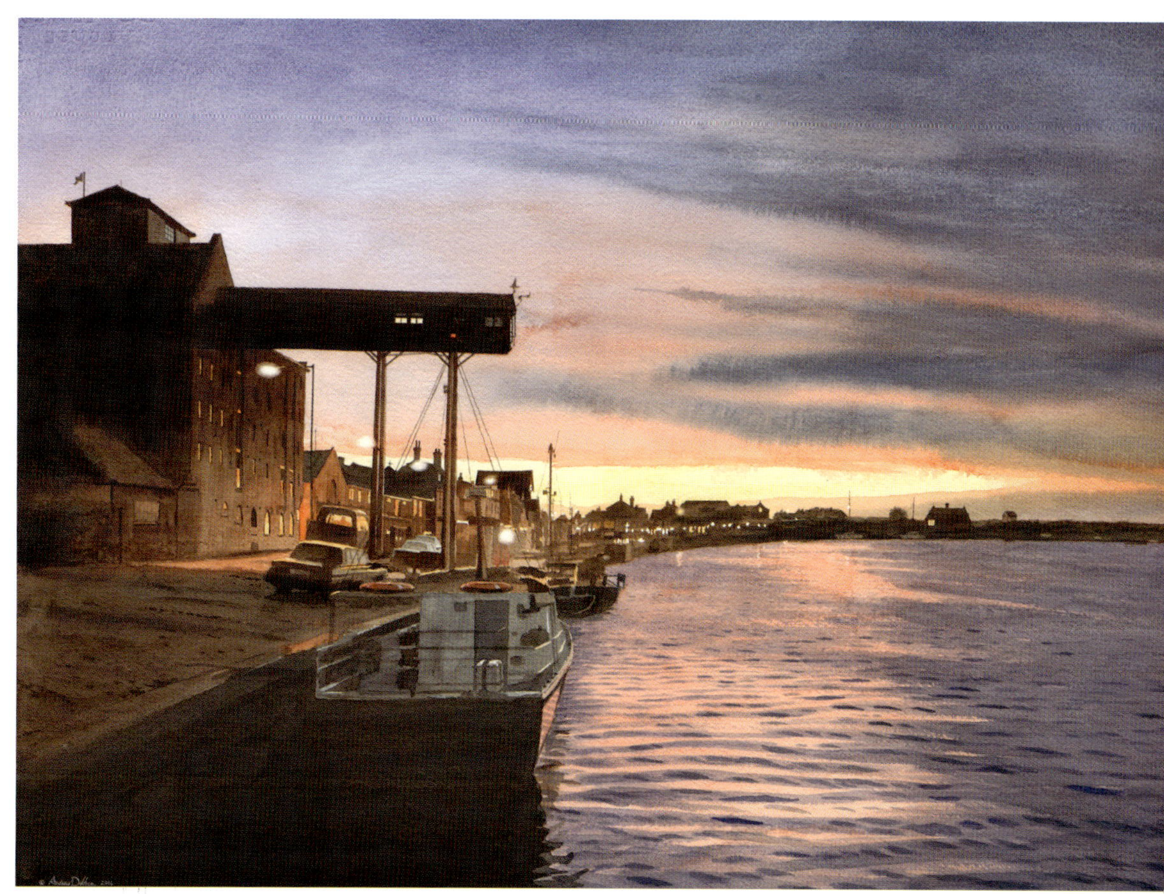

Wells Quay Sunset 29" x 21" 2004

Wells Quay at Dusk II   29" x 21" 2003

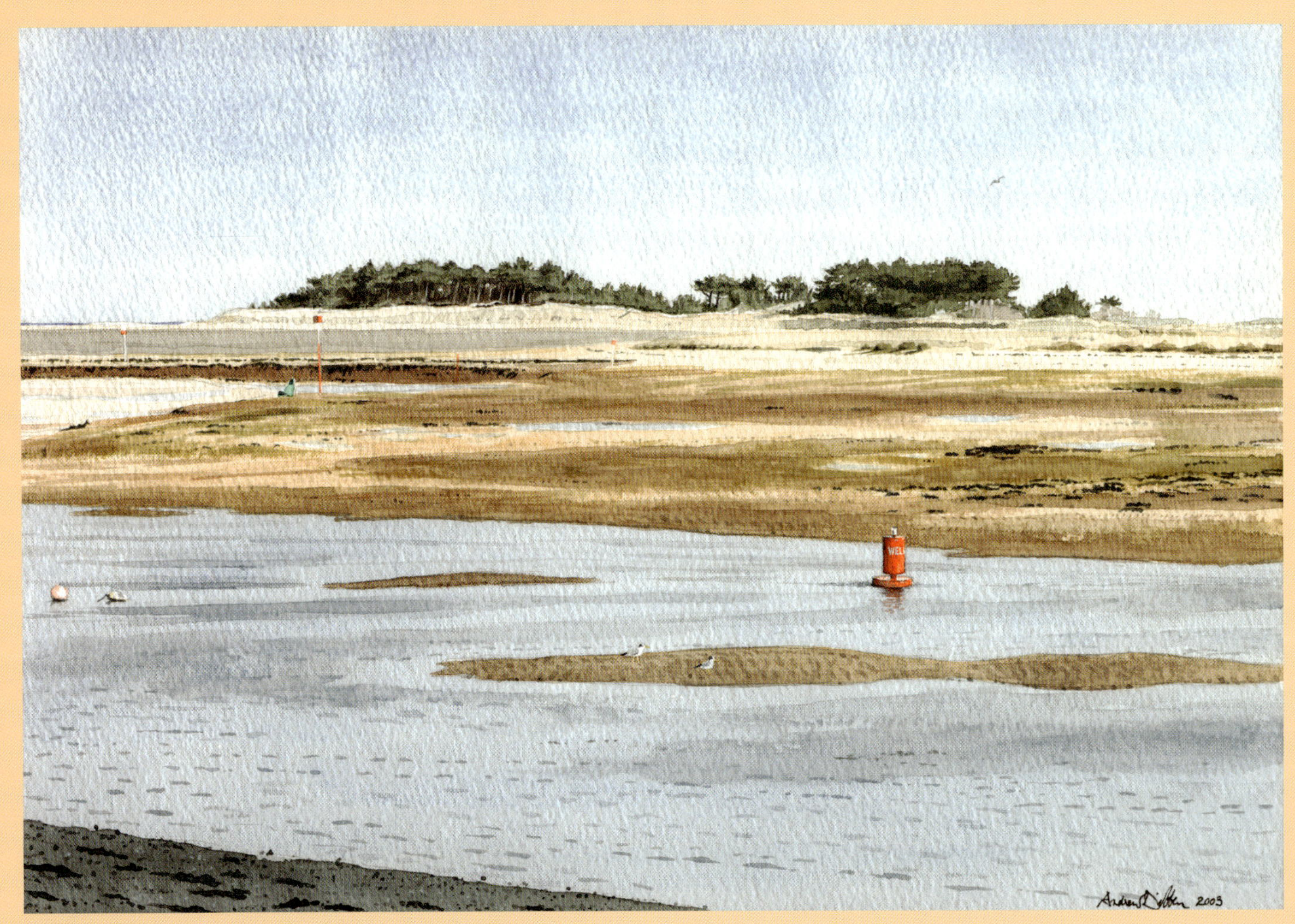

East Hills, Wells, from the Channel 9" x 12" 2003

THORNHAM

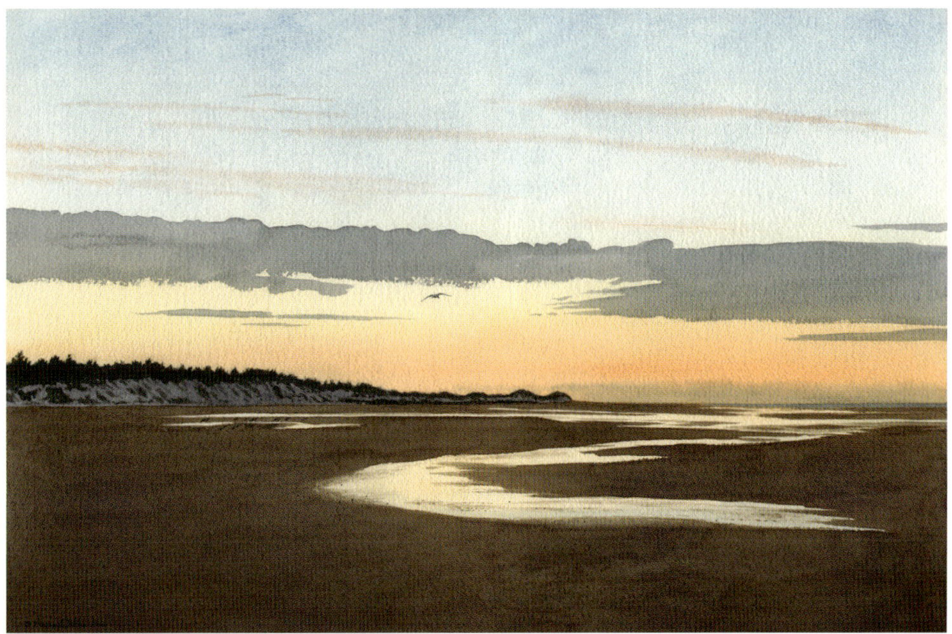

Red Streaks – Thornham Beach (22" x 14") 2004

This series of pictures of Thornham was painted following a trip there at the end of January 2004. We had booked to stay overnight at the wonderful Lifeboat Inn, but then began to worry slightly over whether we would actually be able to travel there when snow was forecast. Sure enough, when the day prior to our trip arrived, it brought quite heavy falls of snow, together with strong gusting winds, causing deep drifts in places. Friends advised us that that they had heard on the radio that some roads in west Norfolk were impassable!

On the day, temperatures had risen slightly, and some of the snow in our garden had melted, so we set off intrepidly, armed with boots, shovel, etc. There certainly was more snow in west Norfolk, but the roads *were* usable with caution.

Late in the afternoon, after arriving safely at the inn, we set off on an unforgettable walk along the raised bank, ice crunching under-foot, and down on to the beach. Only a handful of other walkers were about; the scenes were extraordinary, with quite deep snow covering the marshes and dunes, and snow even on parts of the beach. The wind gusted strongly, whipping up ghostly eddies of sand which rushed around us just above the beach, cutting power-ful ripples in the pools of stranded water. We were treated to a wonderful Norfolk sunset, after which we retreated hastily to the cosy warmth of the roaring log fires in the inn.

The next day we walked to the beach again in daylight and investigated the unfortunate sperm whale, all 60 feet of it, which had been washed up at the Scolt Head end of the beach.

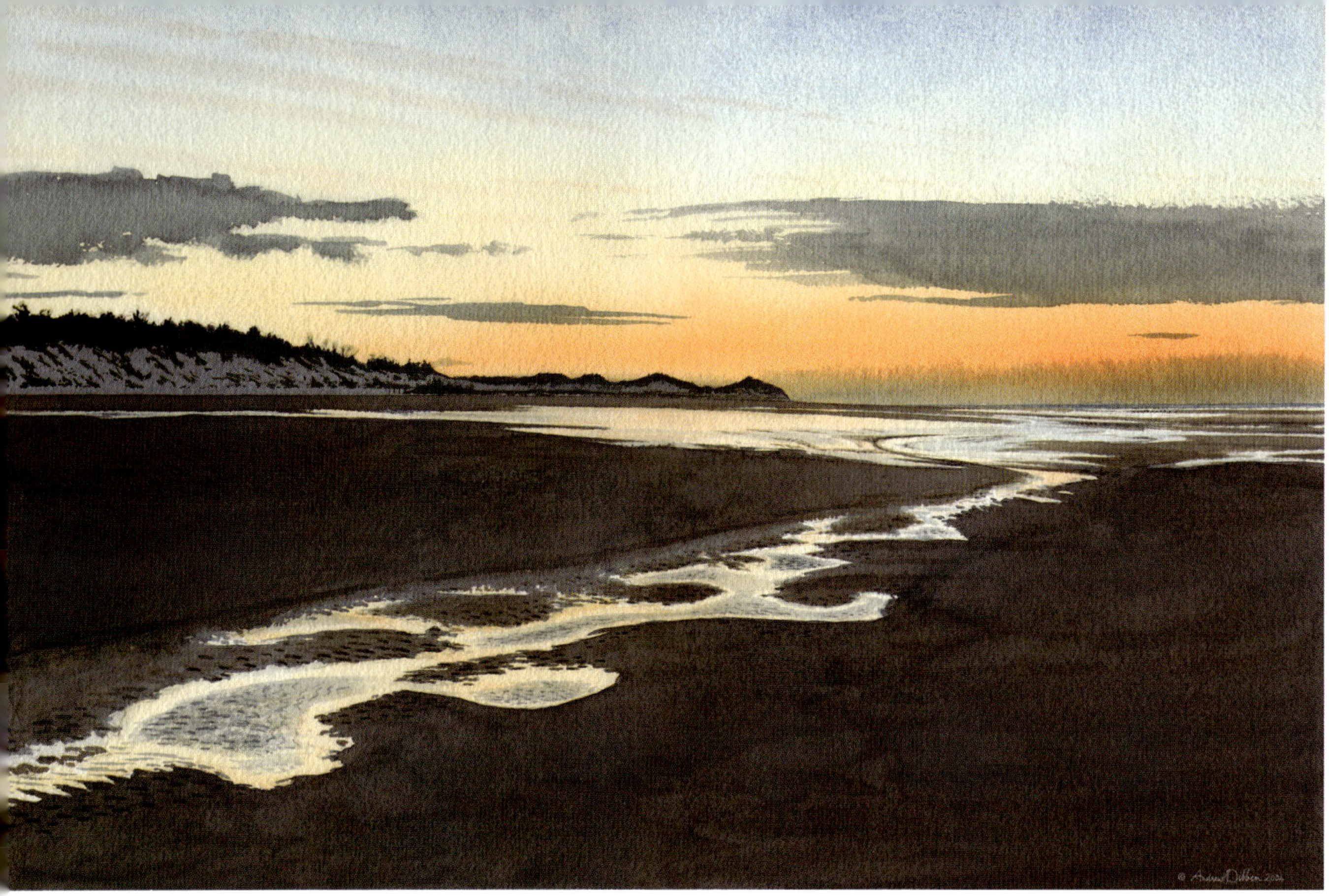

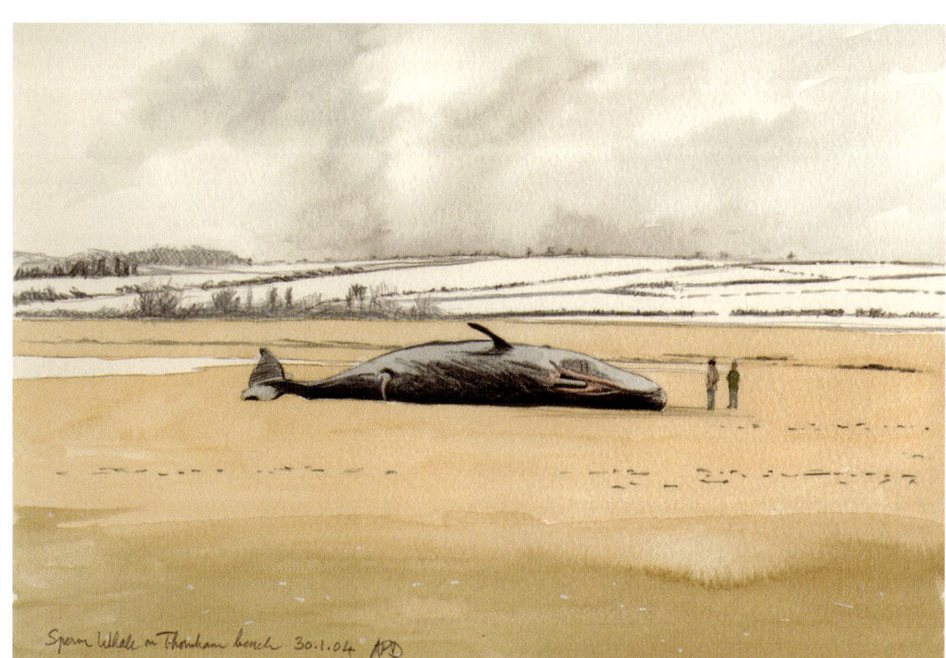

Snow in the Dunes, Thornham
14½" x 21½" 2003

Sperm Whale, Thornham Beach
7" x 10" 2004

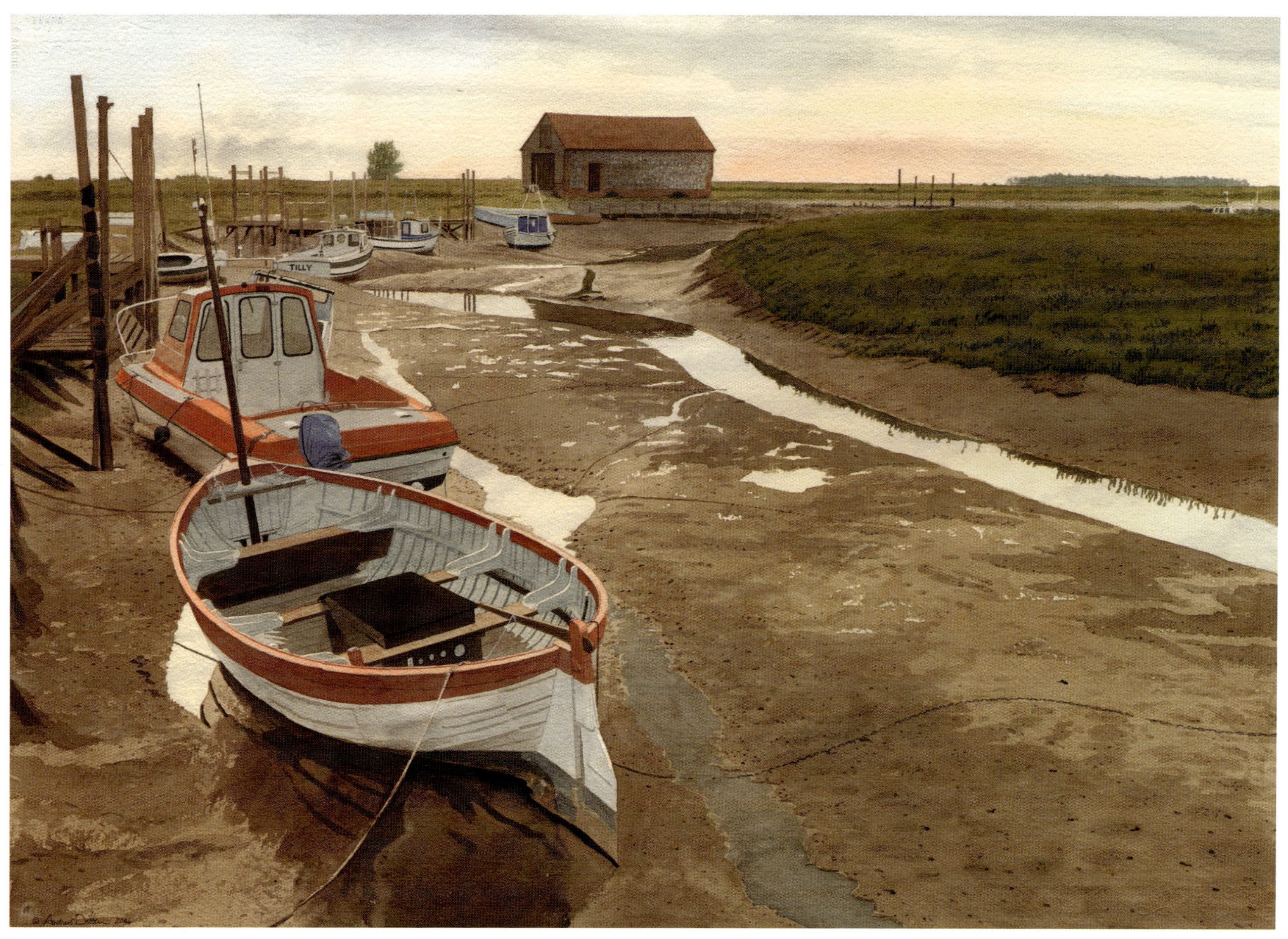

Before Dark – Thornham Creek and Coal Barn (29" x 21") 2004

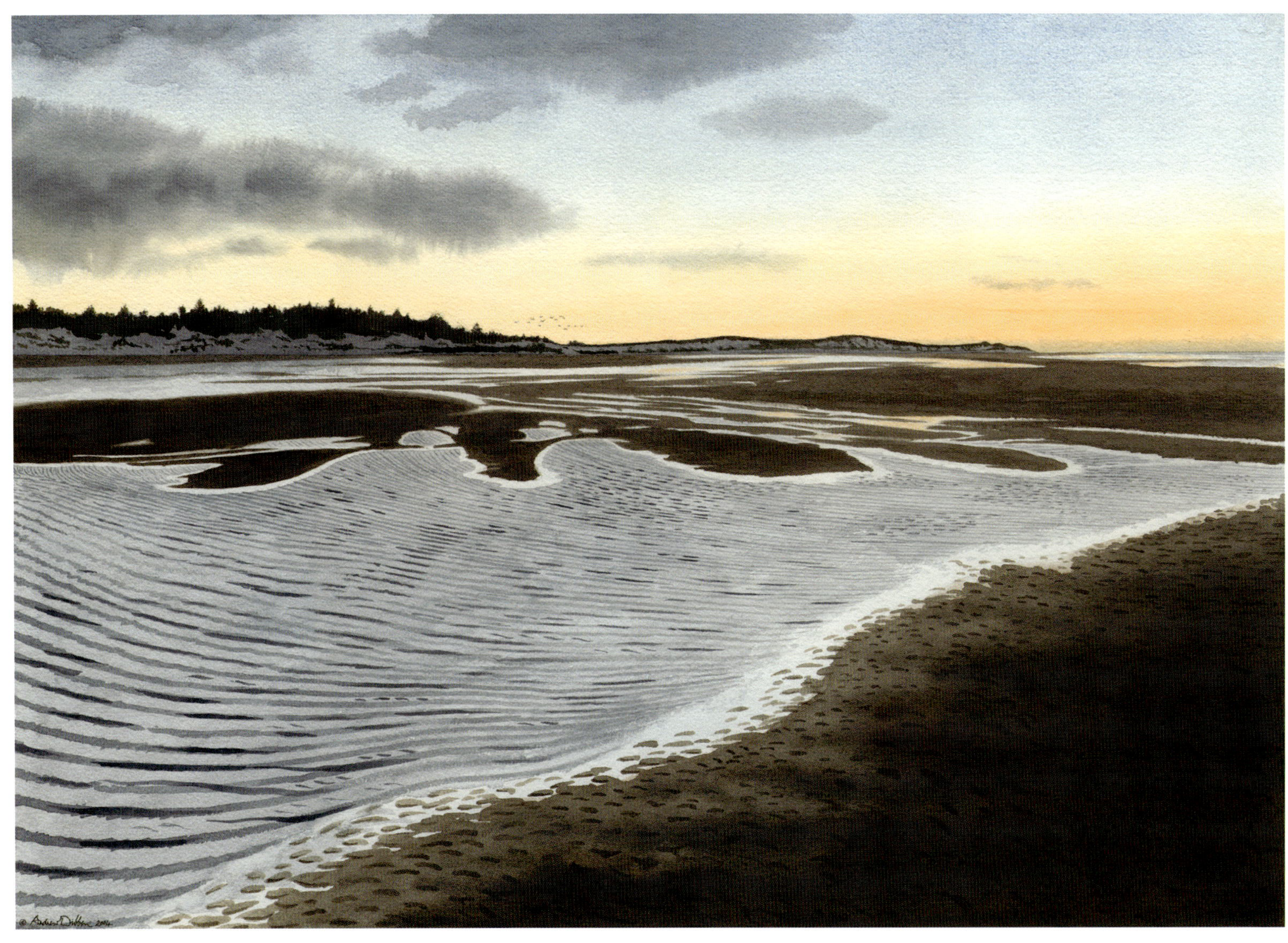

North-Westerly Force 6 29" x 21" 2004

Opposite: *Marauder, Thornham Beach* 29" x 21½" 2004

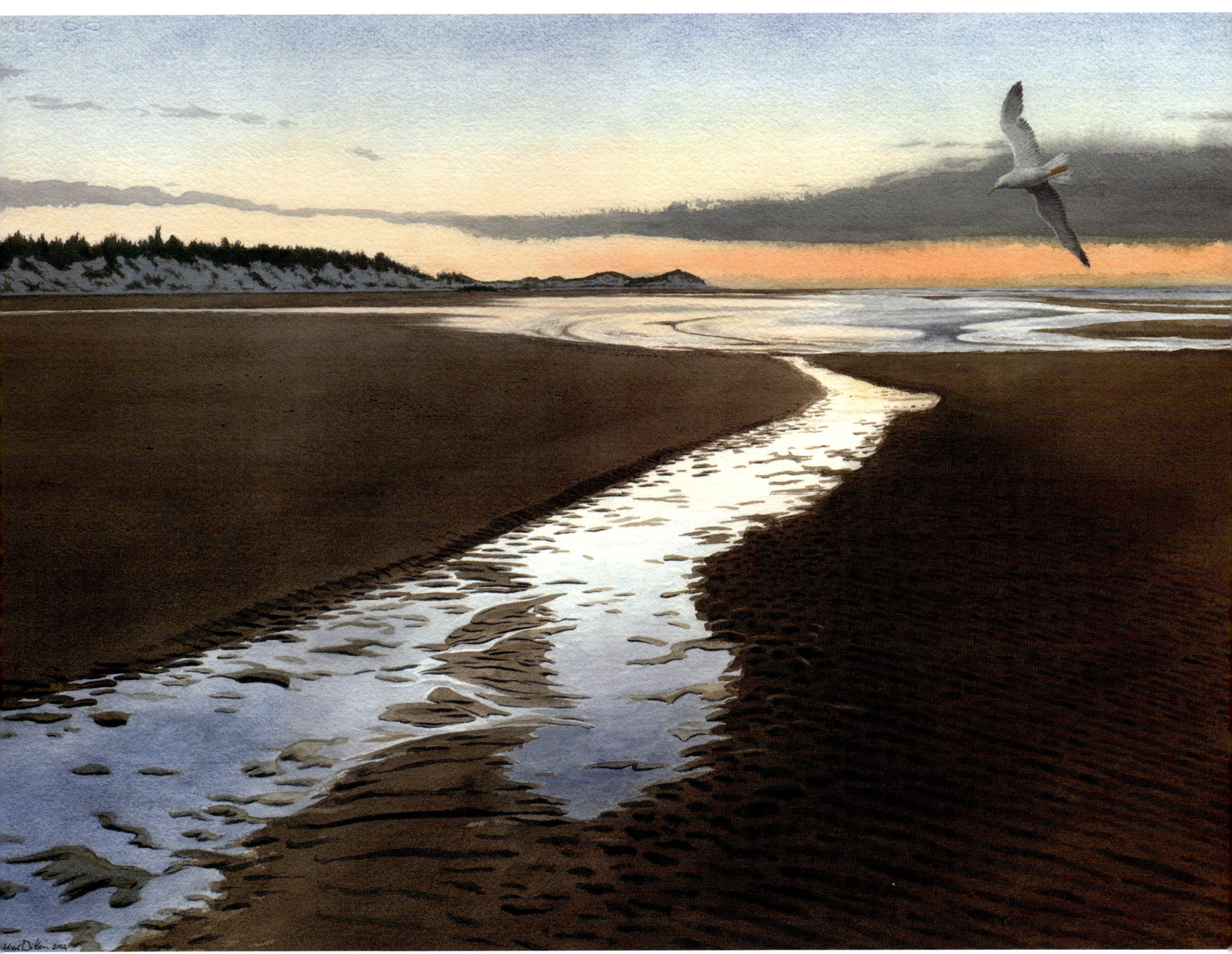

SUNSETS DE-BUNKED

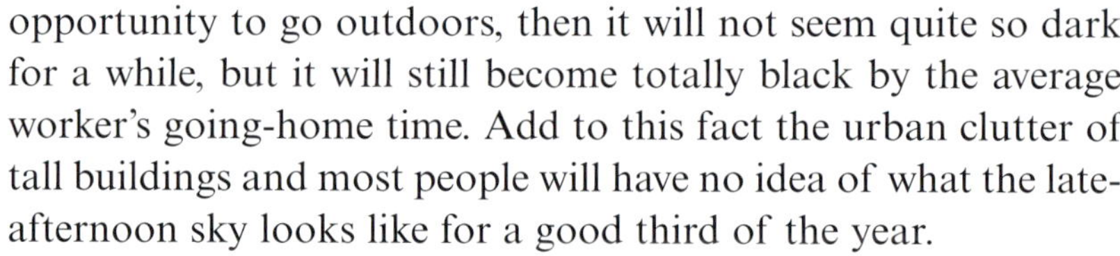

I was a little taken aback recently when an acquaintance remarked that you don't see good sunsets in winter. This idea is probably a symptom of the modern urban lifestyle that so many of us lead. Consider: the average person, working indoors, may be totally unaware of what the weather is doing outside, and from within a well-lit building the outside world appears to be getting dark by about 3.45 in mid-December. If you have the opportunity to go outdoors, then it will not seem quite so dark for a while, but it will still become totally black by the average worker's going-home time. Add to this fact the urban clutter of tall buildings and most people will have no idea of what the late-afternoon sky looks like for a good third of the year.

I cannot make any pretence of being a naturalist, not even an amateur, but I do have the opportunity to be outside more than many. So let me reassure you: striking sunsets happen in all seasons! The important ingredient is cloud, but of course, you don't want the thick covering blanket of horizon-to-horizon cumulus that can so often be a feature of winter skies. Although these conditions can protect us from frosts by trapping warmth below the grey quilt, they also prevent much sunlight from filtering through. Ideally, there should be a clear backdrop of sky, with a weather system of some kind coming in from the west, or a scattering of clouds over the whole sky. That way, the refraction of sunlight can do its thing, as it shines at a shallow angle through the atmosphere, and utilises the clouds as a giant broken projection screen. It may seem that I have just destroyed the romance of sundown, but I like to understand what is happening, and still never fail to be amazed by the spectacular and magical effects that our sun and cloudy atmosphere regularly produce. At times, it is not so difficult to understand that our ancestors sometimes believed that the morning or evening sky was an omen of future events!

And now, here is a challenge for all: the next time you are somewhere where you will be able to see the sun setting over the sea, look out for the 'green flash' phenomenon. This is a momentary flash of green light, seen just as the top edge of the sun's disc vanishes below the sea. Happy hunting!

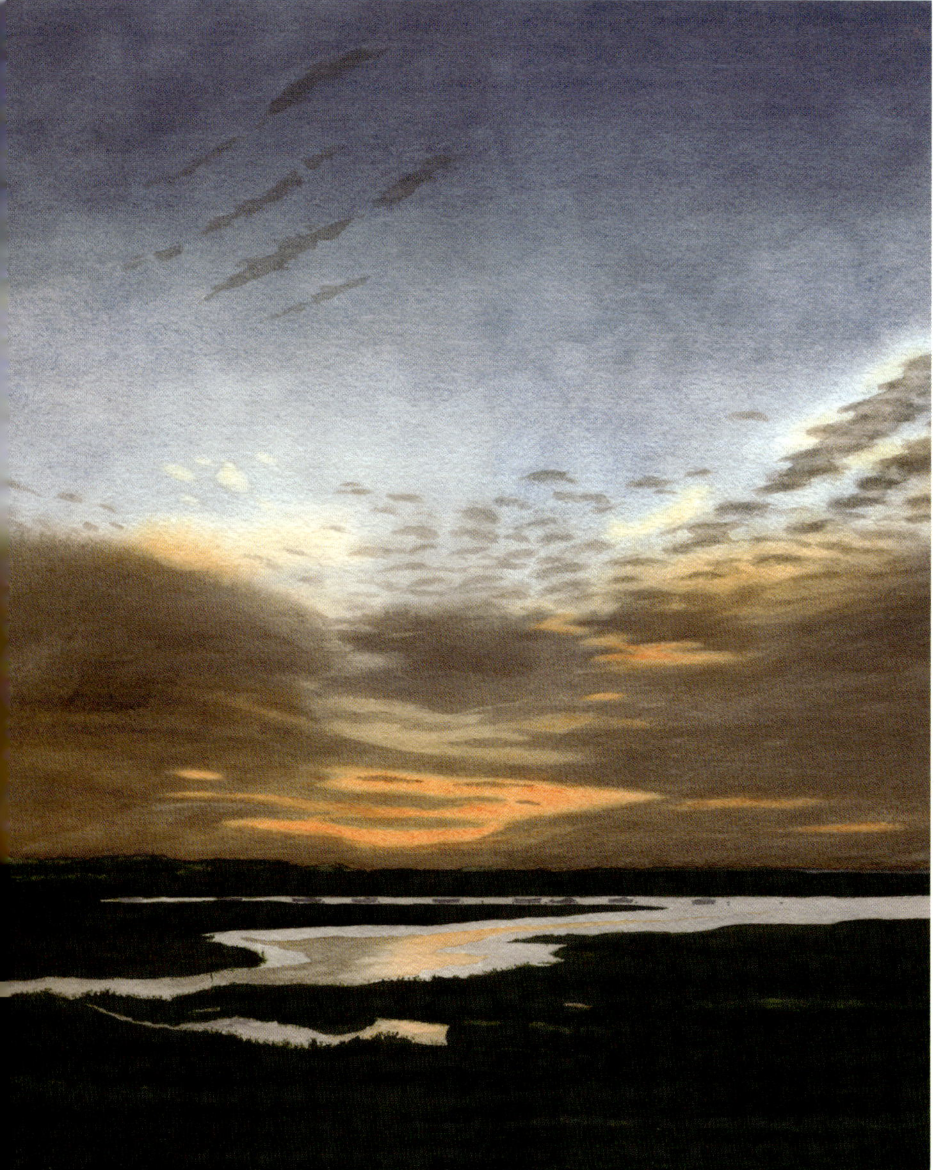

The Fiery Blanket 21" x 17" 2003

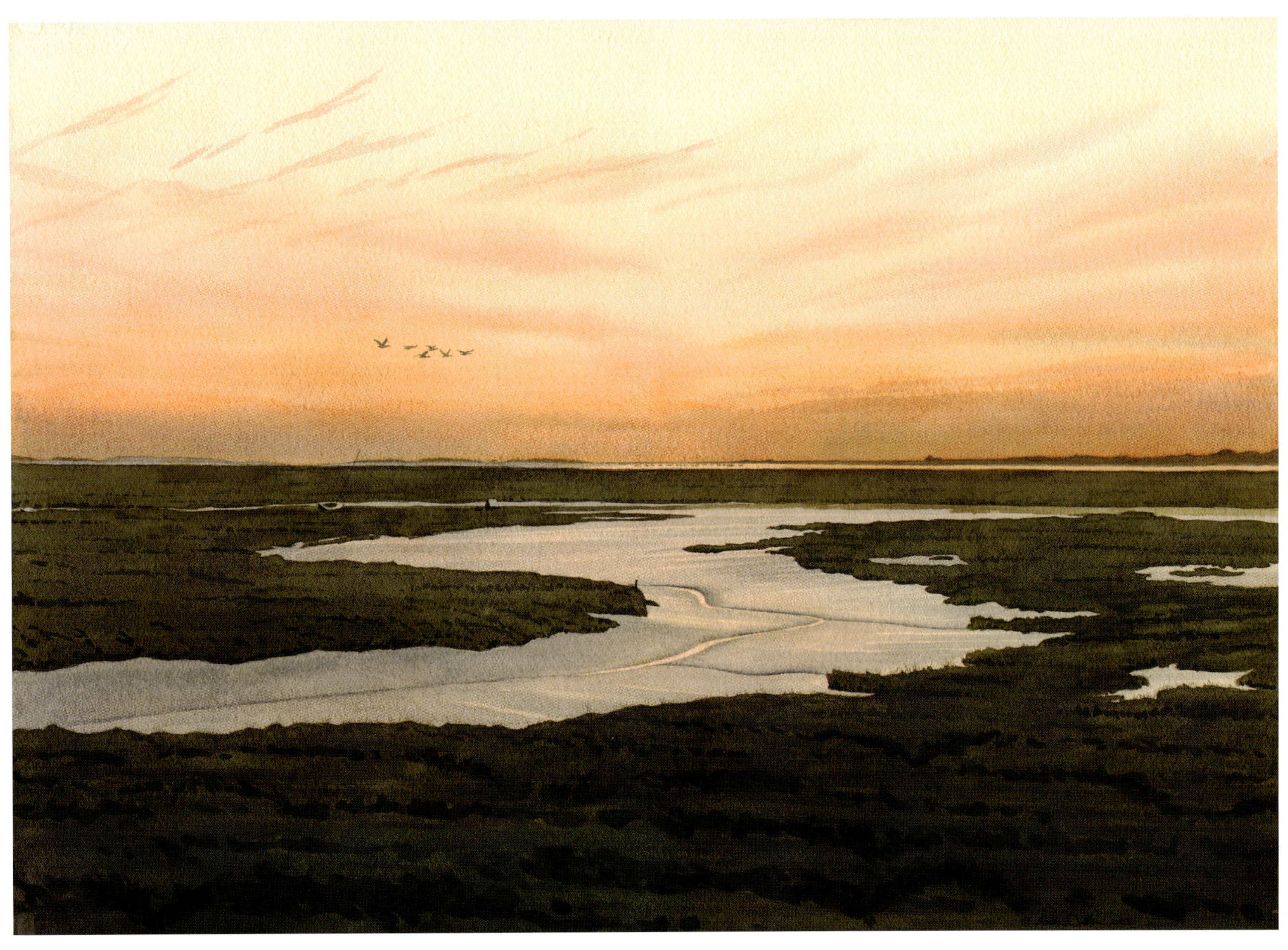

Blakeney Sunset III 29" x 21" 2002

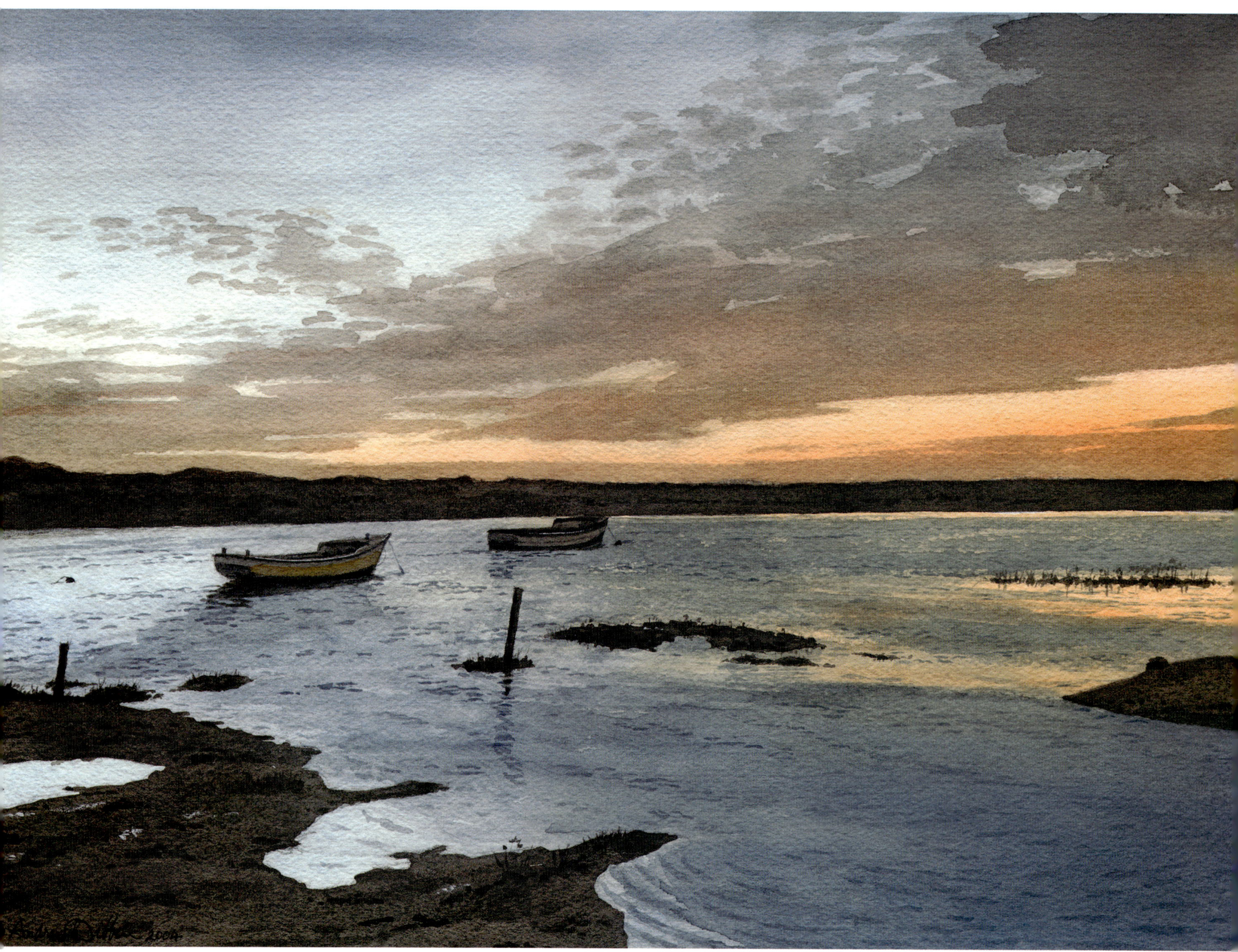

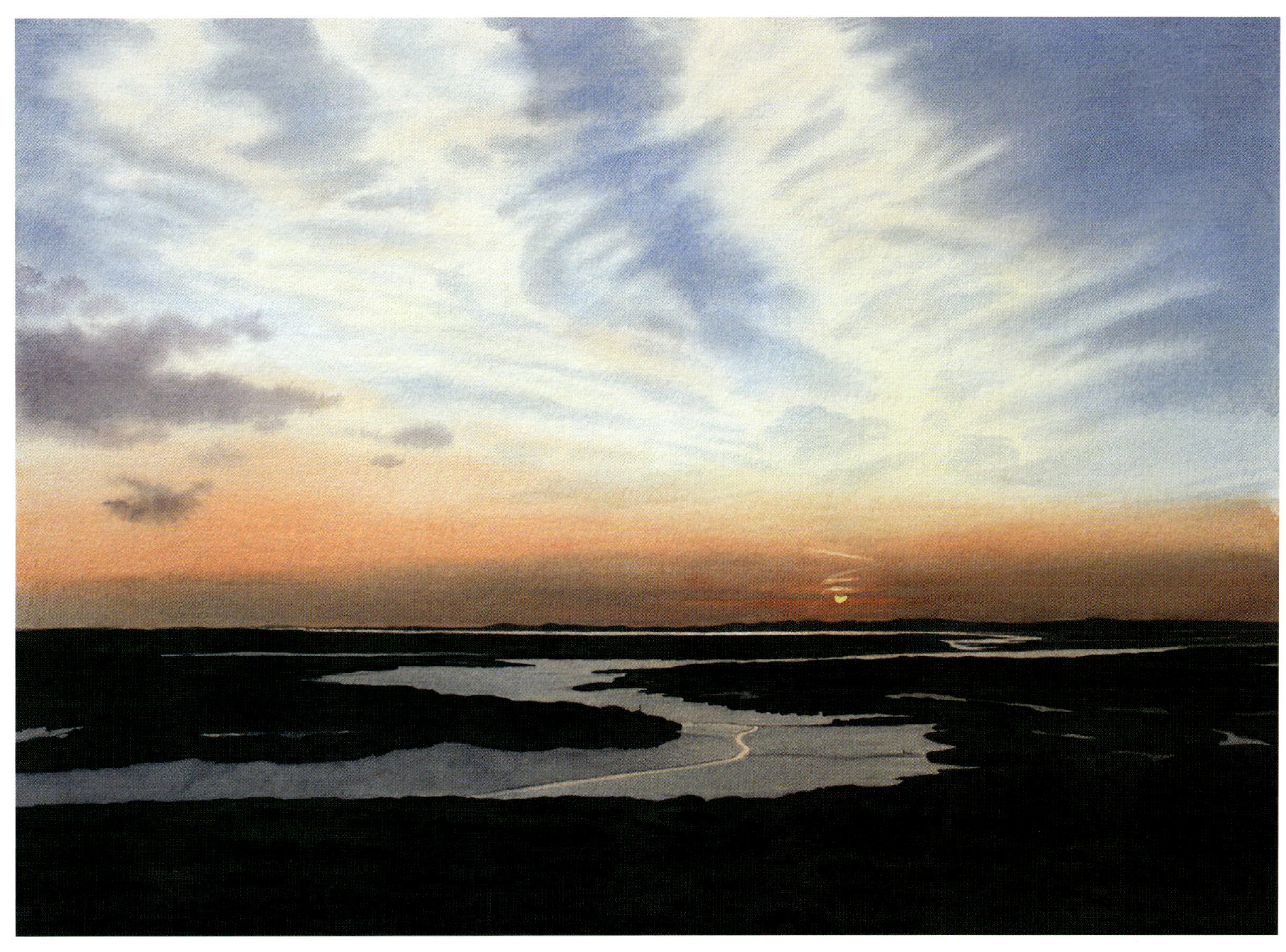

Blakeney Marsh Sunset 29" x 21" 2003

Opposite: *Blakeney Creek – Two Boats* 9" x 12" 2004

OVERY STAITHE – CREEK AND MUDFLATS

If I am travelling westwards along the coast, I always feel that I have arrived somewhere special and very different when I reach Burnham Overy Staithe. It is at Overy that the limestone begins, for one thing. It seems extraordinary that in this county of rich red brick and pantiles there should be a corner where so much construction is of white stone; have we arrived near Portland or the Cotswolds? What is this place? No, it is still Norfolk, but a different Norfolk which feels more exotic thanks to this superb building material, and that other luxury – space. For this north-western corner of Norfolk is more open and depopulated than the central and eastern parts, and I hope that it will always remain so.

This is a great place to walk. On a summer's evening, there is nowhere better to walk out than along the raised flood defence bank, taking in the peacefulness of the marshes, the amazingly polished appearance of the mudflats at the creek's edge – as long as you don't touch them! – with only the footprints of wading birds spoiling the illusion, then a climb over the sand dunes until the beach and sea are revealed at last. Westwards, there is a lovely walk along the edge of the marsh as far as Brancaster.

The area of the Burnhams produced some of the greatest sailors the country has known. Horatio Nelson, later Viscount Nelson, needs little introduction, but there was also his protégé William Hoste, from nearby Tittleshall, and Captain Richard Woodget, from Burnham Norton.

William Hoste was appointed Captain's Servant to Nelson aboard *Agamemnon* at the age of 13. He served at the battles of Cape St Vincent, 1796, and Tenerife, 1797, following which he was promoted to Lieutenant. He was appointed Acting Captain of HMS *Mutine* in 1798 at the age of 18, and, following intrepid service in the Adriatic and Mediterranean, became Sir William Hoste.

Captain Woodget became renowned as the most successful captain of the tea clipper *Cutty Sark* in her wool trading days, setting some of the fastest passage times ever between Sydney and London. He had three sons, all of whom became steamship captains (one of them having served as an apprentice under his father aboard *Cutty Sark*,) and retired to a farm at Overy Staithe.

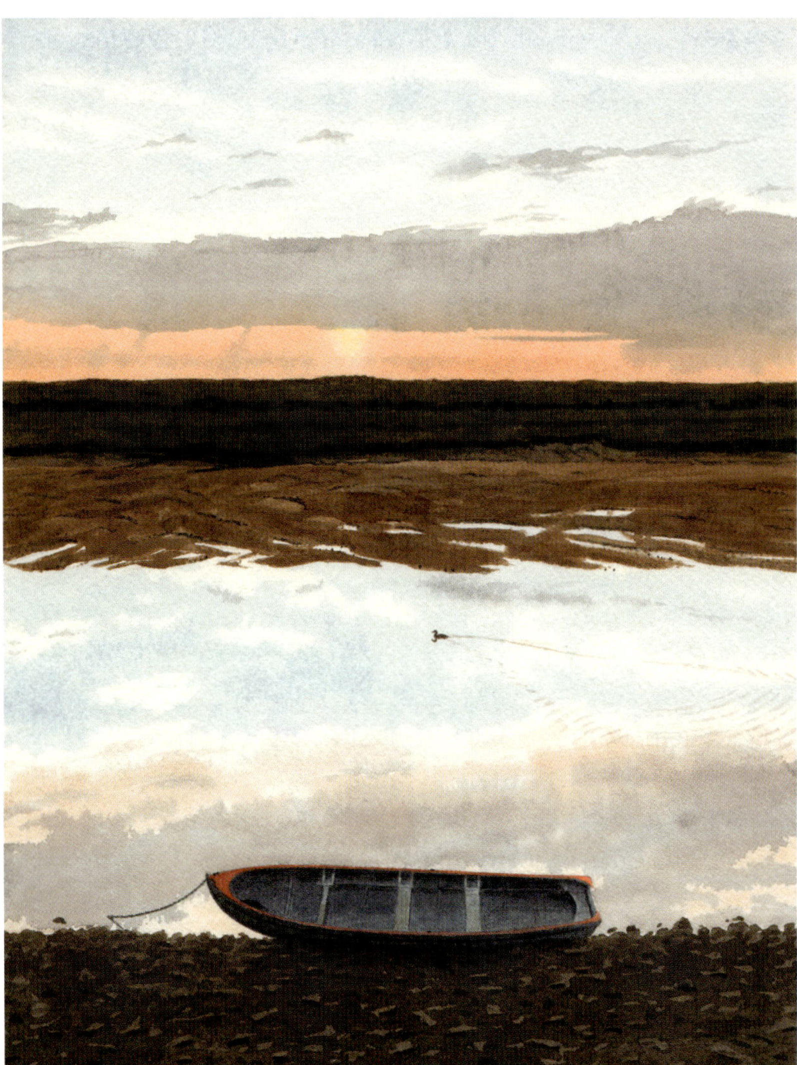

Still Evening, Burnham Overy 11" x 14" 2003

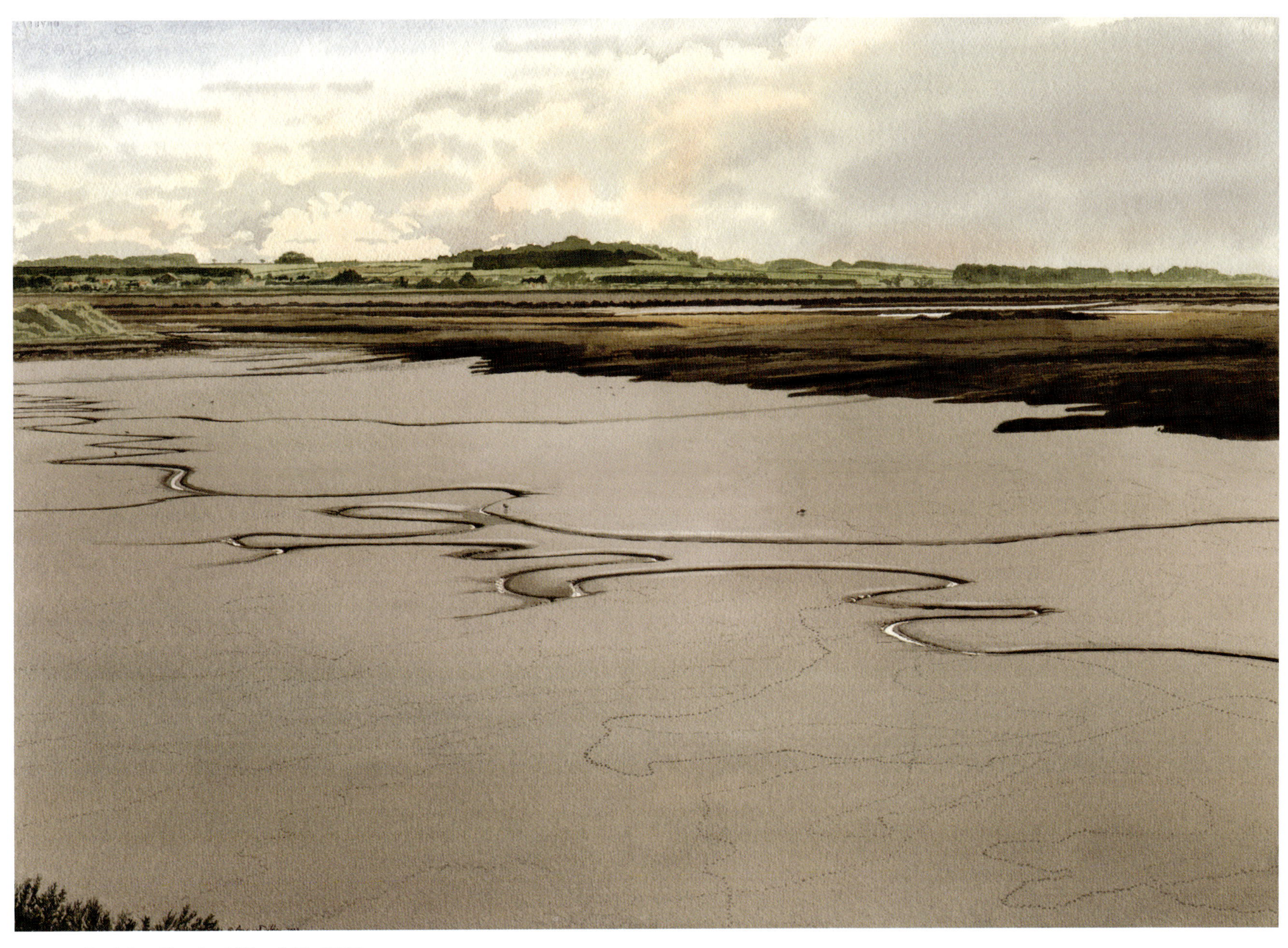

Overy Staithe Creek 29" x 21" 2003

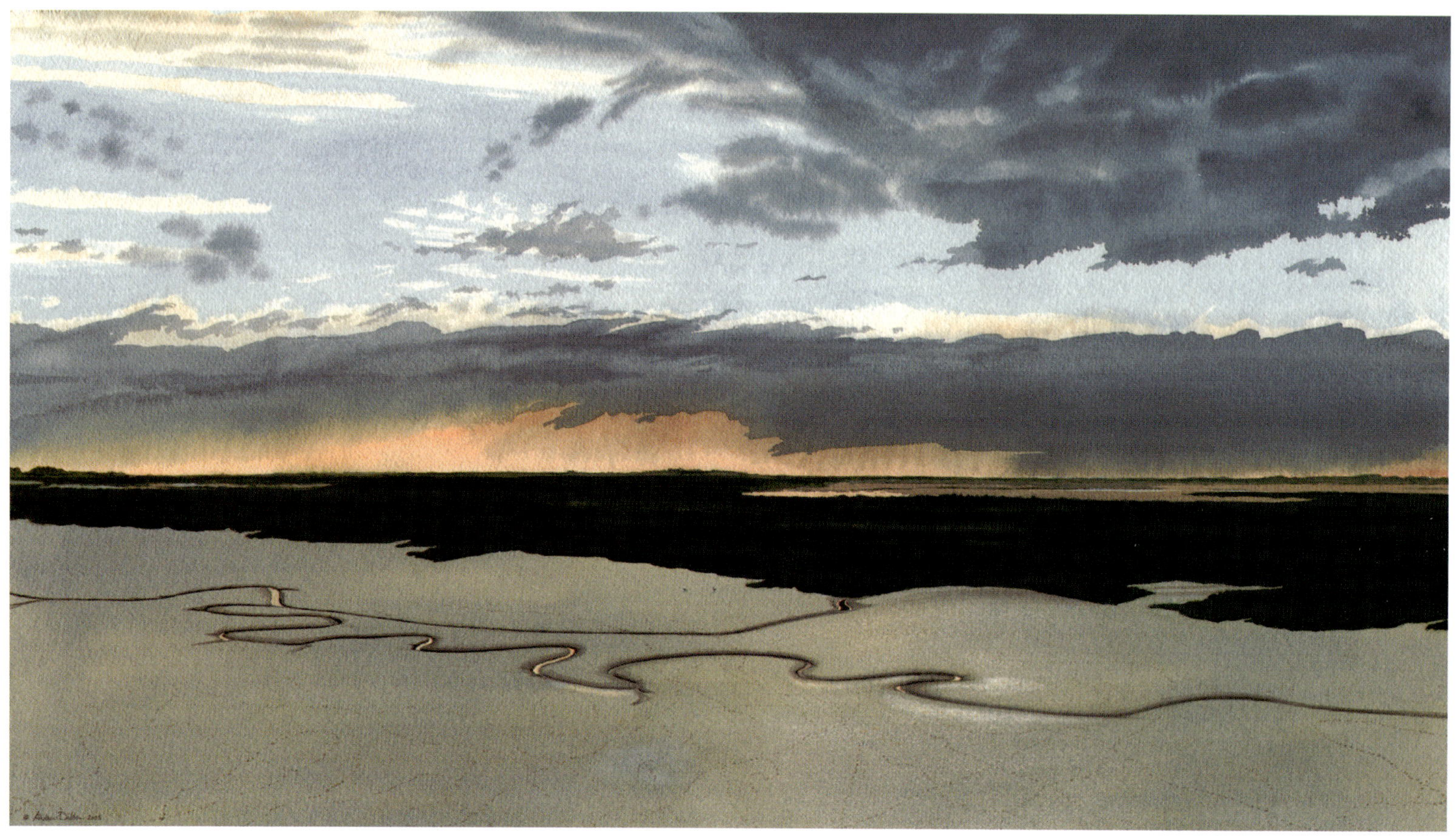

Overy Creek and Marsh 29" x 17" 2003

Walking westwards from the village of Overy Staithe, you pass the striking black-painted windmill, and then can either continue along the edge of the marsh to Brancaster or, returning to the road, admire the watermill and adjoining cottages.

During the season frantic activity begins quite suddenly when the tide starts to flood, dinghy sailors appearing from nowhere and rushing to get their craft afloat and make the most of the few hours of deep water.

It is fascinating to imagine some of our great maritime heroes learning to sail in these creeks; the young Horatio Nelson and William Hoste hauling their boats ashore at the end of a day's adventures. Captain Richard Woodget raced small boats hereabouts until he was quite elderly, and undoubtedly taught his sons to sail here.

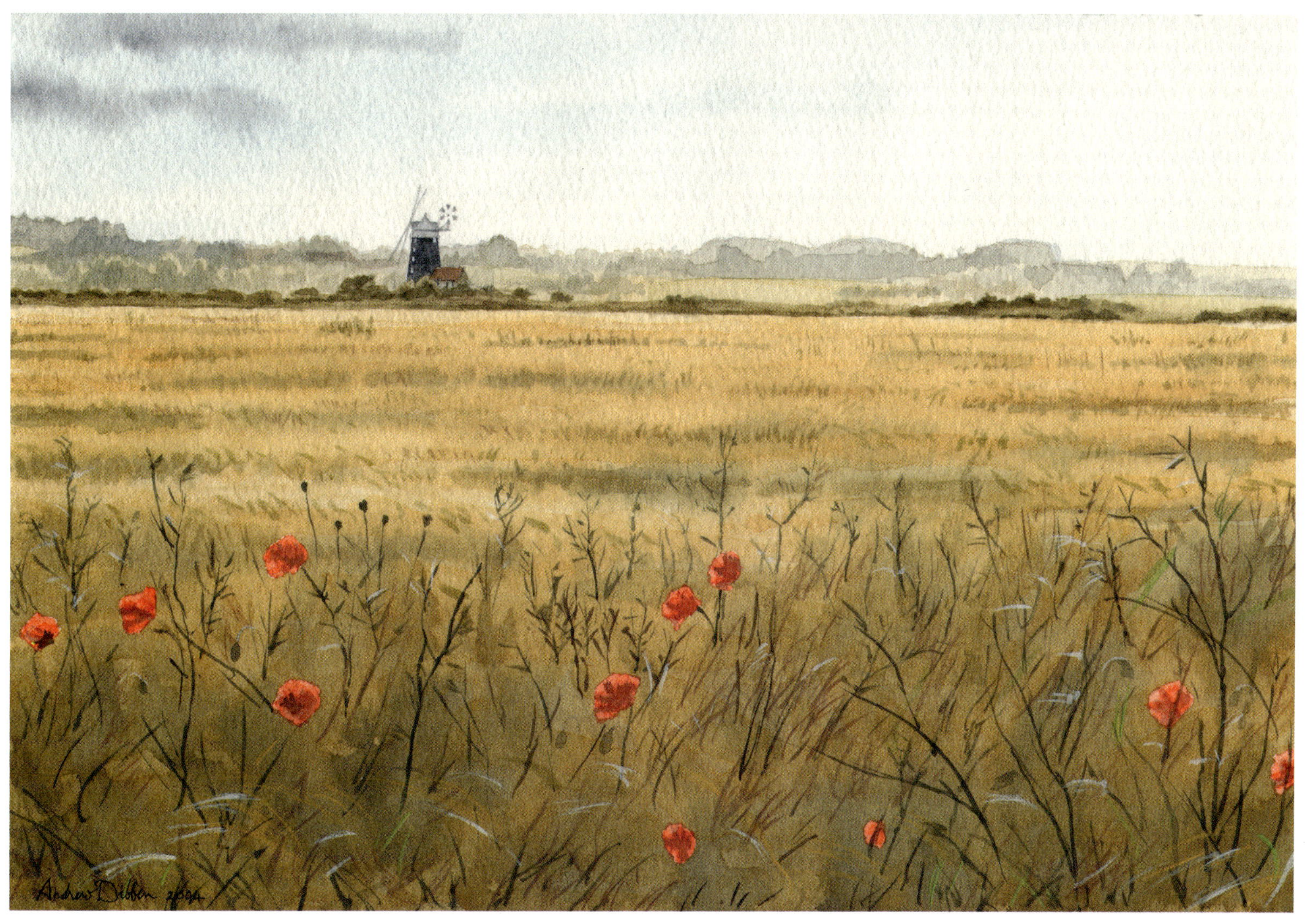

Overy Staithe Mill and Poppies 7" x 10" 2004

Just to be awkward, I have included here two paintings of Overy Staithe windmill that have absolutely no water in them! The windmill at Overy is virtually next door to the watermill on the River Burn, so there is water nearby, and I had every intention of doing another little picture of the windmill from the marsh, where the river starts to become brackish, to prove this point. I also had plans to produce a picture of the watermill, but time conspired against me. Maybe next time!

Overleaf: **Overy *Staithe Windmill from near the Watermill*** 10" x22" 2003

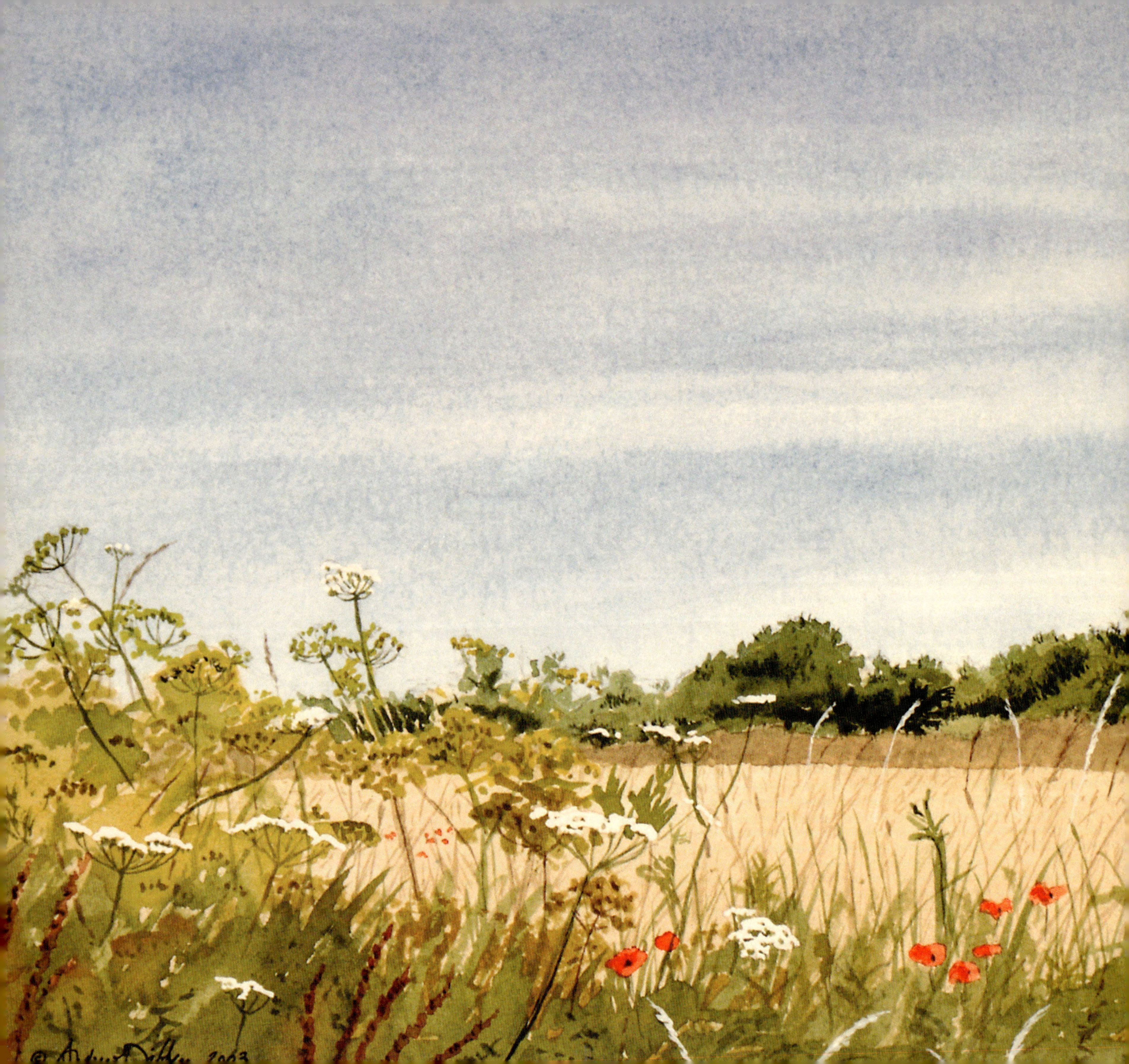
© Andrew Dibben 2003

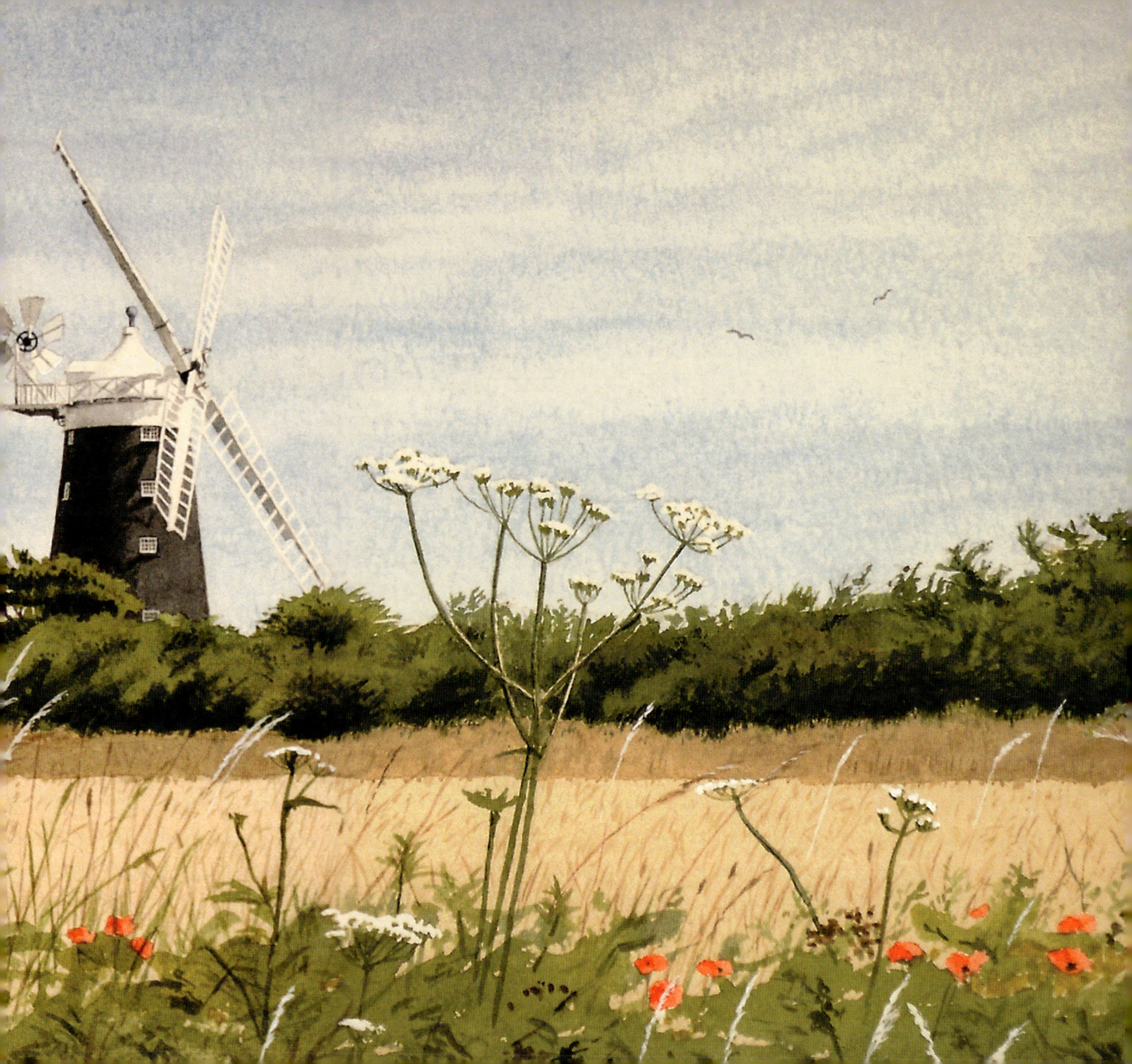

PEACE, PERFECT PEACE

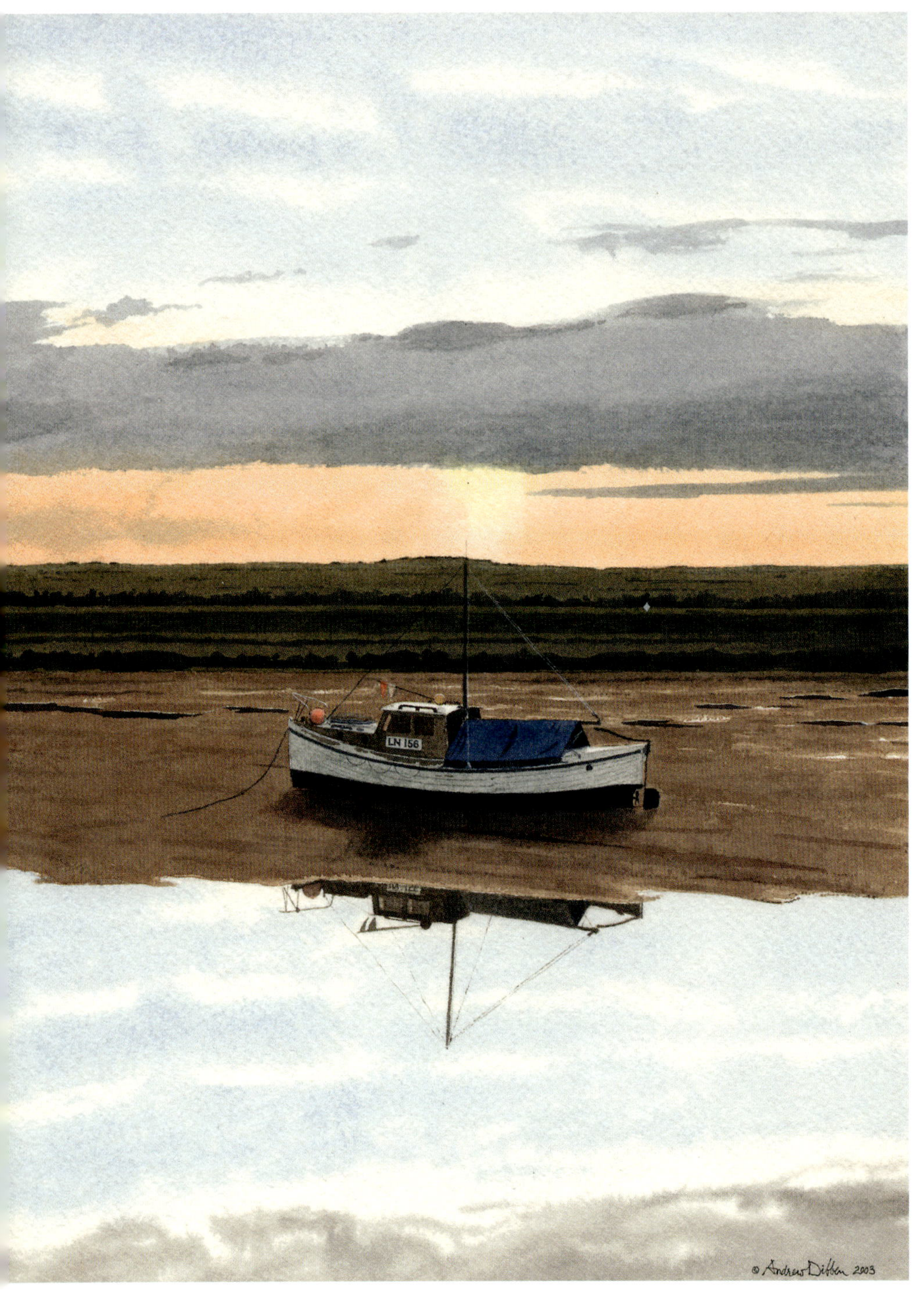

The sun goes down on a still evening at the edge of one of north Norfolk's creeks; there is hardly anywhere in the world more peaceful and quiet. The salt marsh seems to disappear into the distance, bounded only by the sky, and maybe a low rim of dunes. The only sound is the occasional call of a curlew or some other wading bird; a group of gulls flying over to roost for the night is completely soundless, while a flock of geese only produces a gentle wheezing sound from their wings as they pass overhead. Even man's boats seem to fit in quite naturally in this scene that has not changed radically in thousands of years.

But now this environment, and also the Norfolk Broads, are under threat because of our desire for *things*, our need for gas-guzzling machines, for products – even just exotic vegetables or fruit - that have to be transported thousands of miles by air, our need to fly to a theme-park 3500 miles away for a four-day stay, our need to fight wars. I am guilty of some of these things, as are all of us; politicians need to set us an example, and probably to make some very difficult and unpopular decisions.

Burham Overy Harbour 11½" x 14½" 2003

Opposite: ***Two Shelduck, Overy Staithe*** 11½" x 14½" 2003

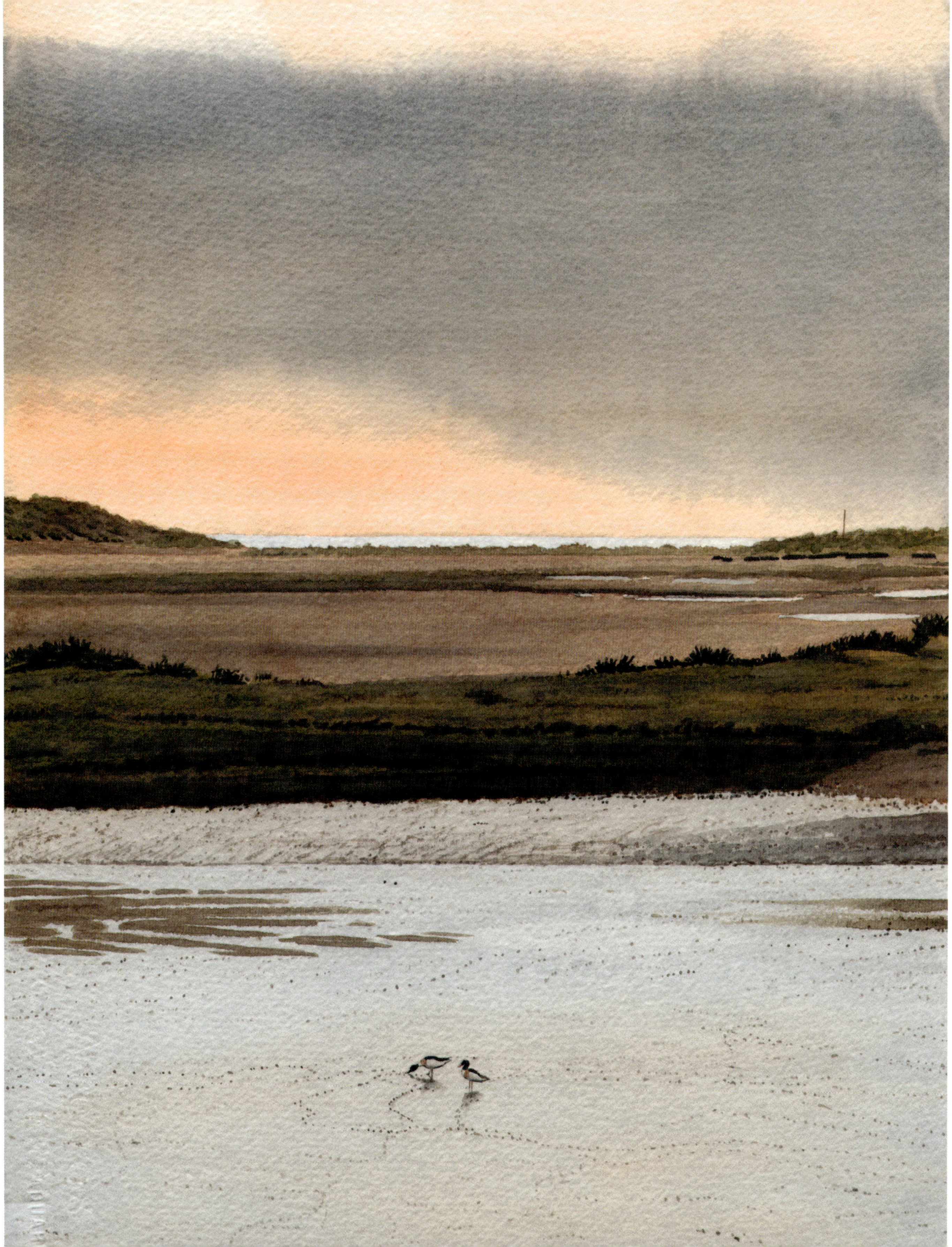

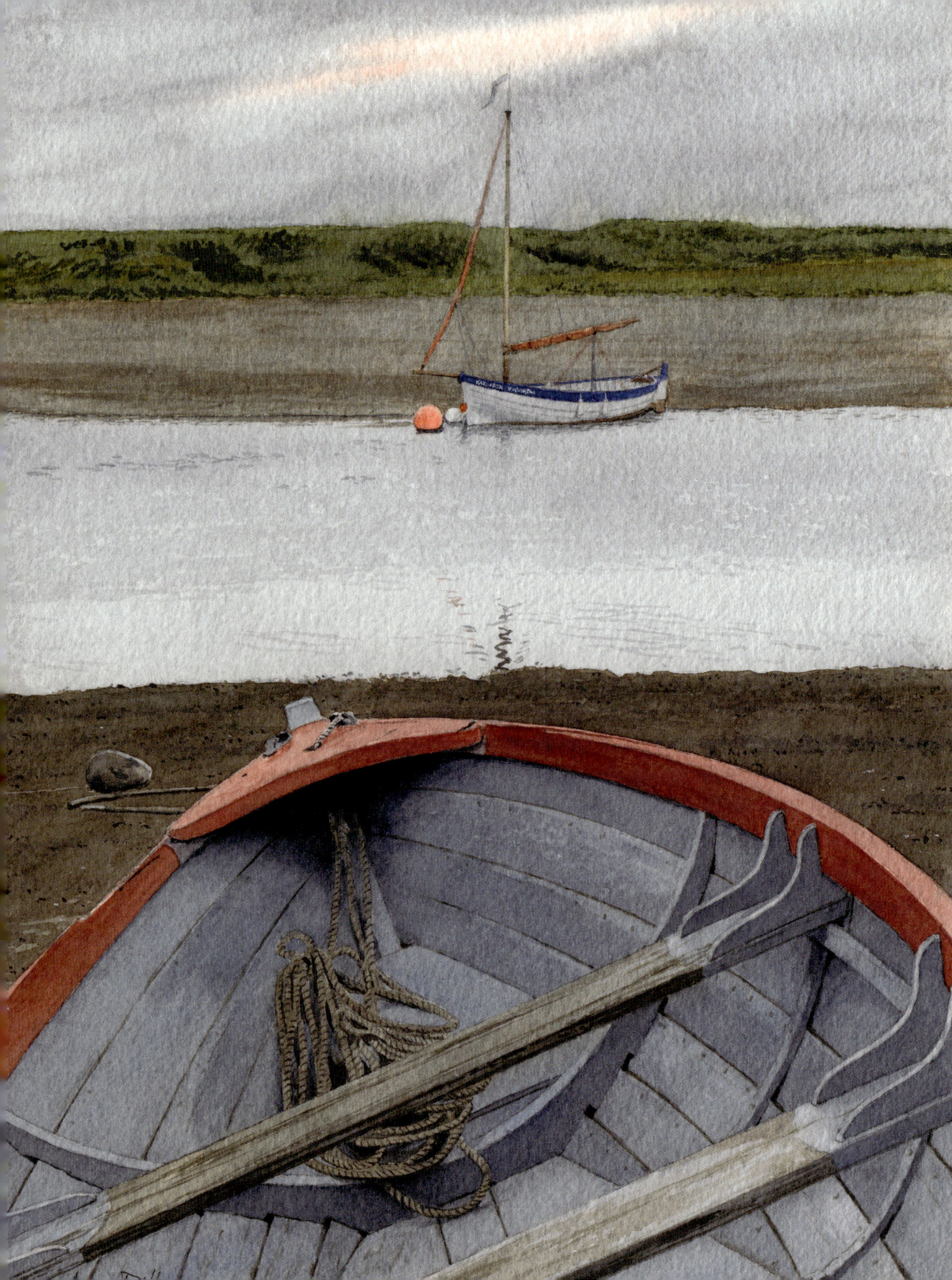

Pink Gunwhales
11½" x 14½" 2003

IN SEARCH OF THE ABSTRACT IN NATURE

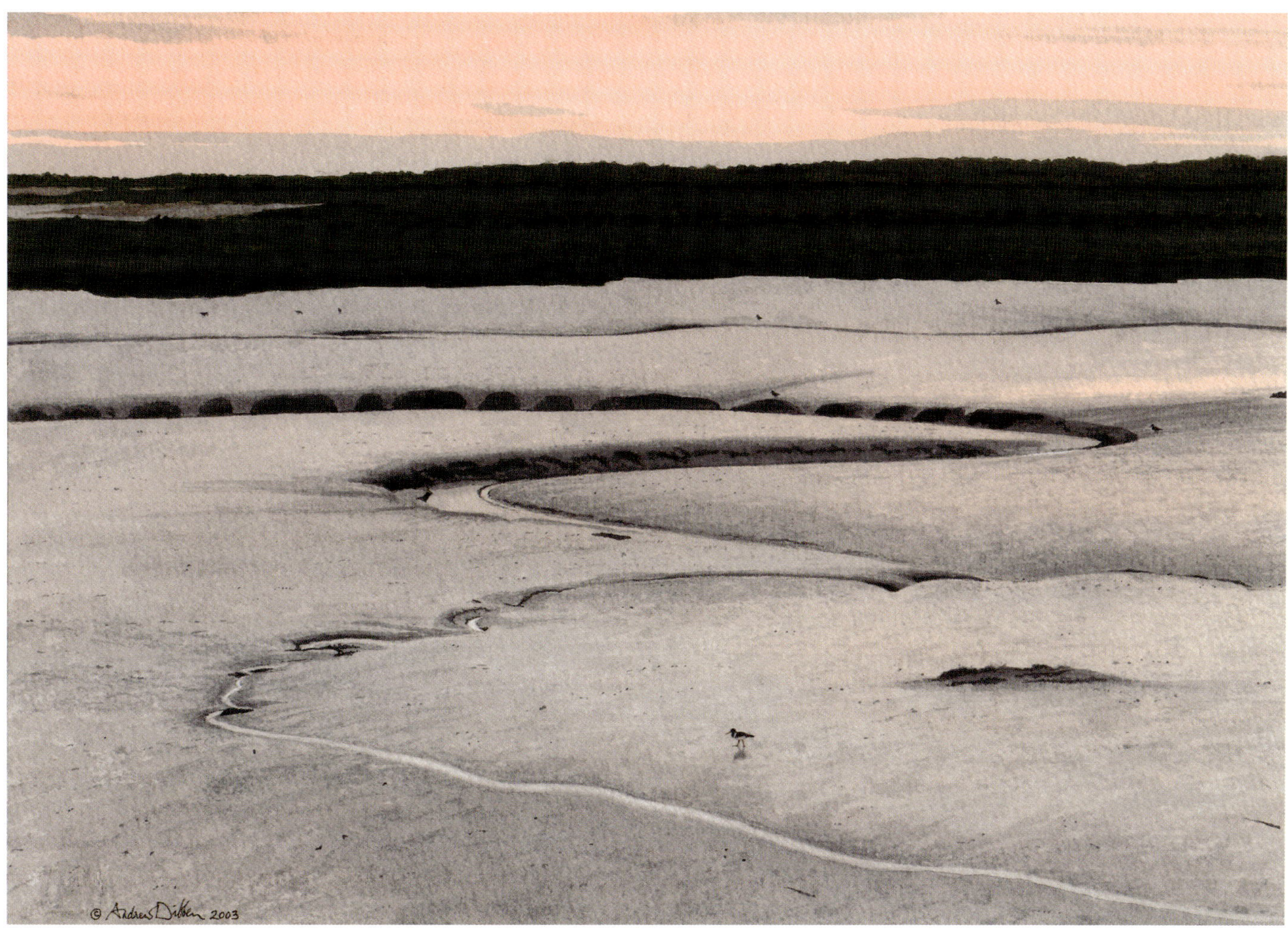

Pink Sky, Overy Creek 14½" x 11½" 2003

It struck me two or three years ago that my quest for simpler shapes within the context of the Norfolk land-scape could perhaps most easily be found among the mud flats of the salt marsh creeks, and also at low tide on our flattest and widest beaches. This series of three paintings explored this abstract theme in the most successful way, I feel; and yet, those who know the Overy marshes seem to recognise them immediately when they see these pictures!

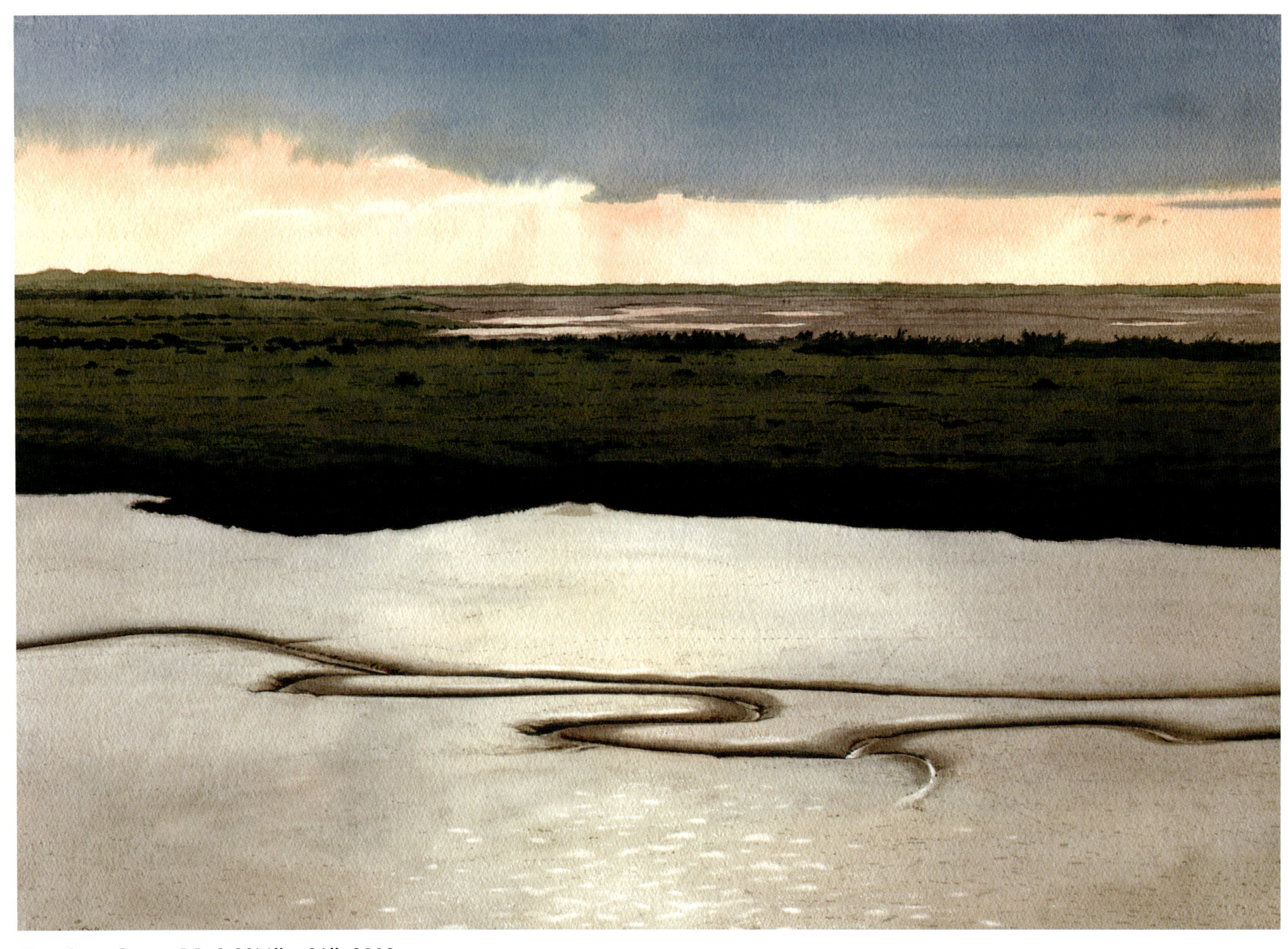

Burnham Overy, Mud 29½" x 21" 2003

Opposite: ***Creek Meanders*** 29½" x 21" 2003

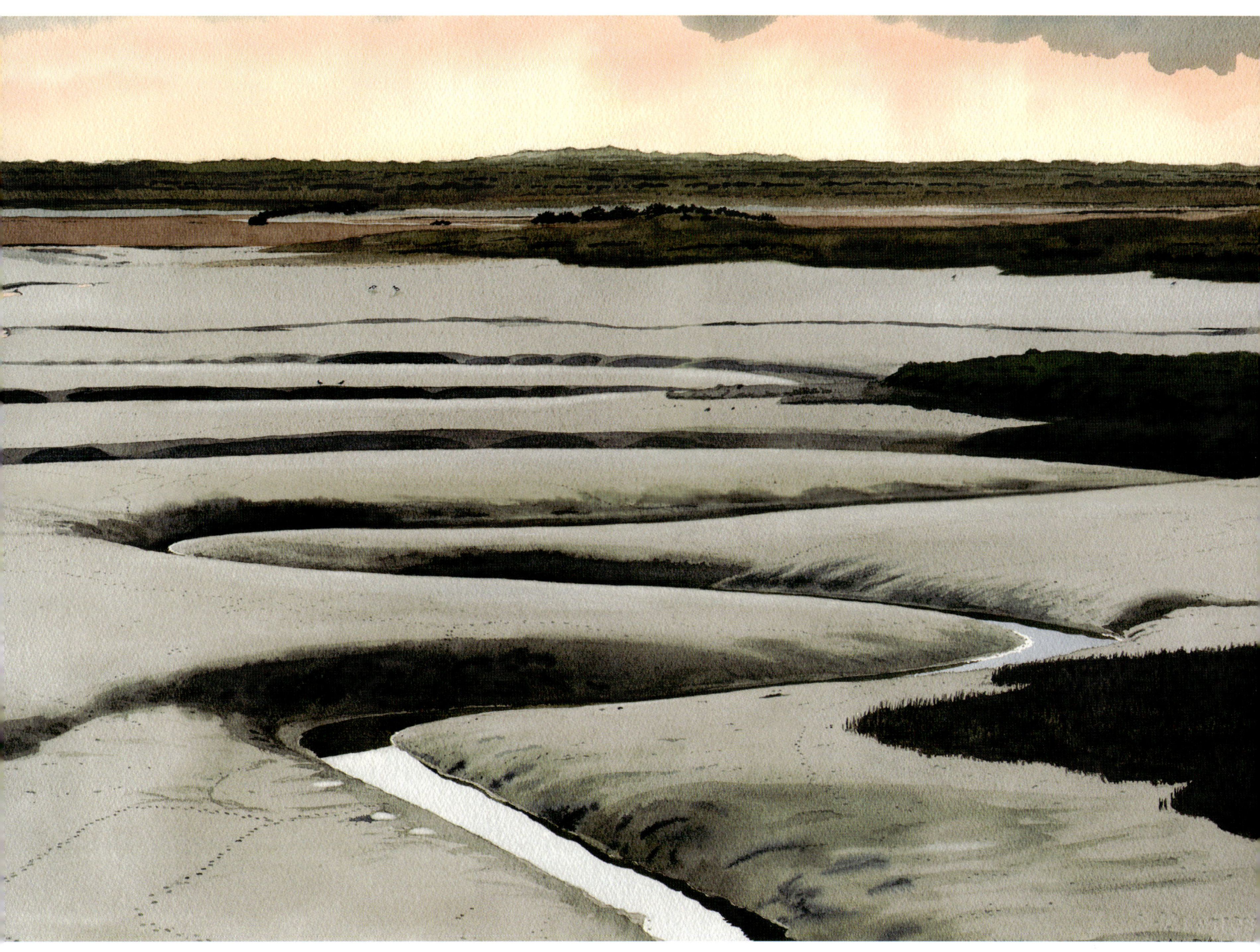

HUNSTANTON CLIFFS

What a remarkable place this is! I am surprised that more fuss is not made of Hunstanton's cliffs, for they are quite unique. They are a Site of Special Scientific Interest on account of the unusual and visible geology, with its overlying strata of white and red chalks, and the brown sandstone known hereabouts as Carrstone. In the village of Old Hunstanton all three materials are used in some of the cottages to beautiful effect. These rock layers formed the old sea-bed and, as a result, the fossils of many ancient sea creatures can be found fairly easily.

The colours of the rock are just wonderful, particularly on a sunny day, and the sea's action has crumbled and ground the rock into some interestingly coloured sand too. It is a delight to walk along the beach here among slabs of fallen rock of different colours. Thinking about this point, it occurred to me that in fact there is nowhere else in Norfolk that you can do this. Although West Runton beach has a large field of massive flints strewn over a chalky bedrock, somehow the effect is not quite the same. I recently noticed that Weybourne cliffs also have a base composed of chalk, with sand over the top, but in the main, Hunstanton has the only rock cliffs in Norfolk, and virtually the only exposed visible rock in the county. In fact, you have to travel quite a long way to find the next piece of rock cliff in England; there is none until you reach Yorkshire, travelling northwards, or Kent in the opposite direction; but here we have this little one-mile stretch of the most beautiful scenery, perversely facing west on the east coast!

High tides at Hunstanton can reach the foot of the cliff at one point, so there has been no opportunity to 'civilise' the spot with a promenade, ice cream kiosks, litter bins and benches. Thank goodness the wild appearance is retained. It is strange to think that the built-up suburban part of the town is only a couple of hundred yards away from the edge of the cliff, up above you, as you walk along the beach here; you could think yourself to be a hundred miles from the nearest town, because the slightly convex curvature of the coastline prevents you from seeing along the full length of the cliff. I was at the town end one wild and windy night, just after dark, and the feeling of isolation was reinforced; there is no artificial light beyond the end of the promenade, and suddenly it becomes untamed and potentially hazardous territory.

Opposite: *Hunstanton Cliffs, Summer's Day* 26" x 19½" 2004

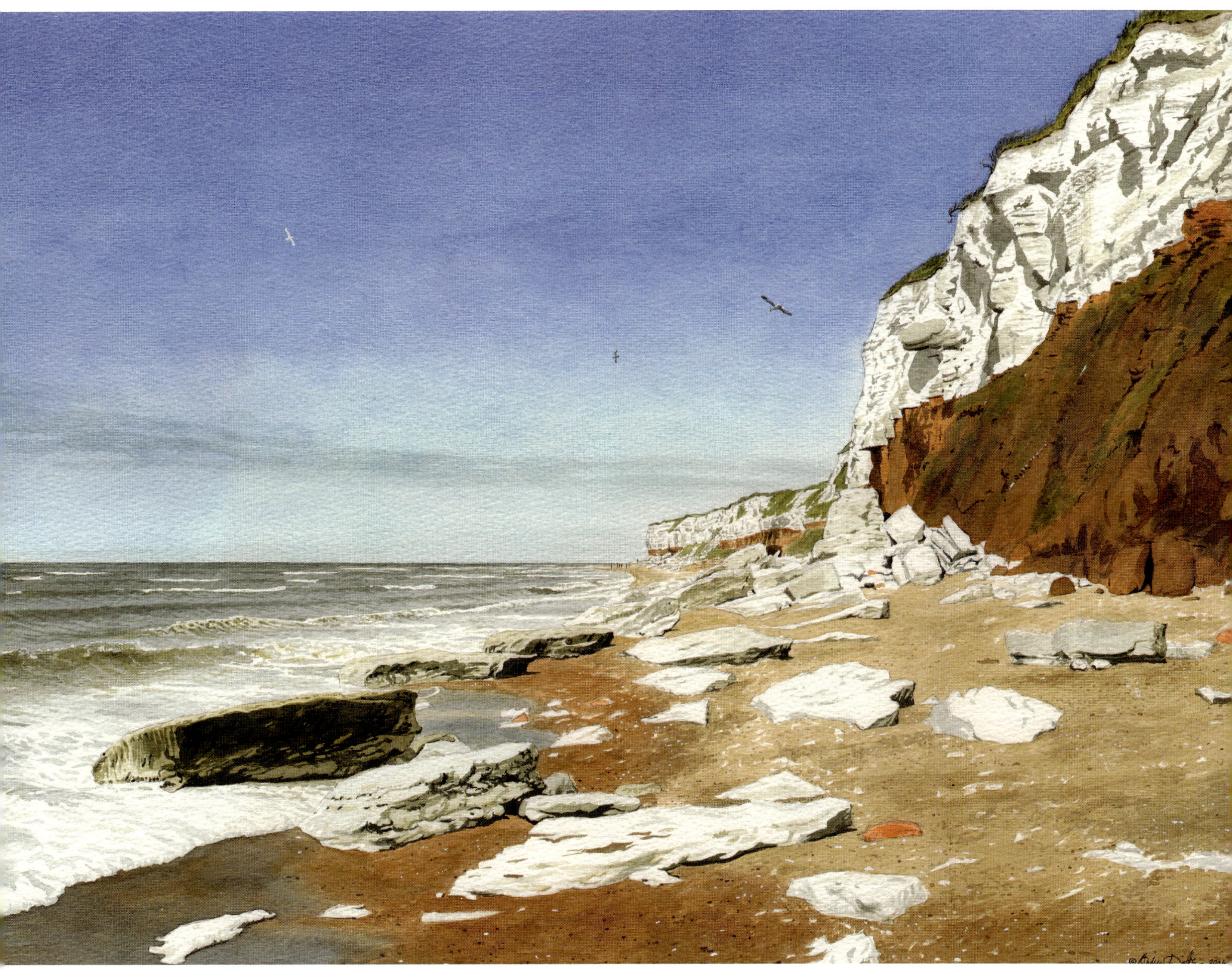

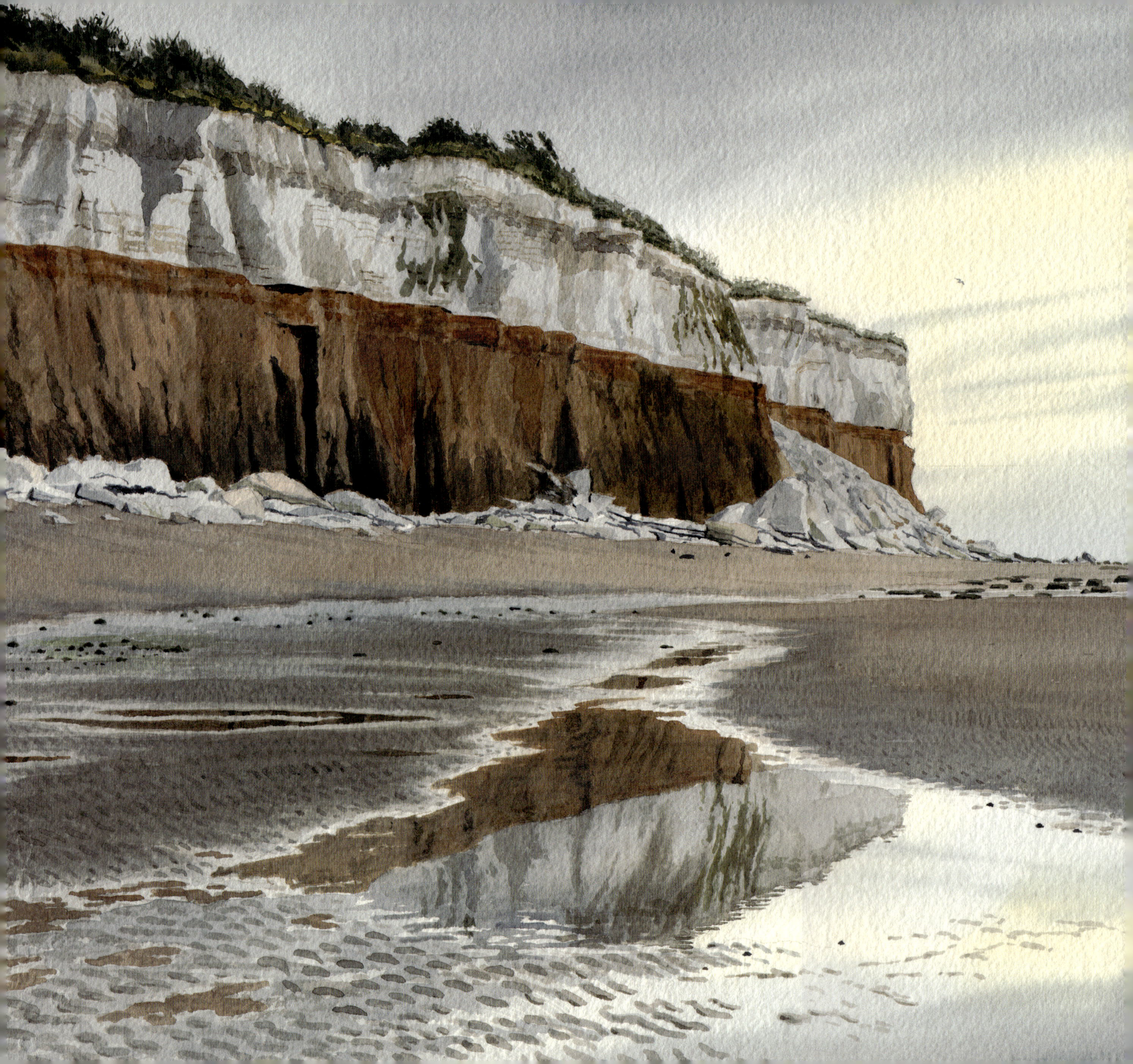

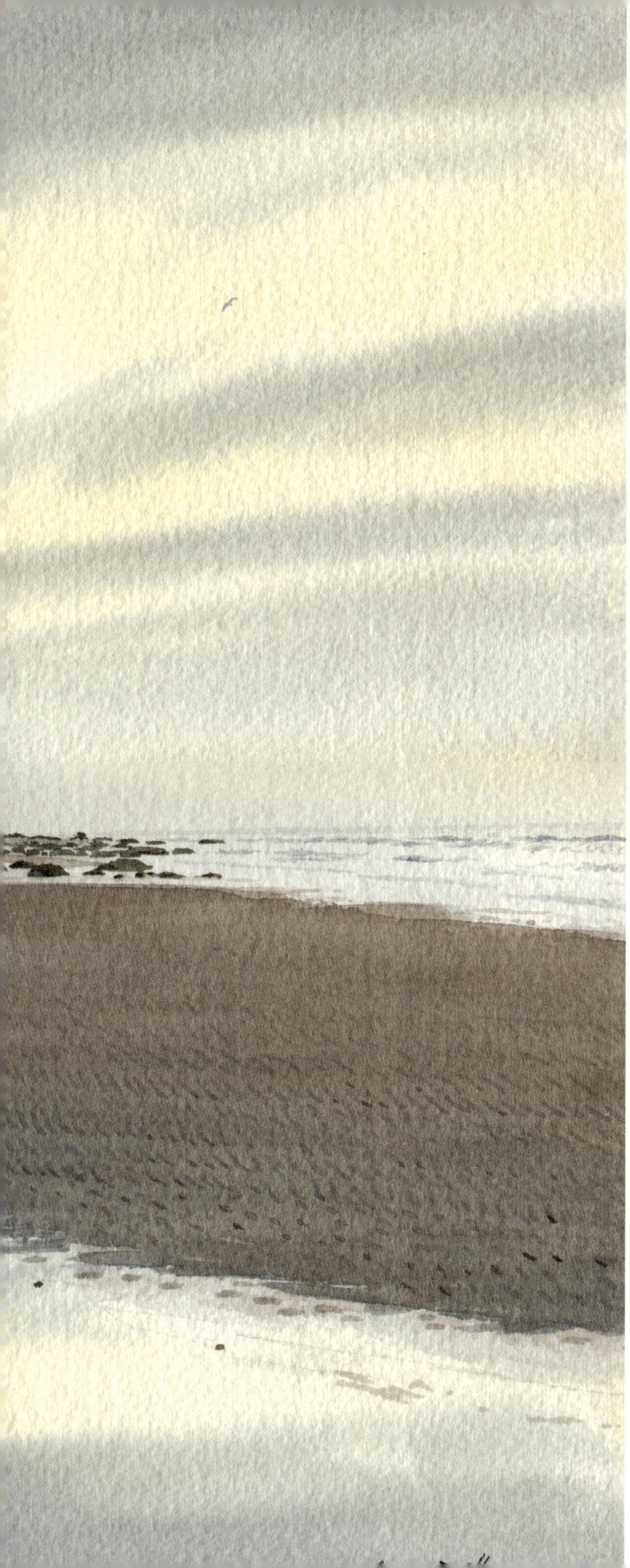

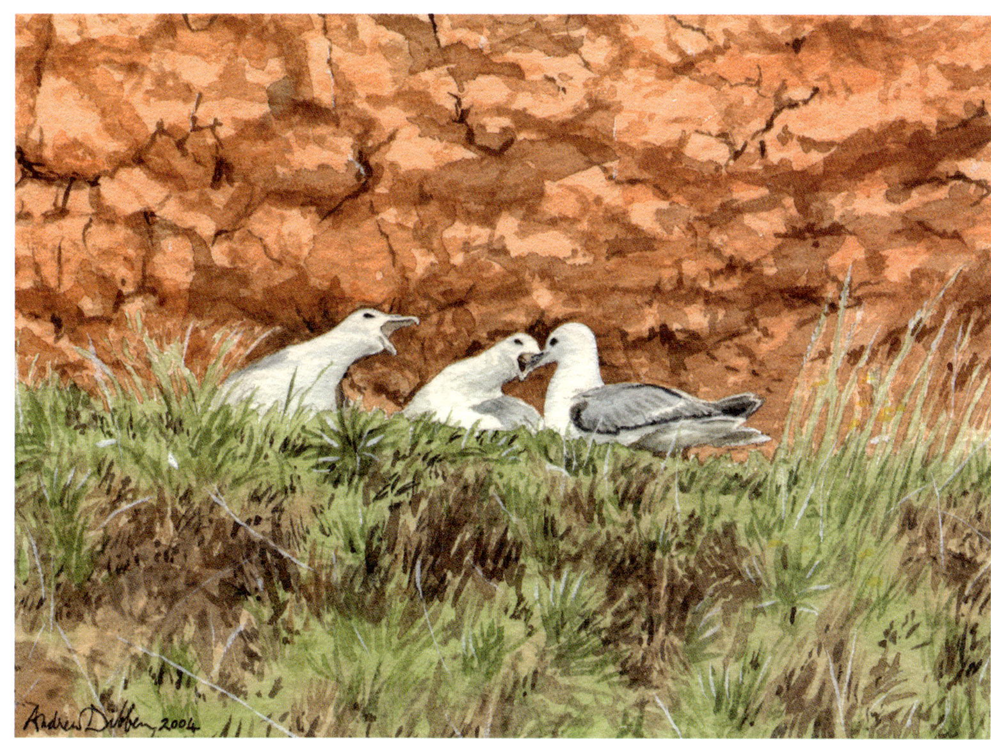

Fulmars on Hunstanton Cliffs 7¹⁄₂” x 5¹⁄₂” 2004

Hunstanton cliffs and beach is one of the best spots in this area to see fulmars. They nest on ledges in the cliff face, and as this is not very tall, it is possible to see the birds at relatively close quarters. Strictly speaking, they are not gulls, but part of the petrel family, and have a noticeable tubular nostril on top of their bill. In flight, they are less slender of body and wing than most gulls, but still very graceful flyers.

Reflections, Old Hunstanton Cliffs 21¹⁄₂” x 14¹⁄₂” 2004

WHEN WATER CHANGES STATE

When the temperature drops below 0°C, water changes state to form frost at ground level, and snow in clouds. The bland scientific fact does no justice to the extraordinary visual transformation of the landscape, which is an event of amazing beauty, although some inconvenience too!

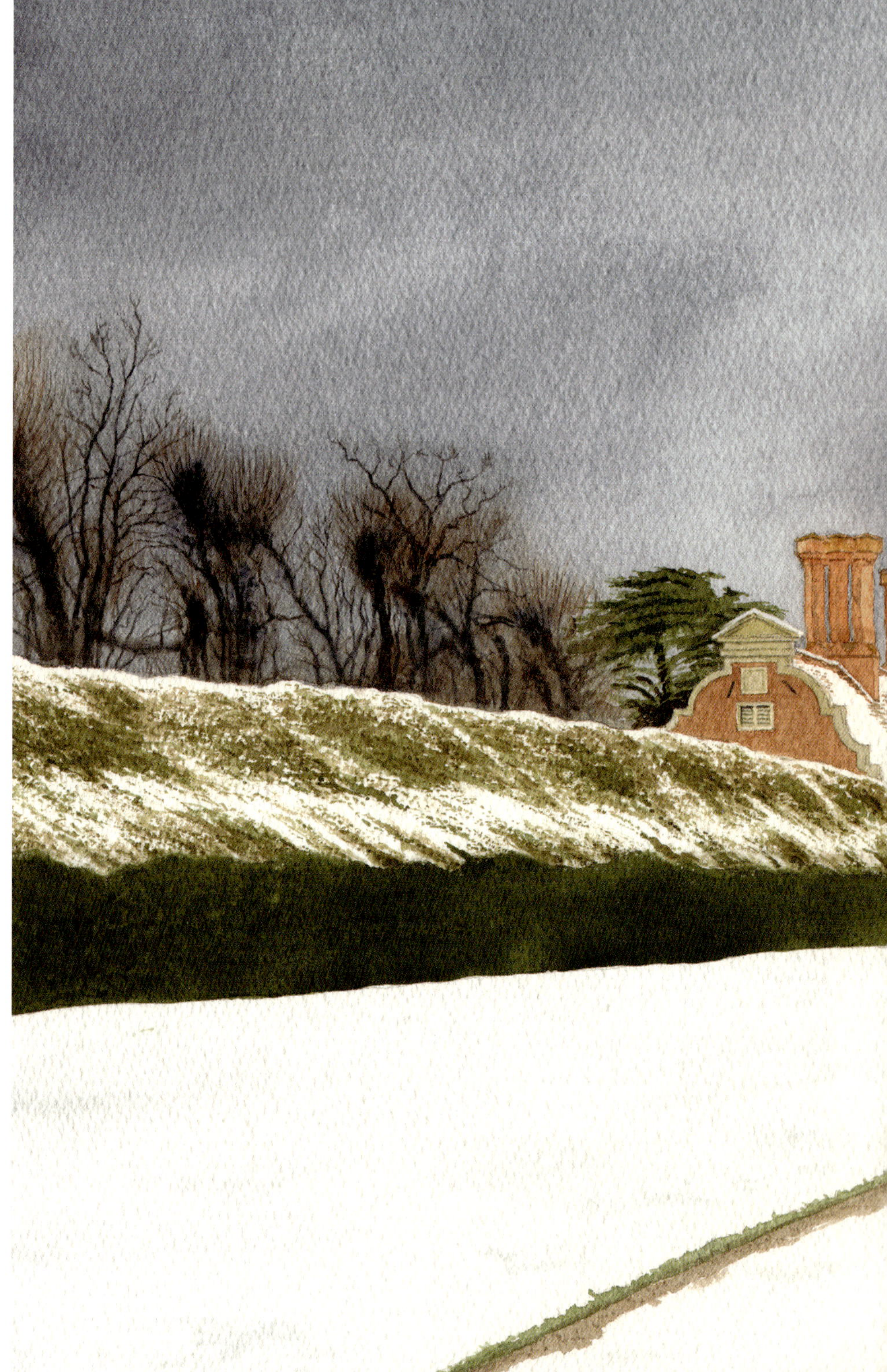

Blickling Hall, Winter 29" x 18" 2003

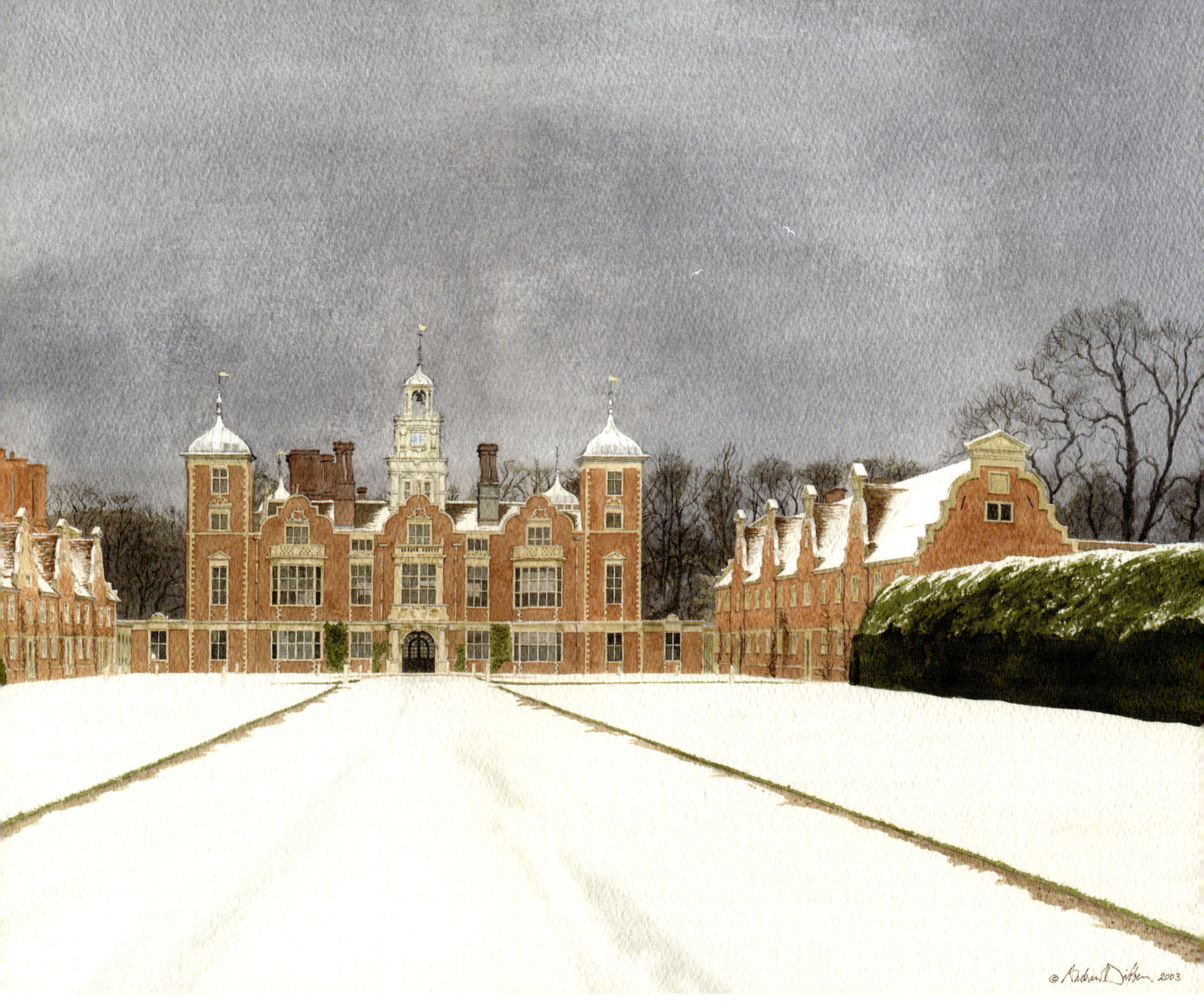

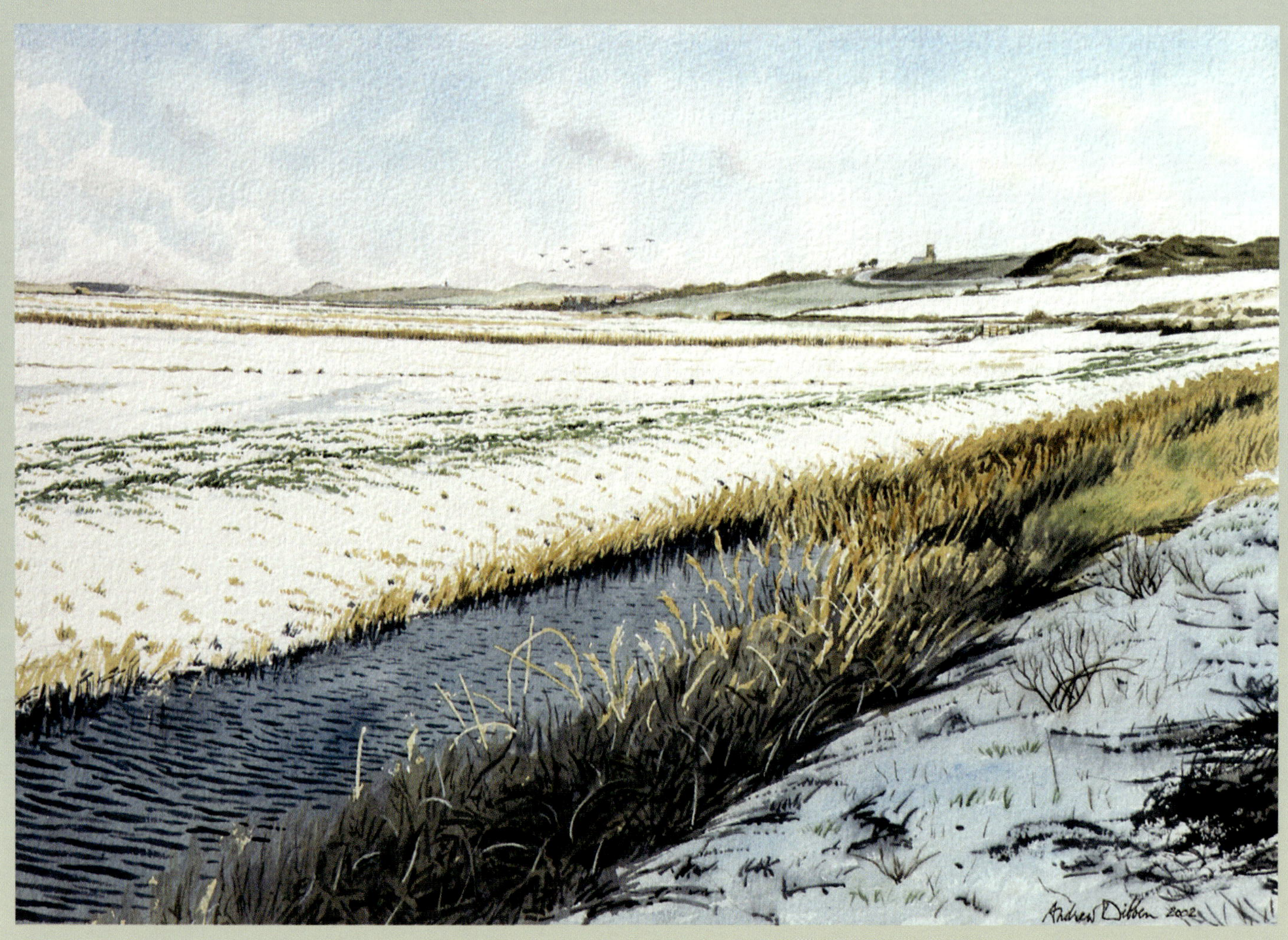

Towards Salthouse – Snow 10" x 14" 2003

MARSH

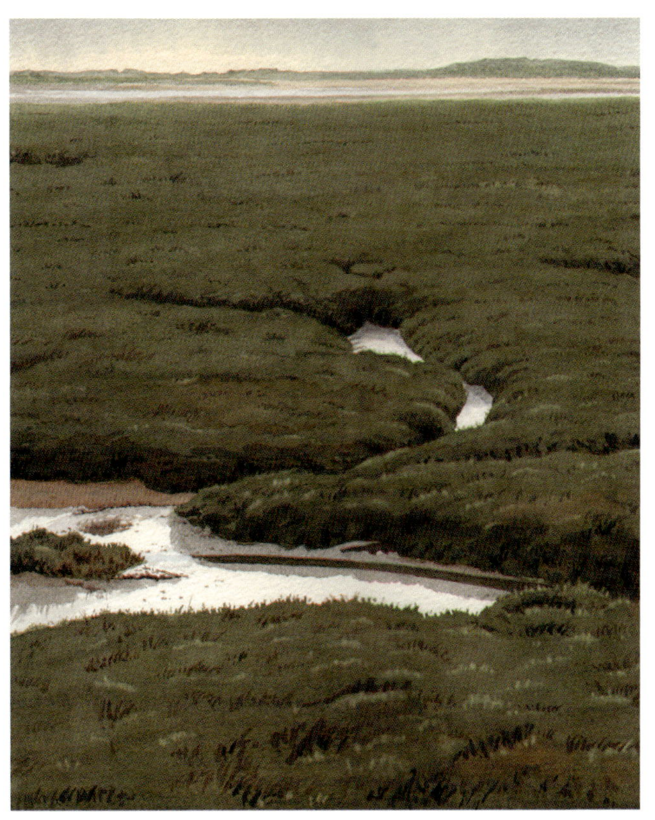

HIGH SUMMER ON THE SALT MARSH

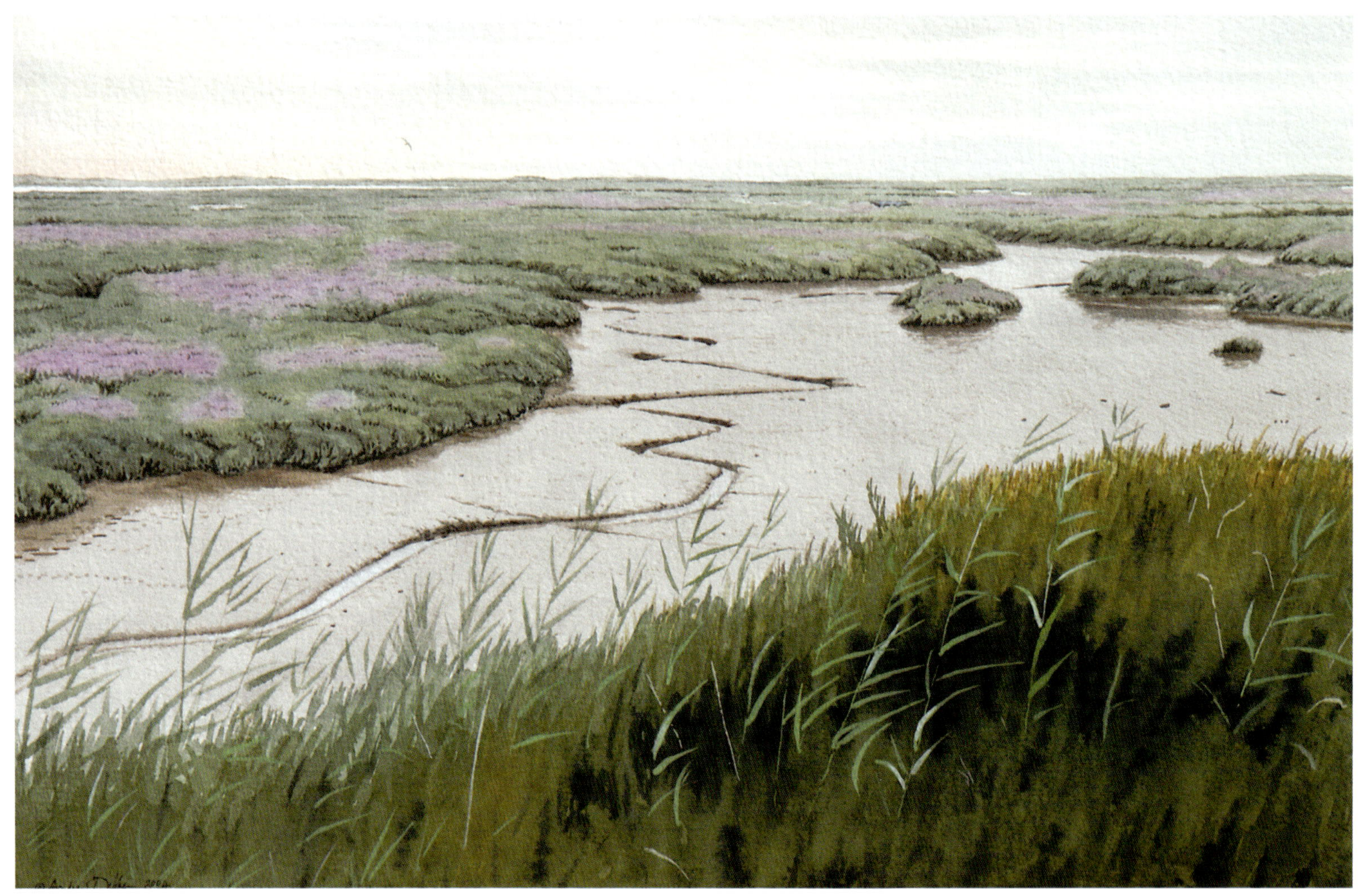

The Marsh Fringe, Brancaster 21½" x 14½" 2004

Opposite: *Brancaster Marsh, Sea Lavender* 21½" x 14½" 2004

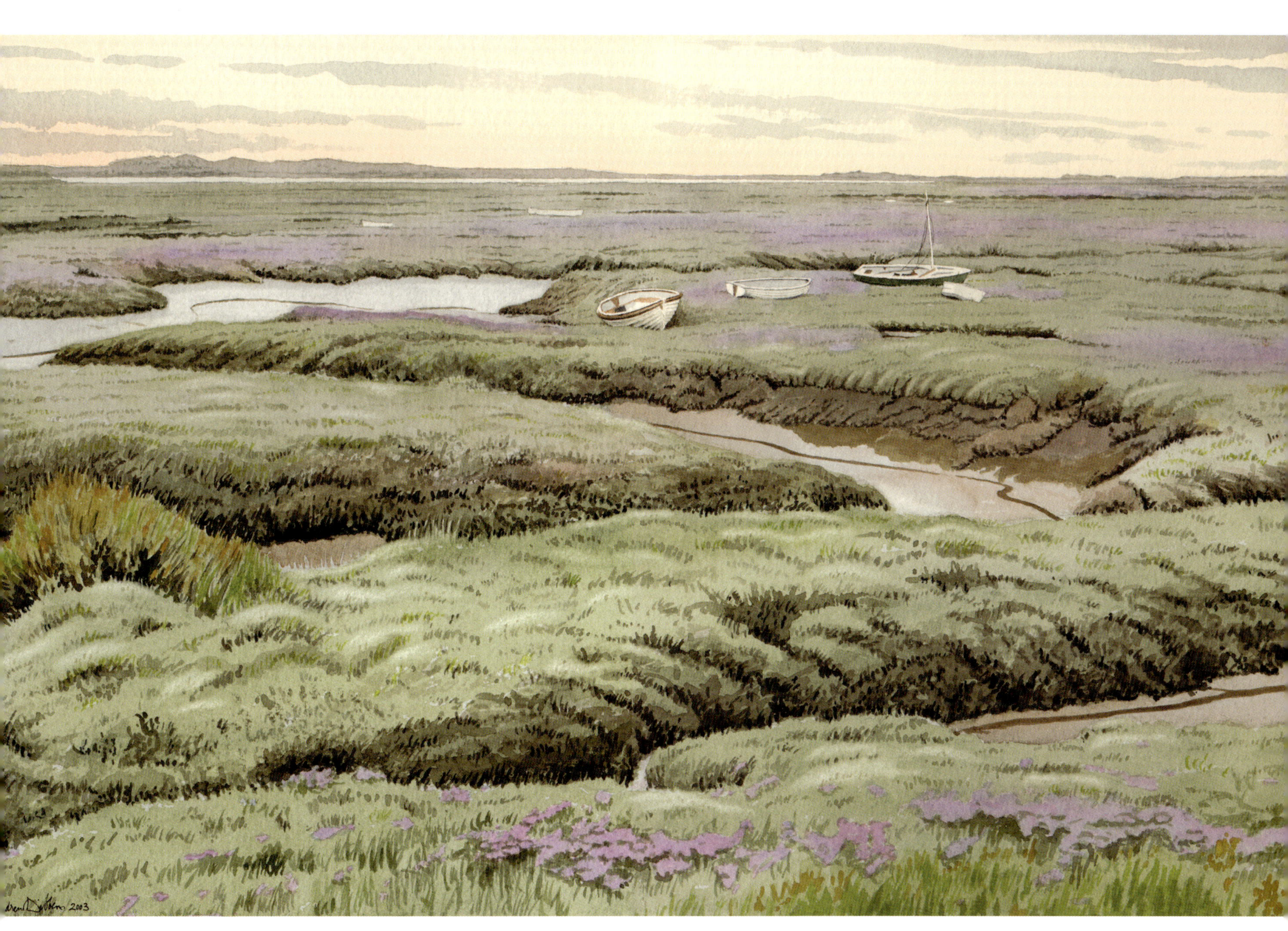

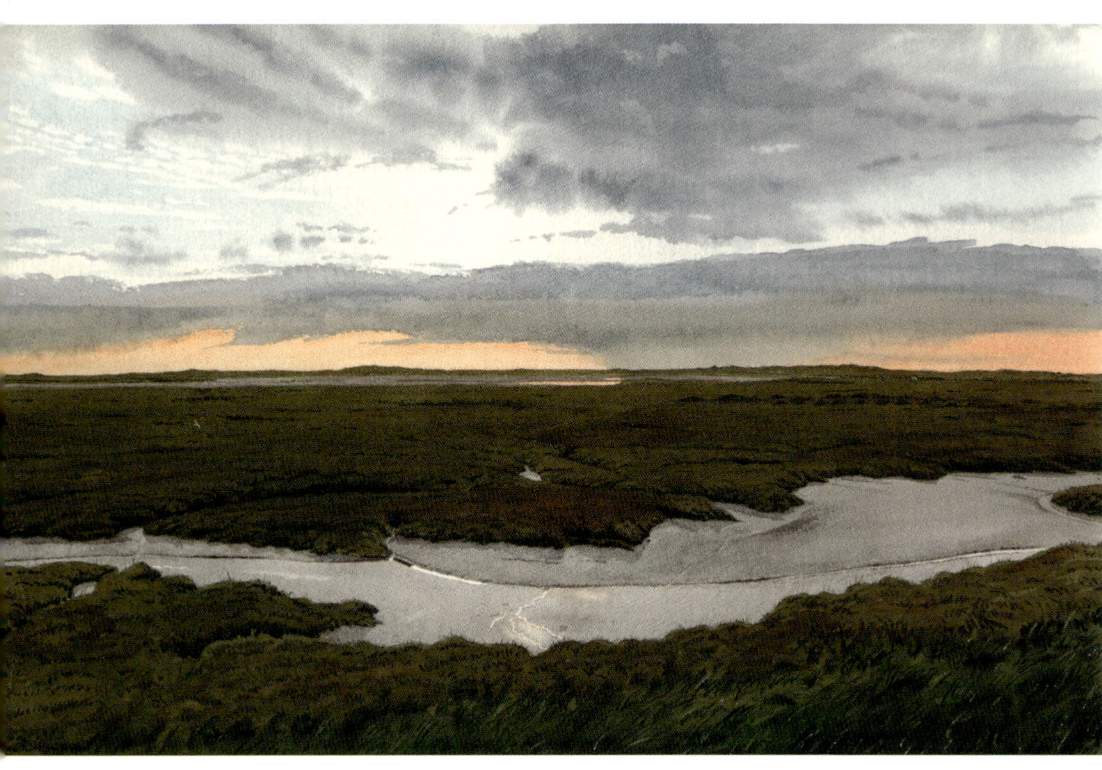

Burnham Overy Marsh 21" x 14" 2003

Burnham Overy Marsh 2 21" x 14" 2003

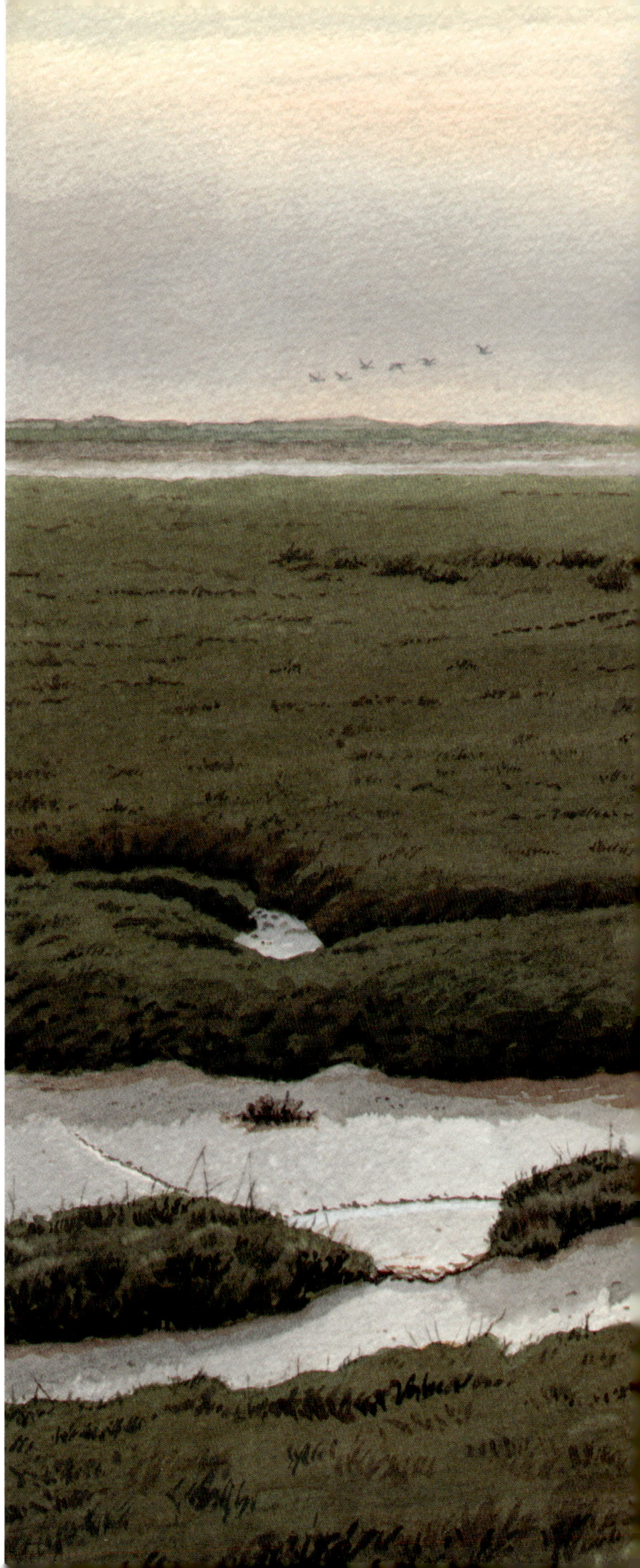

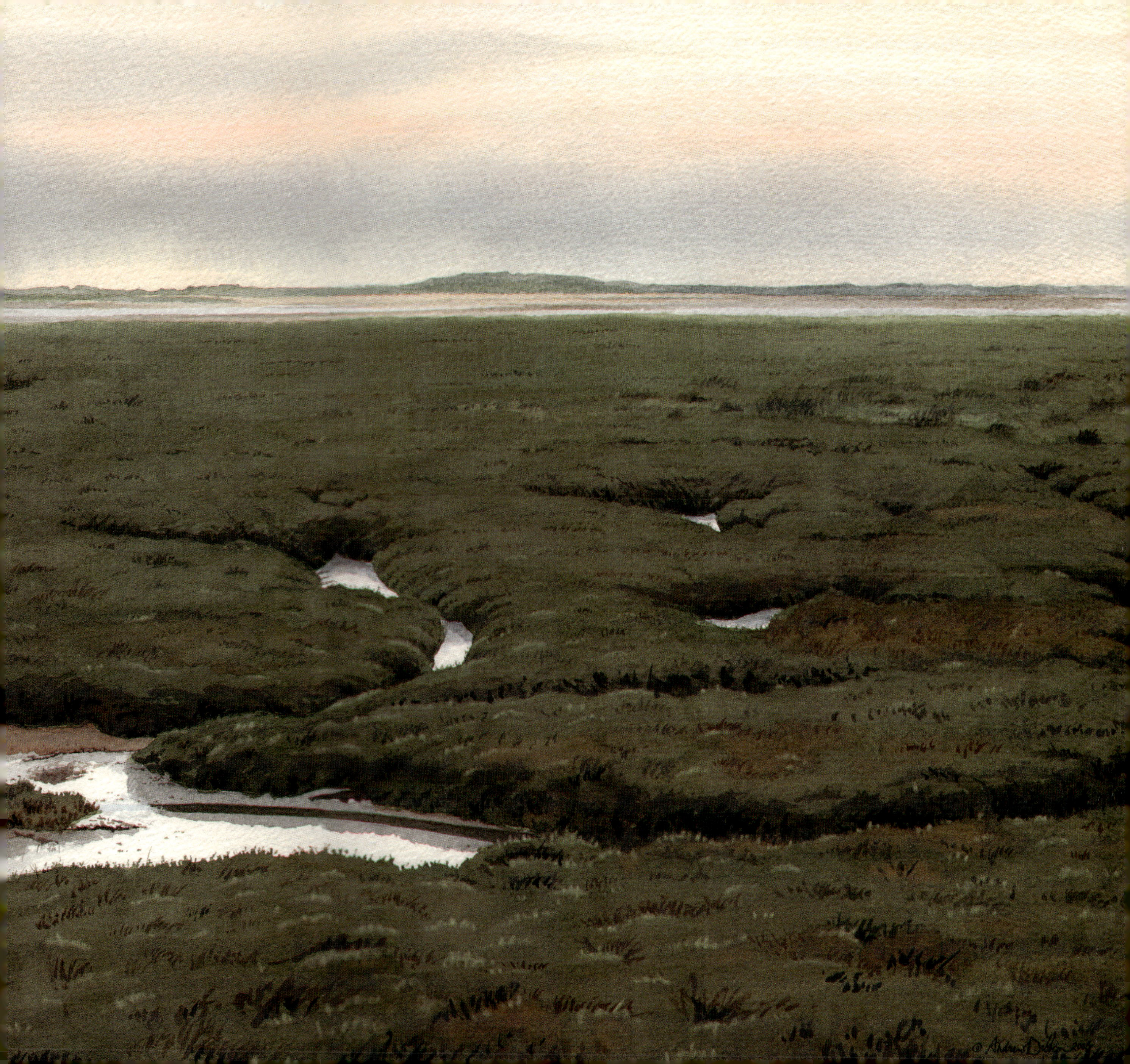

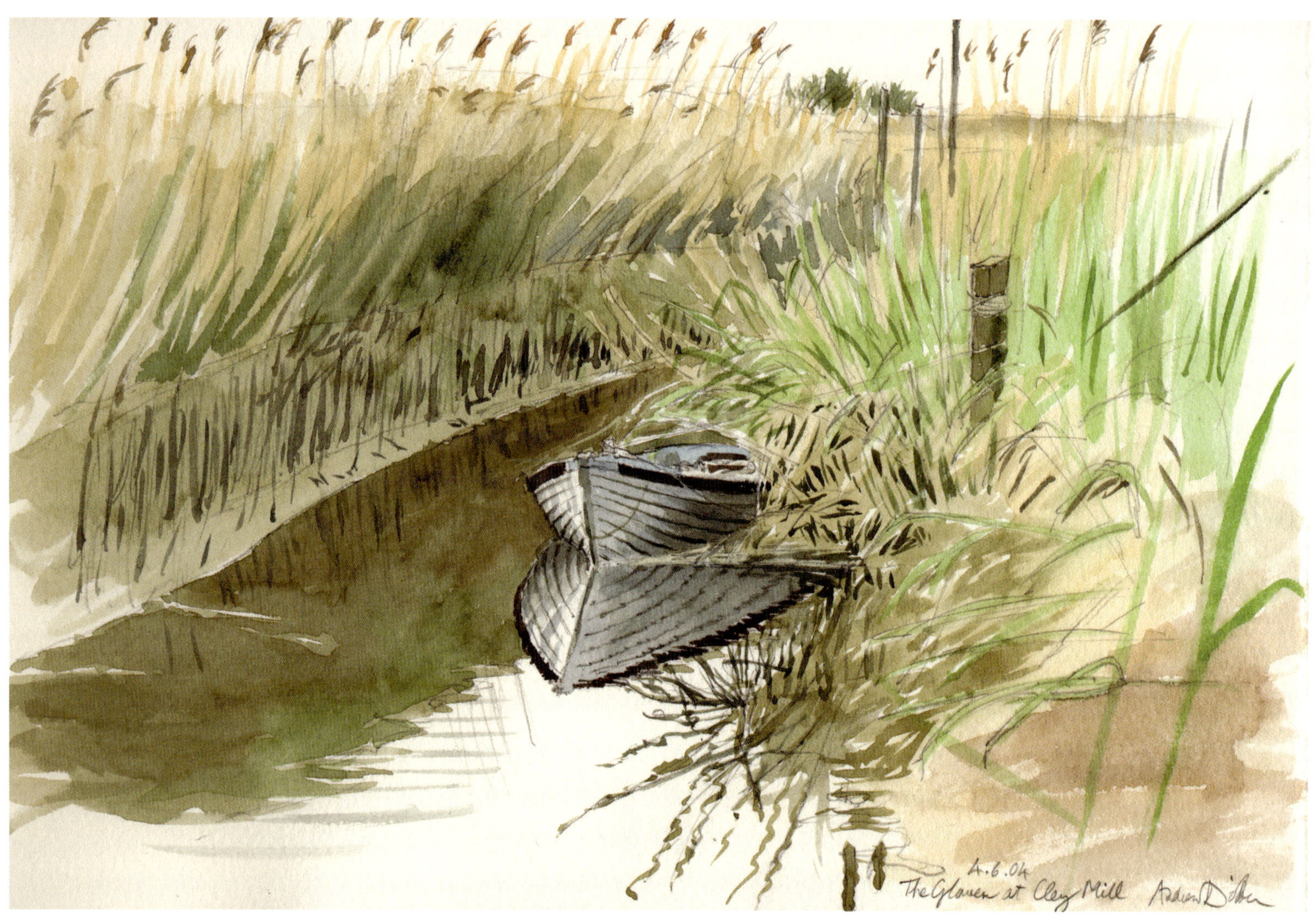

The River Glaven at Cley (From Sketchbook) 7" x 10" 2004

Opposite: **Cley Sunset – Winter** 14½" x 21" 2005

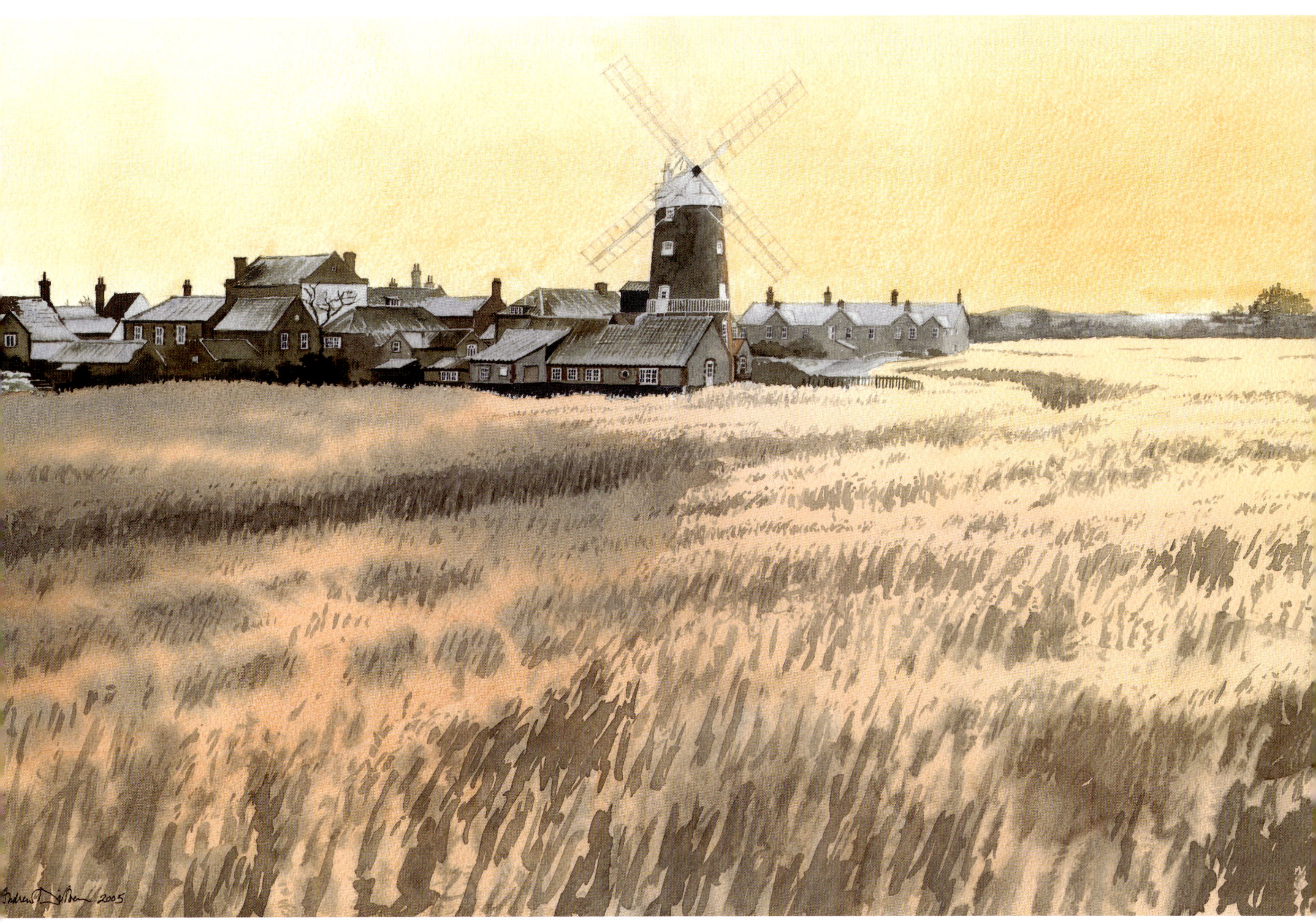

MORSTON HARBOUR

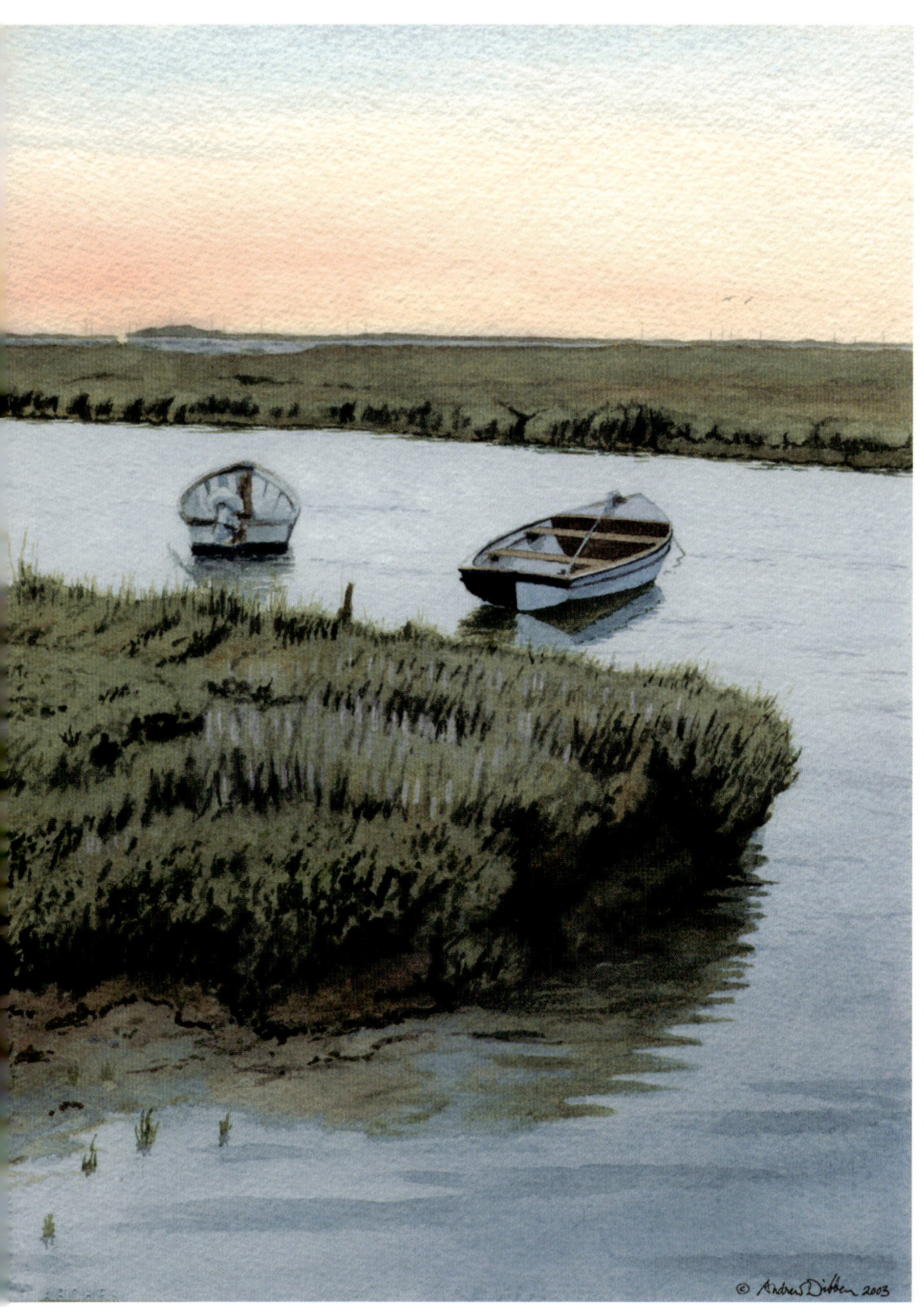

Two Boats, Clear Sky 14½" x 10½" 2003

Morston is deservedly popular with those who like boats and water. For many visitors their first experience of this spot will be when they take a seal-viewing trip from Morston on a day when the tides do not permit sailings from Blakeney Quay.

The creek offers sheltered moorings for working boats as well as pleasure craft, with lovely views over the marshes towards Blakeney village and its lofty church tower, as well as seawards to the Point.

This set of three paintings resulted from a visit to Morston harbour made almost on the spur of the moment as I was passing through the village. The sun was setting and it was a lovely still evening, and it seemed there was not another soul around. The flooding tide was still flowing quite strongly, although it had nearly reached its highest level, and a group of boats swung slowly to and fro at their moorings. Looking into the distance, it was possible to make out Blakeney harbour, and then I realised that several boats in 'the pit' were showing anchor lights; there were probably people out there eating their evening meals while admiring the gentle sunset, and watching the last few marsh birds returning to a roosting place. I was particularly pleased with the third picture, 'Lights on the Anchorage'; it seems to have achieved a very serene and tranquil feeling. There is something quite timeless about this kind of scene, with small working boats awaiting their owners' return, and untidy piles of fishing gear at the water's edge. It could be found at almost any seashore around the world, although a nautical expert would undoubtedly be able to identify the location, within say a hundred miles, by the landscape and the type of boat and crab-pot, which are most definitely English.

Opposite: **Mussel Boat and a Crab-Pot, Morston** 14½" x 10½" 2003

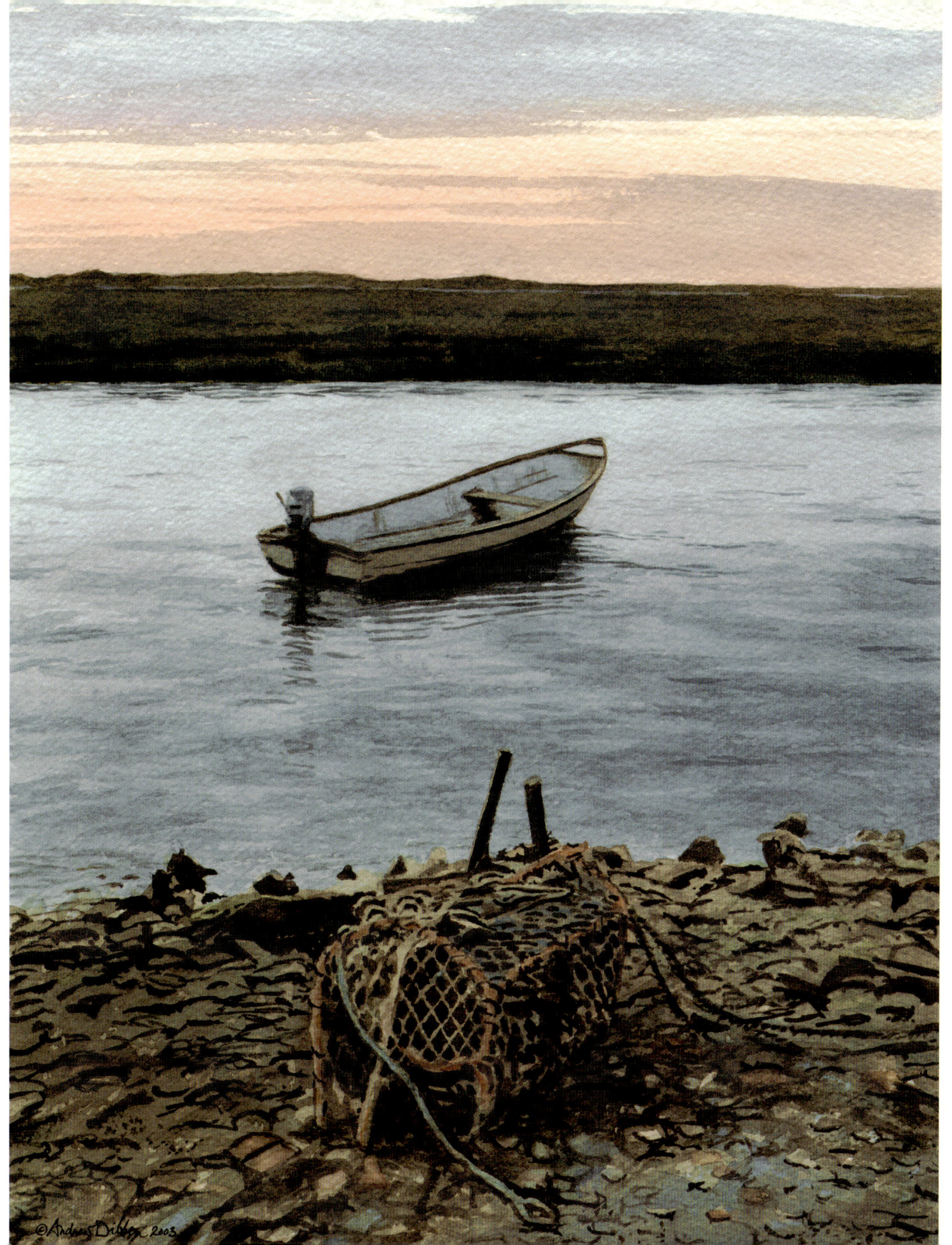
©Andrew Dibben 2003

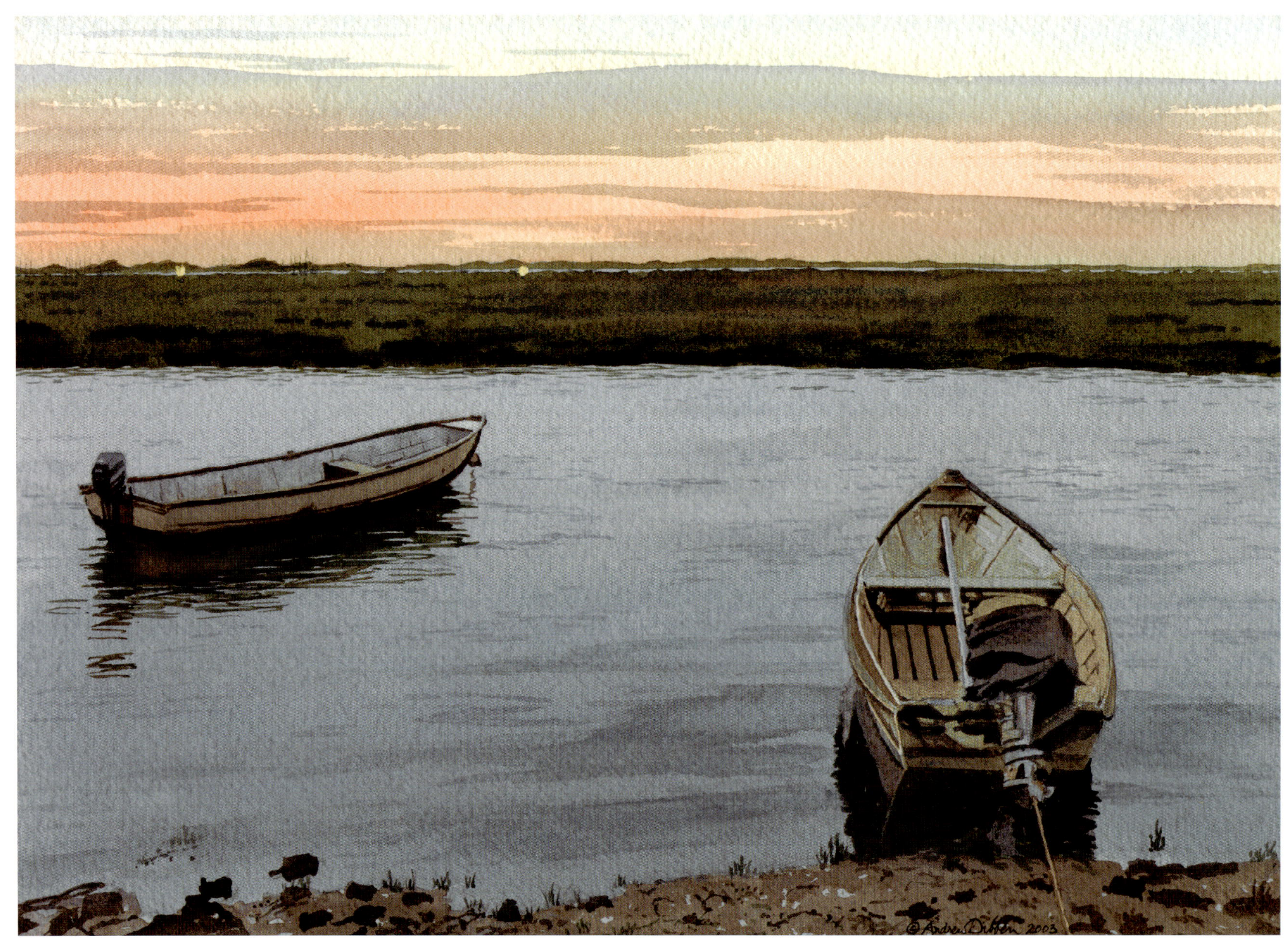

Lights on the Anchorage, Morston 10½" x 14½" 2003

DISTANT WATERS

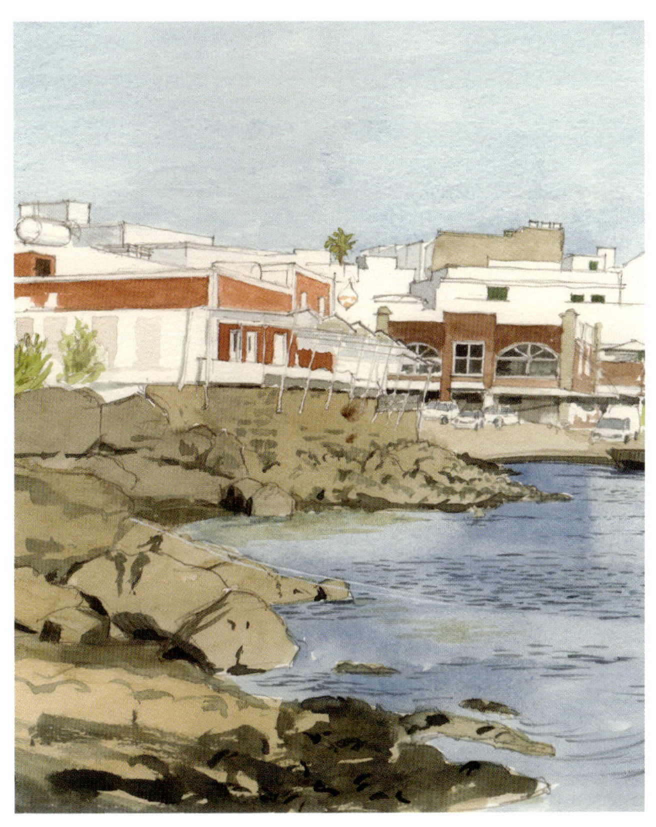

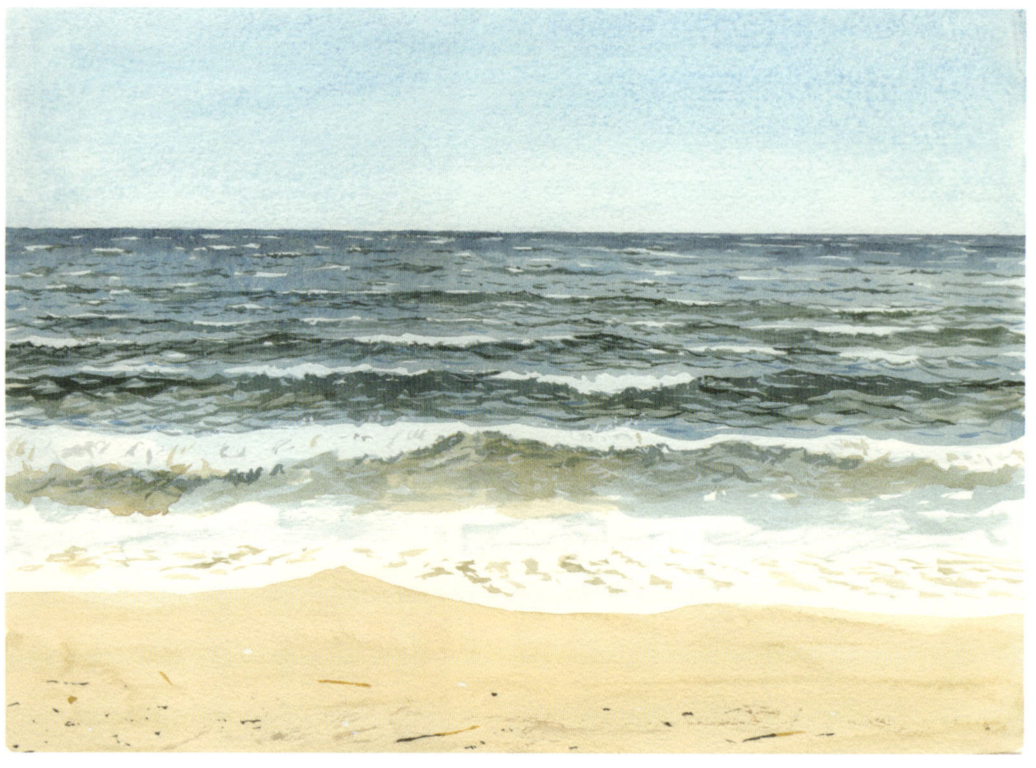

Nerja Beach (from sketchbook) 14" x 10" 2004

I have been fortunate enough to travel to a number of countries during my life. The desire to travel was sown at a very early age by my mother who took my brother and I back and forth between Britain and France every year to visit our grandparents, sometimes even twice a year. After my grandfather died, my mother was anxious to take Grand'mère to lots of places, to make up for having to stay at home for many years looking after the old gentleman. Having been quite an adventurous man in his younger days he frequently suffered from bronchitis in his later years. He had been cured for good of the travel bug during a visit to England just after the war, when he declared that he had never felt so cold in his life; he couldn't understand why English houses didn't have central heating, and vowed he would never return, not even for his only daughter's wedding! So, after his death, my brother and I accompanied my mother on epic voyages to show Grand'mère the sights of Europe.

I still enjoy travel; now, it is usually undertaken as a holiday but nevertheless I rarely go away without drawing and painting equipment, even if it only results in one solitary sketch! I always take a camera with me also, and usually take hundreds of photos; it would seem that the urge to make pictures is very deep-seated! It occurred to me that the problem with using a camera is that, each time you press the shutter button, in effect you are saying 'I'll paint this one later!' And of course, it rarely happens. In a way, photography is just far too quick and easy! That will not stop me doing it though.

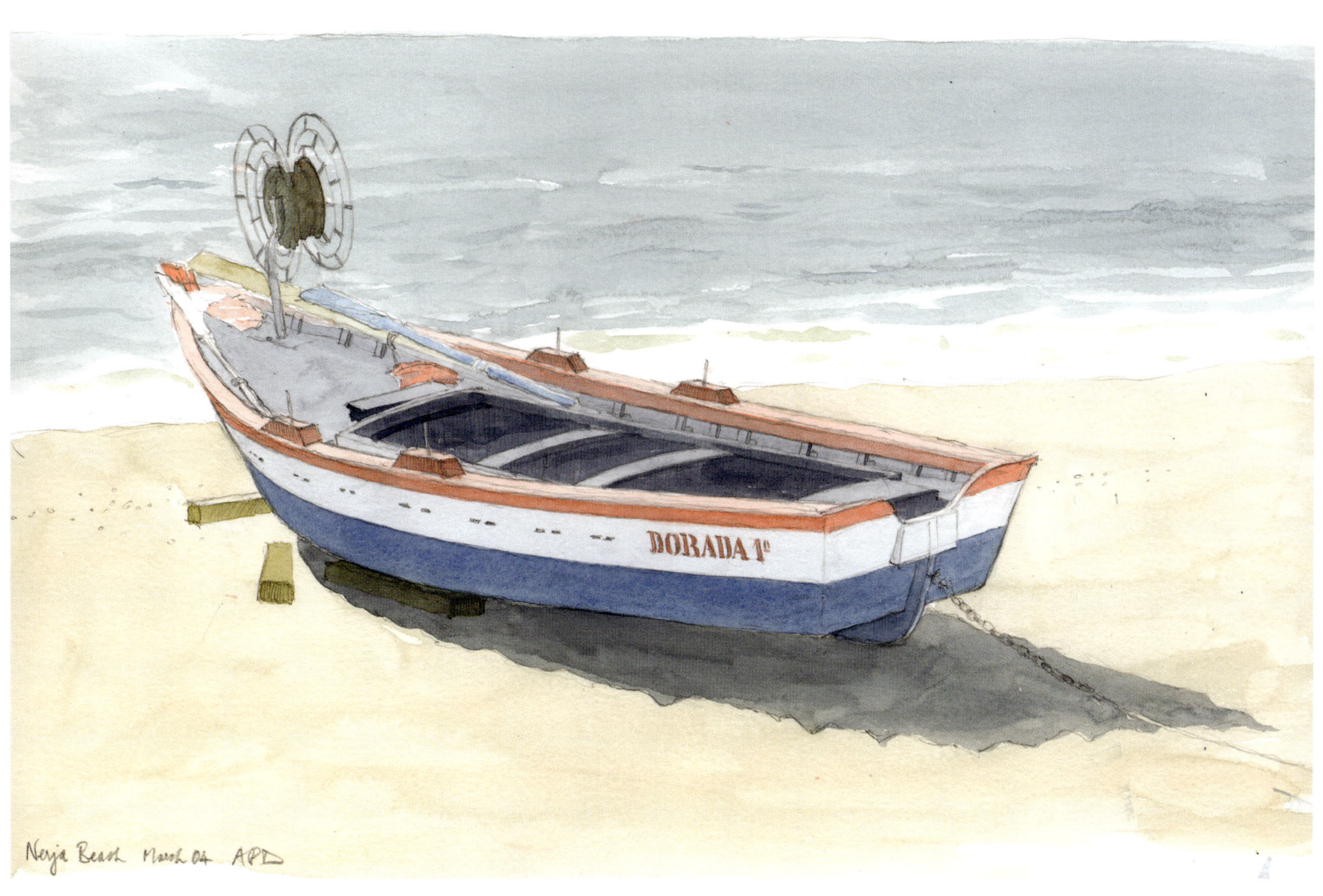

*Fishing Boat (***Dorada I***) on Nerja Beach* 14" x 10" 2004

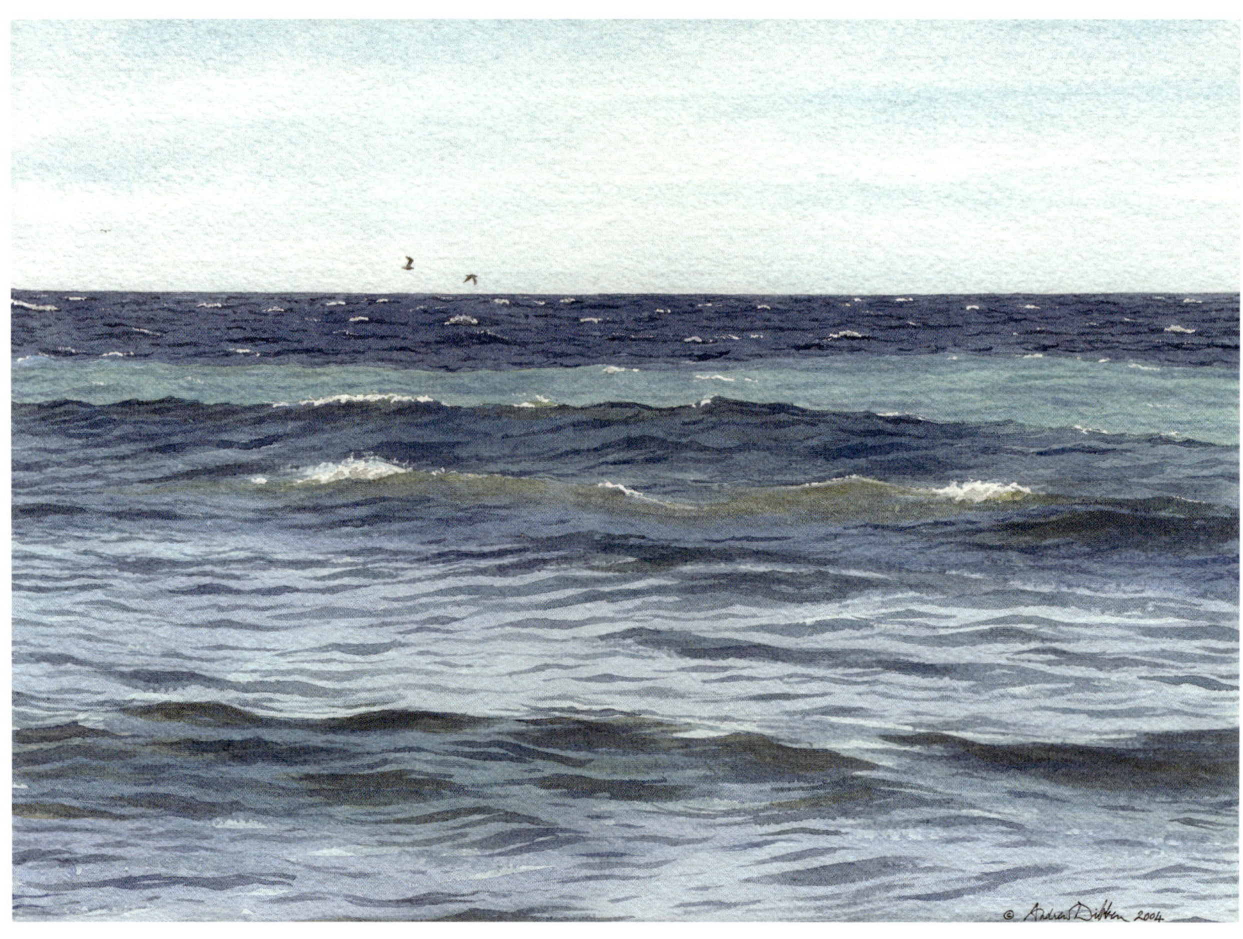

Mediterranean 2 14" x 10"

In March 2004, we flew from Norwich to southern Spain, to the eastern end of the Costa del Sol where there are still some delightfully unspoilt stretches of coastline. The Mediterranean Sea was a beautiful colour, quite different to the North Sea. The southern North Sea is relatively shallow, and bounded in most parts by sandy coastlines; this results in sand and silt being churned up by the action of waves and tides, resulting in the greyish colour we so often see. I spent several afternoons in Spain sitting on the beach, just painting the sea.

The other picture here is one of a handful painted during a holiday on the island of Lanzarote, in the Canaries. I found the landscape here absolutely fascinating, with its desert-like and moonscape areas, as well as the slightly sinister dormant volcanoes. It was also a revelation to learn about the artist César Manrique whose influence was so enormous and beneficial to the island; he prevented the spread of high-rise hotels and apartment blocks almost single-handedly, and left a legacy of world-class visitor attractions.

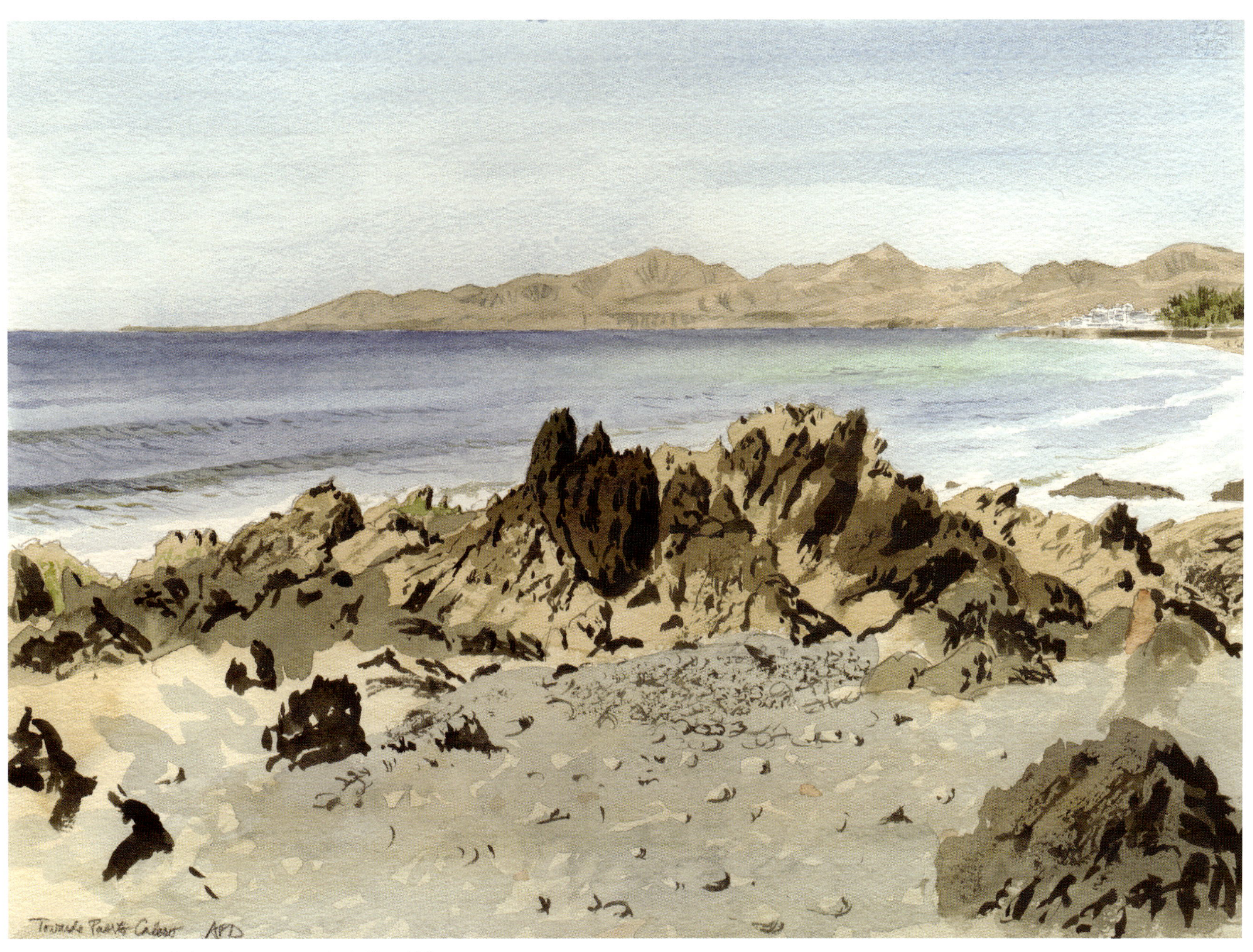

Towards Puerto Calero (Lanzarote) 14" x 10"

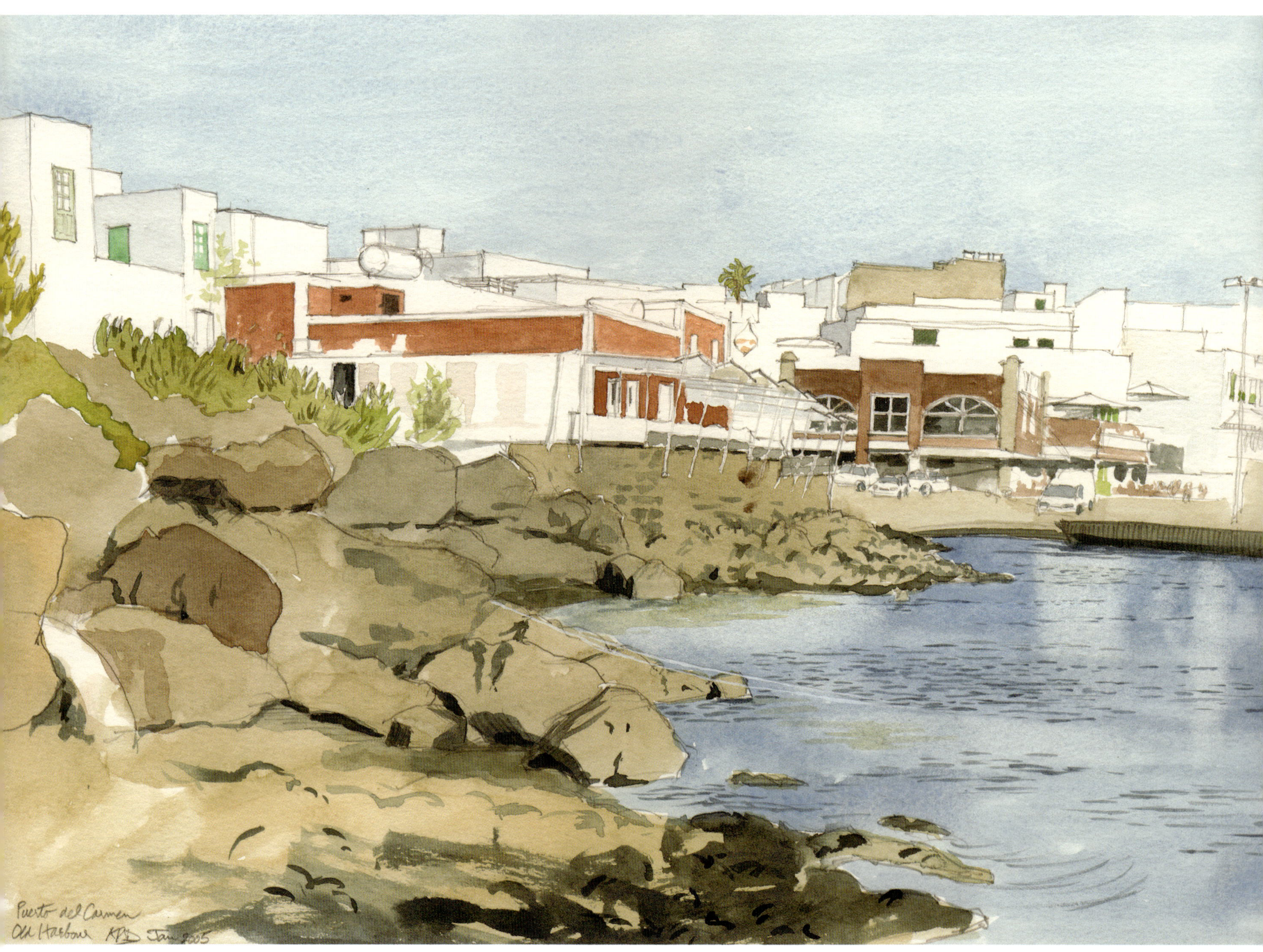

Puerto del Carmen
Old Harbour KAD Jan 2005

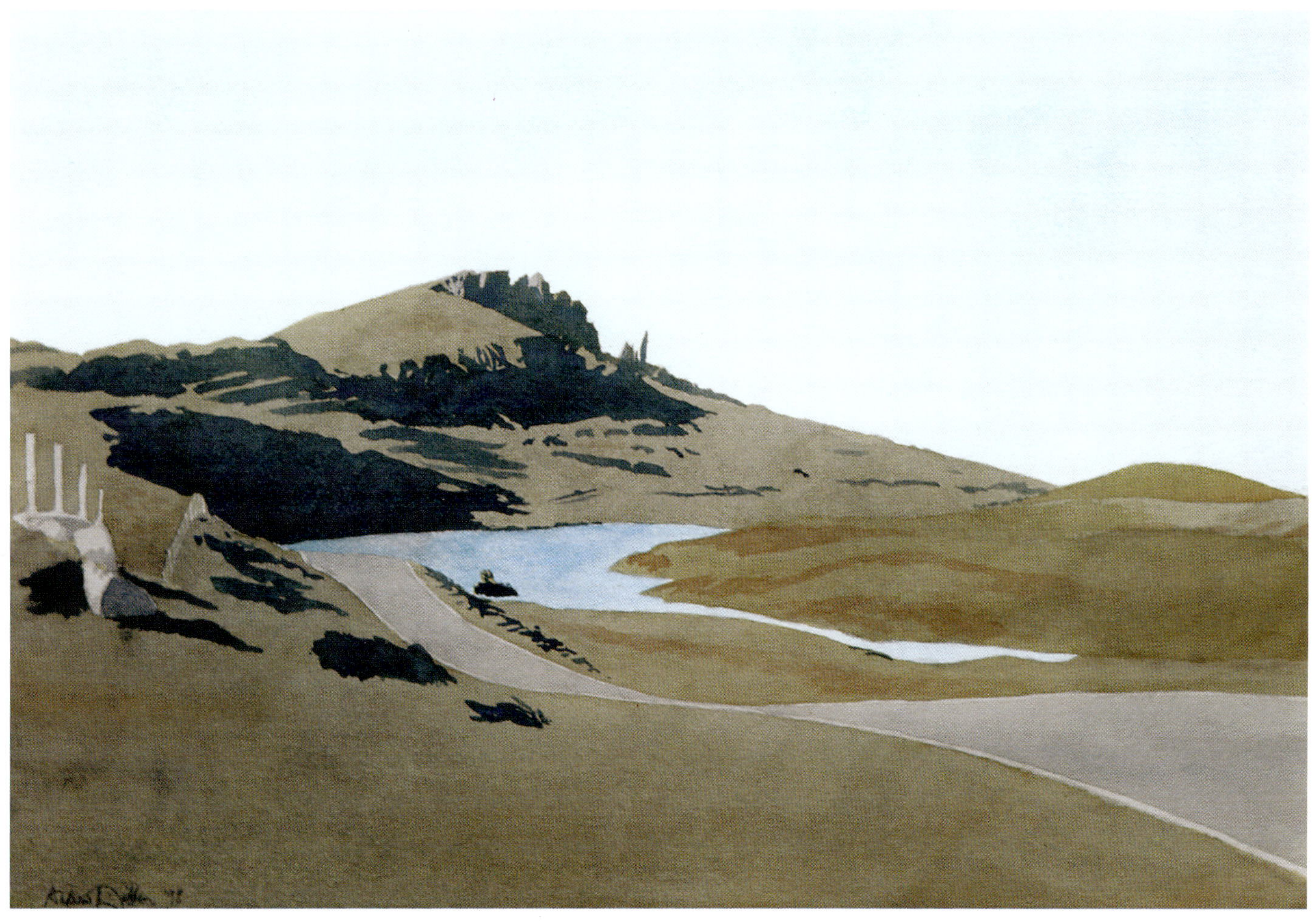

The Old Man of Storr Isle of Skye 16" x 12"

Above is a small painting of the Old Man of Storr, a huge rock needle on the Isle of Skye. This was one of the results of a painting trip to Scotland in 1998. I was totally bowled over by the scenery on Skye, which is among the most spectacular in the whole of Britain, and condensed into quite a small area.

Opposite: ***The Old Harbour, Puerto del Carmen*** (Lanzarote) 14" x 10" 2005

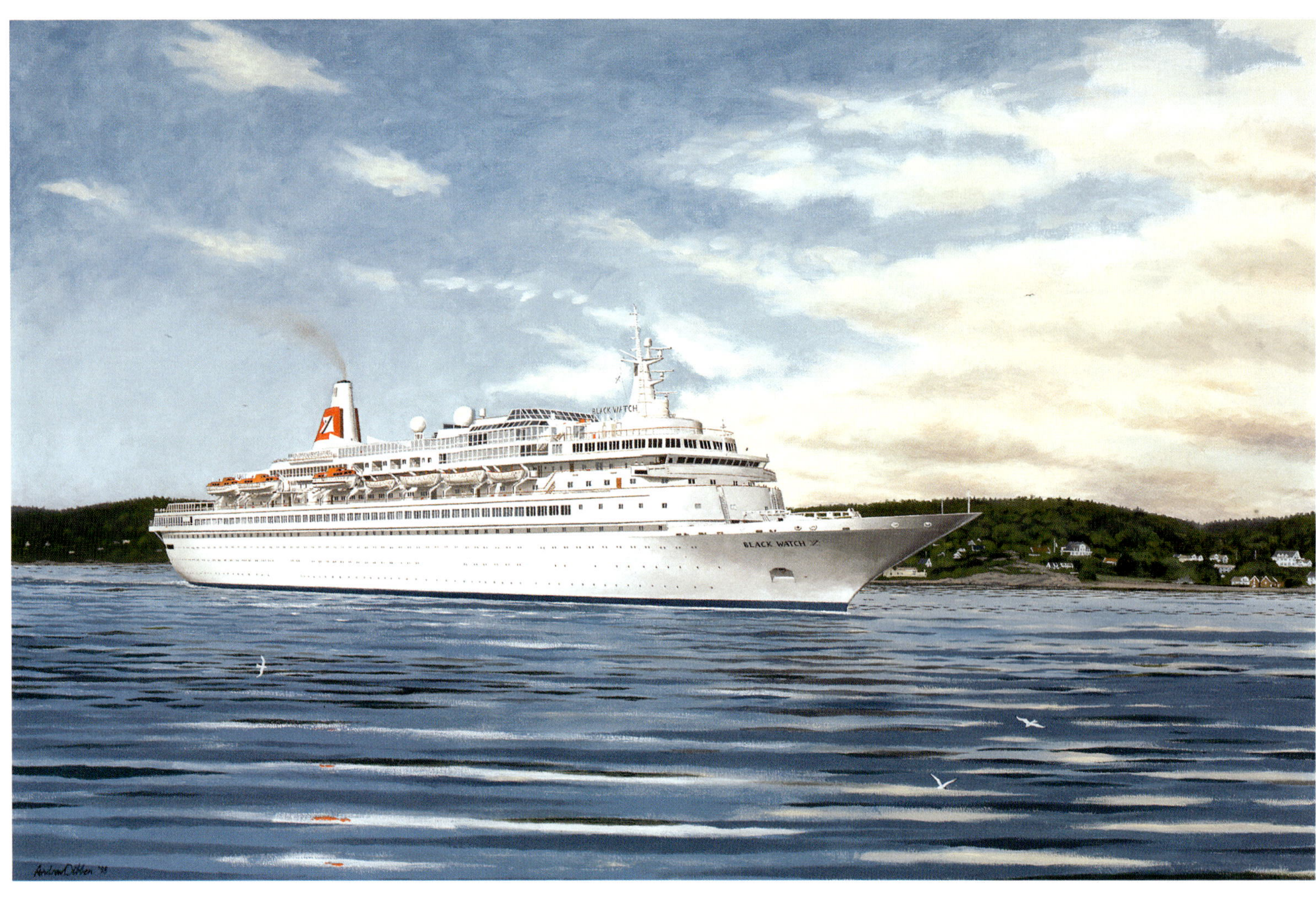

_M.S._ Black Watch (Fred Olsen Cruise Lines) Oil on canvas, 36" x 24"

This is an unusual painting of mine, in that it is an oil, commissioned by Fred Olsen Cruise Lines. This proved quite a difficult project as I had to wait for photographs of this part of the Oslofjord to be taken specially by one of the on-board photographers when one of their ships passed this spot. Mr Olsen wanted the village of Hvitsten included in the painting because the Olsen family owns most of the houses depicted, as well as the former school-house. When the long-awaited photos finally arrived, I was dismayed to find that the only opportunity to take them in months had come on a day of thick cloud cover and unremitting rain. The shots were as grey and lifeless as anyone could imagine! With much perseverance, I managed to come up with this result, which I felt was quite good in the circumstances. I never heard the client's opinion, which may be just as well!

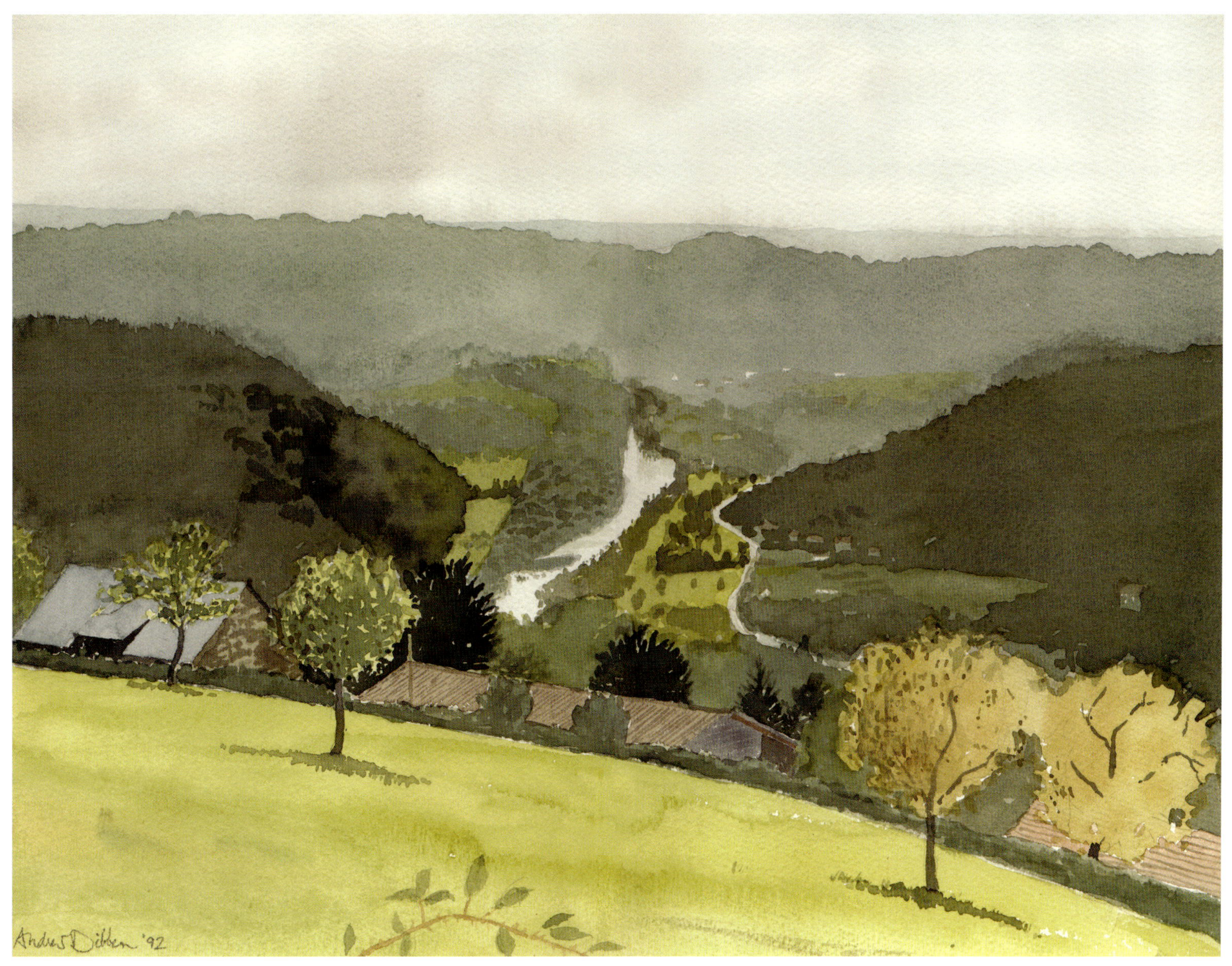

The Dordogne near Beaulieu-sur-Dordogne 9" x 12" 1992

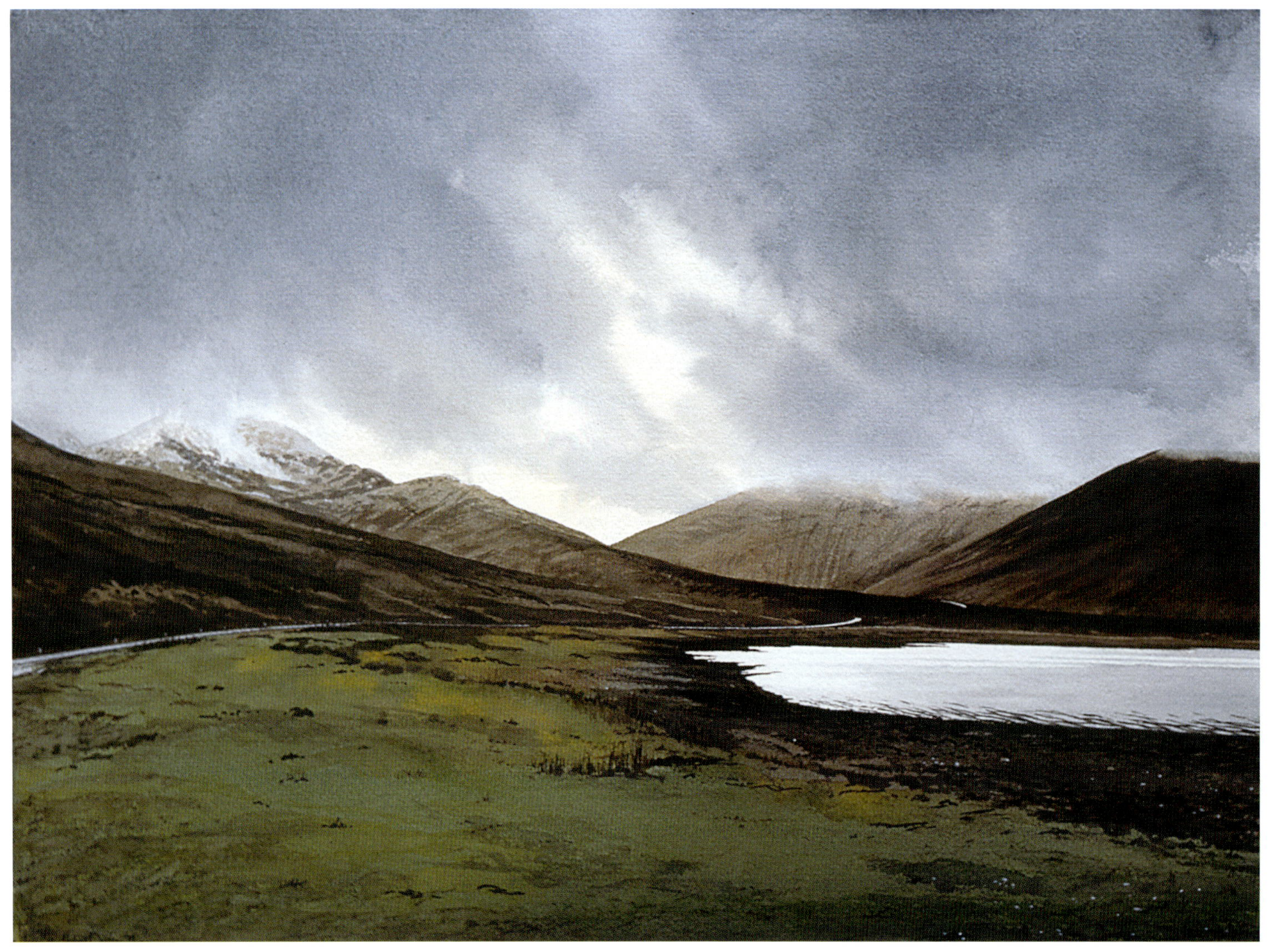

Above: ***Runrig Country: Marsco and Loch Ainort*** 29" x 21" 1999

Scotland has always drawn me, with its beautiful rugged coastline and numerous sea and fresh-water lochs. Maybe it's to do with the blood link; my paternal grandmother came from the little village of Craigie, near Dunfermline. The above painting was titled in honour of the band Runrig, one of whose songs is called 'Moonlight on Marsco'; Marsco is the large, snow-capped mountain in the background of this view of the east coast of Skye.

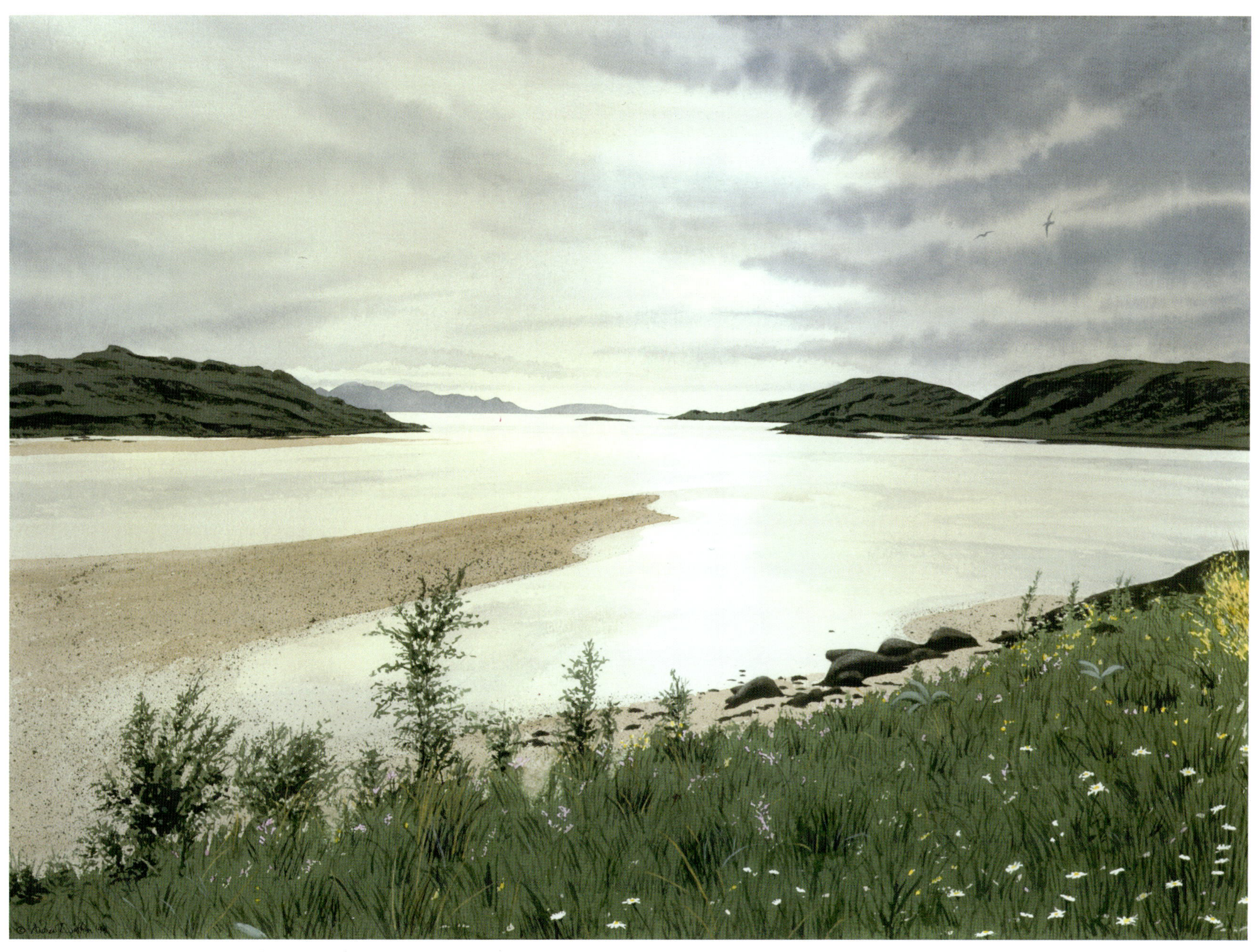

The River Morar Estuary, Near Mallaig 29" x 21" 1999

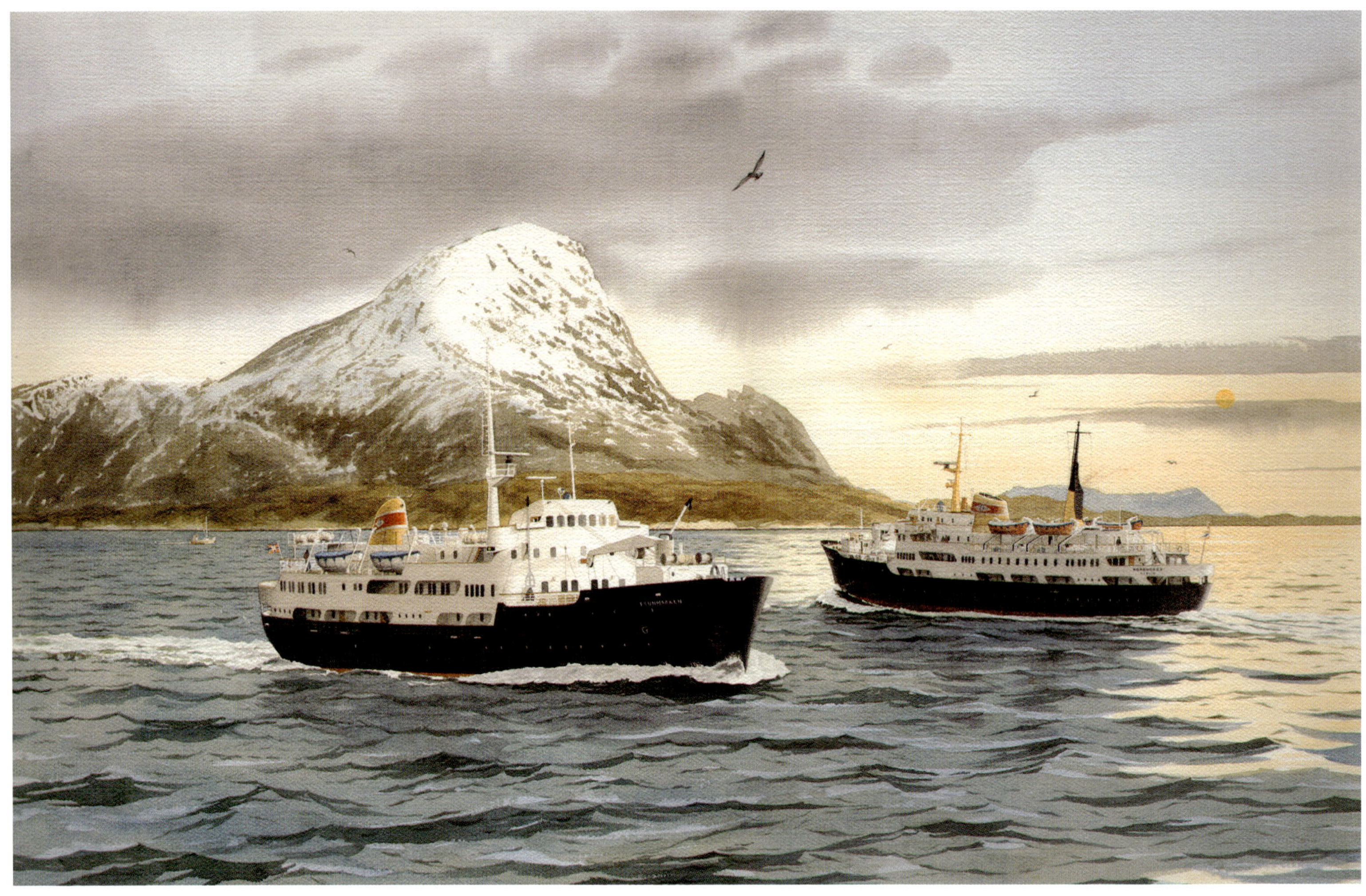

Arctic Encounter – M.S. **Finnmarken** *and* **Nordnorge** 39½" x 22" 1992

Another country that draws me is Norway, with its majestic mountain lined coastline, and beautiful fjords. I travelled along the whole coast from Bergen to the Russian border in 1992 in order to carry out a commission from one of the companies operating the Norwegian Coastal Voyage ships. This large painting was one I did for myself after producing five for the company, and shows two of their ships passing near Harstad, close to the Lofoten islands. Opposite is a typical early morning view from one of the ships in a serene location in southern Norway, while the next painting was done following another trip, in 1999, and shows the scene as a ship leaves the Nordfjord at 11.45pm on a misty July evening.

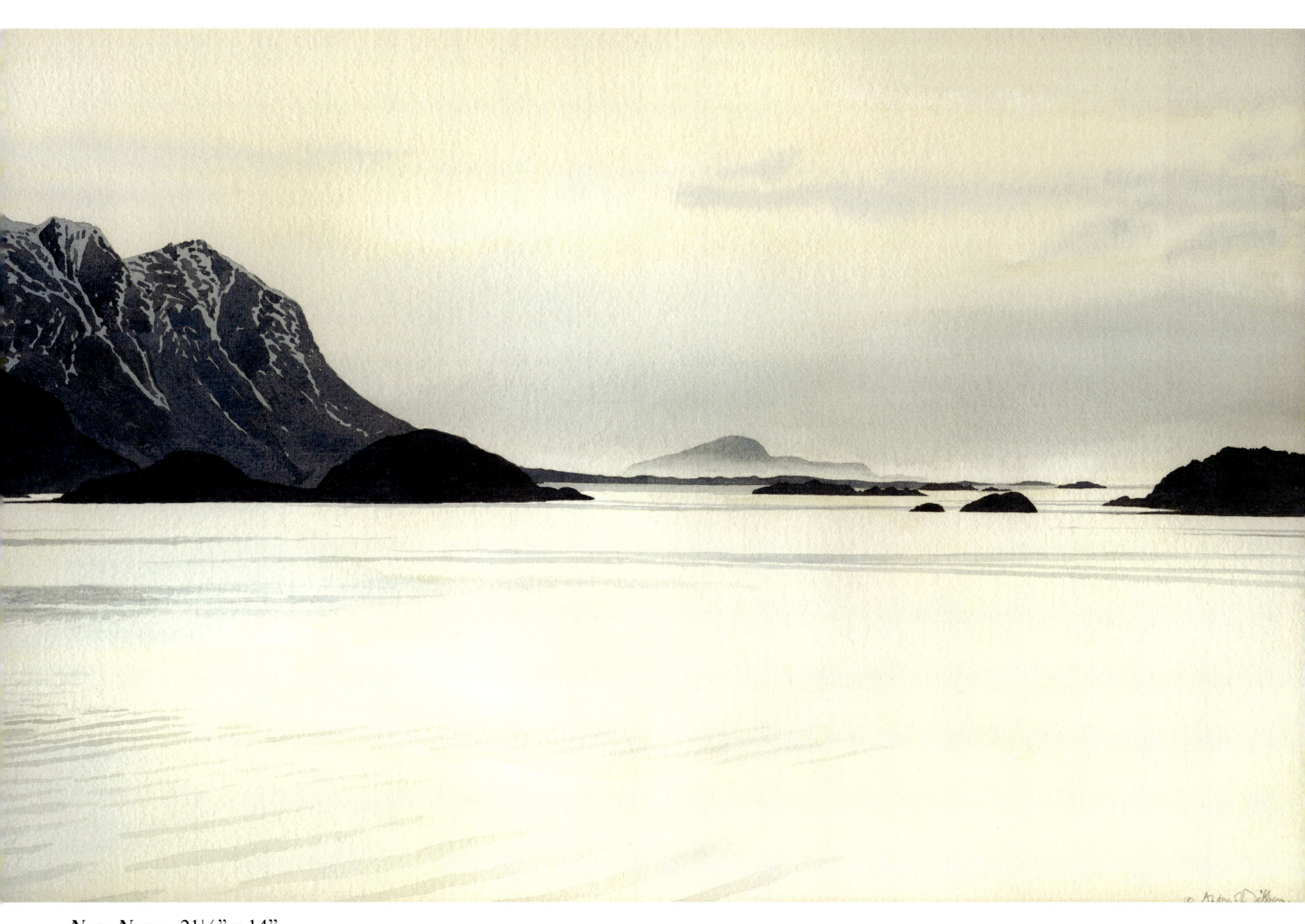

Near Nesna 21½" x 14"

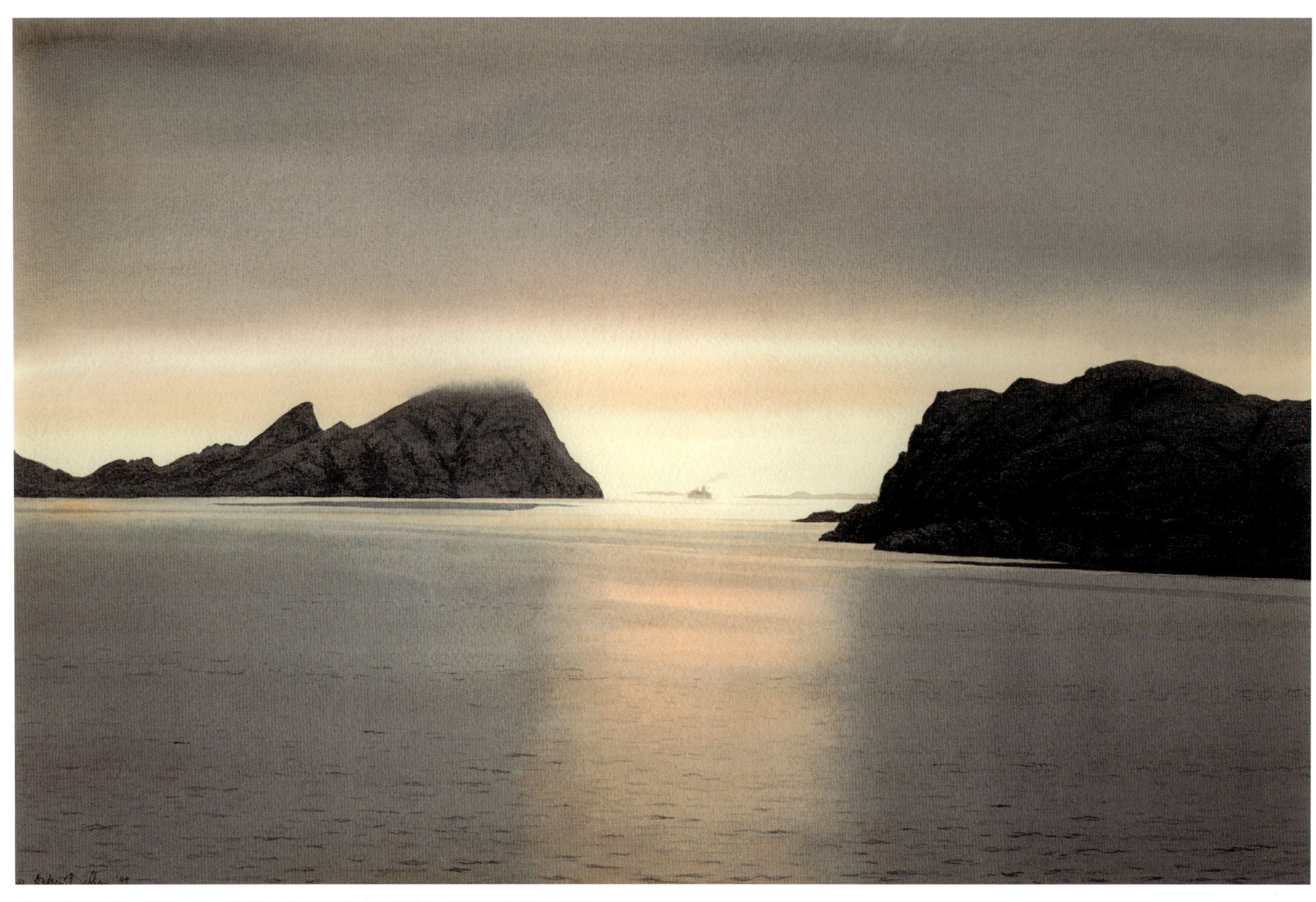

Leaving The Nordfjord, 11.45pm, July 1999 20" x 14" 1999